World University Library

The World University Library is an international series
of books, each of which has been specially commissioned.
The authors are leading scientists and scholars from all over
the world who, in an age of increasing specialisation, see the
need for a broad, up-to-date presentation of their subject.
The aim is to provide authoritative introductory books for
students which will be of interest also to the general
reader. The series is published in Britain, France, Germany,
Holland, Italy, Spain, Sweden and the United States.

Frontispiece The muse of pornography, satirised by Felicien Rops.

VRA   POESIS   MUSICA   SCULPTURA

ΠΟΡΝΟΚΡΑΤΗΣ

Matthew Hodgart

Satire

World University Library

Weidenfeld and Nicolson
5 Winsley Street London W1

© Matthew Hodgart 1969
Phototypeset by BAS Printers Limited, Wallop, Hampshire
Printed by Officine Grafiche Arnoldo Mondadori, Verona

Contents

Introduction   7

1 Origins and principles   10

2 The topics of satire: politics   33

3 The topics of satire: women   79

4 Techniques of satire   108

5 Forms of satire   132

6 Satire in drama   188

7 Satire in the novel   214

  Postscript   241

  Notes   249

  Acknowledgments   251

  Index   252

Introduction

Satire is a word used in various senses: the original meaning in English and other languages is a literary work of a special kind, 'in which vice, follies, stupidities and abuses etc., are held up to ridicule and contempt' (*Webster's New World Dictionary*). It can also be used collectively of all such literary works, and the art of writing them. A third, more modern, meaning is 'the employment in speaking or writing, of sarcasm, irony, ridicule etc., in denouncing, exposing, or deriding vice, folly, abuses or evils of any kind' (*Shorter Oxford English Dictionary*); in other words, the process of attacking by ridicule in *any* medium, not merely in literature. It is a legitimate use of the word to talk of satire in the monologue of a night-club or radio entertainer, in the cinema and television, or in the visual arts (caricature and cartoon).

In this book, however, I confine myself mainly to the first two senses, namely individual satirical works of literature and the art of satire in general, but under 'literature' I include not only the printed book and manuscript, but also folklore or primitive oral traditions of verse and prose. For reasons of space, it is not possible to trace the analogies between literary satire and the other arts; but it is hoped that the illustrations to this volume will suggest some of the more interesting connections. The boundaries of literature are, however, never very clear: drama, as it is usually understood and as I take it in chapter 6, implies a fixed literary text which is used for a stage performance; but there is no absolute dividing line between the 'legitimate' theatre and the improvisations of the mime and the entertainer, which throughout history have been the chief vehicle for satirical comment on the absurdities of the world. The media of satire, like its topics, are often ephemeral: but if there is an art of satire common to all the media its outlines can best be discerned in the greatest works of satiric literature.

Of the many possible topics of satire the pre-eminent one is politics, the most challenging, dangerous and rewarding to the satirist; and this I discuss in chapter 2. There are many other topics which could be illustrated from the history of satire, including literature itself. This I have in general avoided, since in my opinion too much of satirical literature consists of literary in-fighting. Since the poets are an irritable race, they spend much of their time and talents proving how contemptible their rivals are; but with a few exceptions such as Alexander Pope's *Dunciad*, the charm of the literary battle soon fades. Instead, I have chosen the rather archaic topic of women – archaic because the sex-war is no longer a one-sided affair in satirical terms. Although women as a topic seem to have largely disappeared from modern satirical literature they were of vast interest to classical and medieval writers.

There are several dangers facing the writer of a short book of this kind. First, there is the trap of categories. 'Satire', in my view, is not a well-defined category, but a convenient expression to cover a variety of literary works that have many characteristics in common. The same I believe to be true of the accepted genres of literature, such as tragedy and comedy. When I generalise about the aims or techniques of satire, I am not laying down rules, but summarising these characteristics as I have found them; and when I say, for example, that after Aristophanes most comedy diverges from satire, I am not stating this as a logical deduction from the nature of comedy, but merely noting what in my opinion is an empirical fact. If at times I may give a contrary impression and appear to be making normative statements about satire (that is, saying what satire should be, rather than what satirical works are like), I can only plead that shortage of space has made me, like other critics, appear to fall into the trap.

Secondly, it has not been possible to give a full enough treatment to the satirists of world literature. To do so in the space would have meant only a list of names, dates and subjects. There is a vast amount of good satire in every language. I am most familiar with English satire of the eighteenth century but I hope I have not been too parochial in time and place. Every reader will find that some of his favourite satirists have been omitted or discussed too scantily, but this is true of most literary history. Again, space has not allowed me to give full scholarly references for each point: there is however a short reading list and a few notes at the end. There are a great many theories about satire and critical studies of satirists. I have not quoted chapter and verse in every case where I have mentioned such theories and studies, but I hope I have acknowledged my general indebtedness, particularly to the works of Northrop Frye, Alvin B.Kernan and R.C.Elliot.

1 Origins and principles

The perennial topic of satire is the human condition itself. Man, part ape and part essence, is born for trouble as the sparks fly upwards. He is notoriously a weak and mortal creature, and during his brief span of life suffers the heart-ache and the thousand natural shocks that flesh is heir to. His desires, physical and mental, are boundless, and by the nature of things most of them are doomed to remain unfulfilled, those which are fulfilled often having unexpectedly unpleasant consequences. Man is ceaselessly engaged in solving the problems set by nature – but every problem that he solves creates new ones: thus, the conquest of disease leads to over-population and the unhappy survival of the old; the demands of our increasingly complex civilisation lead to more and more tension and frustration. There would not seem to be any conceivable future less problematical than the troubled past, less full of absurdities than the nightmare of history. There are many ways of looking at this life, and satire's is one of them. To respond to the world with a mixture of laughter and indignation is not perhaps the noblest way, nor the most likely to lead to good works or great art; but it is the way of satire. Satire, 'the use of ridicule, sarcasm, irony etc. to expose, attack, or deride vices, follies etc.' (as the dictionaries define it), has its origin in a state of mind which is critical and aggressive, usually one of irritation at the latest examples of human absurdity, inefficiency or wickedness. If the occasions for satire are infinite and inherent in the human condition, the impulses behind satire are basic to human nature. Indeed, they probably go back beyond human nature, to the psychology of our animal forebears. All social animals are aggressive to their own kind: each of their societies possess a hierarchy, sometimes known as a 'pecking order', by which its efficient functioning is maintained. To establish this order, two animals will use 'threat displays' against each other, until the inferior submits to the superior. The human expression of contempt, the curling lip and the mocking laugh, seem to be rooted in such threat displays; and the satiric impulse is probably more closely connected with this kind of aggressive behaviour than with overt attack, such as animals make against other species. The satirist's anger is modified by his sense of superiority and contempt for his victim; his aim is to make the victim lose 'face', and the most effective way of humiliating him is by contemptuous laughter. As is well known, horses and dogs do not like to be laughed at.

That is as far as we need go for the moment into the motivation of satire. It does not, of course, answer two questions: how does satire become art? and how does satire differ from other kinds of literature? It is, after all, only with art and in particular with the art of literature that we are to be concerned. First and most obviously, satire can turn from a state of mind into art only when it combines aggressive denunciation with some aesthetic features which can cause pure pleasure in the spectator. The spectator, indeed, may identify himself with the satirist and share his sense of superiority; but that is not enough. There must be other sources of pleasure in the satire, as for example patterns of sound and meaning, or the kind of relationship of ideas that we call wit, which we can feel as beautiful or exciting in themselves, irrespective of the subject of the satire. But many kinds of denunciation or sermon, however wittily or elegantly phrased, are not generally accepted as satire unless something else is involved. There is an enormous amount of polemical criticism, invective, political journalism and so on which is intensely critical of social and moral conditions, and may be very well expressed, yet fails to enter that realm ruled over by Juvenal and Swift and inhabited by even the minor masters of the art. I would suggest that true satire demands a high degree both of commitment to and involvement with the painful problems of the world, and simultaneously a high degree of abstraction from the world. The criticism of the world is abstracted from its ordinary setting, the setting of, say, political oratory and journalism, and transformed into a high form of 'play', which gives us both the recognition of our responsibilities and the irresponsible joy of make-believe. So with more personal satire: the tension and bitterness evoked by unpleasant personal relationships are transmuted into delight at the creation of a beautifully absurd figure which is both like and unlike the subject. One recognises true satire by this quality of 'abstraction'; wit and other technical devices (discussed in a later chapter) are the means by which the painful issues of real life are transmuted. But even more important is the element of fantasy which seems to be present in all true satire. The satirist does not paint an objective picture of the evils he describes, since pure realism would be too oppressive. Instead he usually offers us a travesty of the situation, which at once directs our attention to actuality and permits an escape from it. All good satire contains an element of aggressive attack and a fantastic vision of the world transformed: it is written for entertainment, but contains sharp and telling comments on the problems of the world in which we live, offering 'imaginary gardens with real toads in them'. It would seem, then, that satire is distinguishable from other kinds of literature by its approach to its subject, by a special attitude to human experience which is reflected in its artistic conventions. It is in fact very difficult to distinguish it clearly from other literary forms on any other basis; first, because it does not clearly form one of the traditional 'genres', and secondly because it may assume a bewildering variety of sub-forms. The traditional genres, such as epic, tragedy and comedy, were long considered to be self-contained and clearly defined. Each grew out of a particular stage of social development: epic out of the 'heroic' society of warrior aristocracy, tragedy out of the religious and moral preoccupations of the Greek city-states. Each was at a later stage established by convention, and codified by literary critics, and imitated by generations of writers so that norms of epic and tragedy were set up and lasted for centuries. No such stabilising process ever affected satire, with the partial exception of Roman formal satire (the loose monologue in verse on a variety of moral topics). This was much imitated, as we shall see, by classicising poets of the sixteenth, seventeenth and eighteenth centuries, but even in these convention-bound centuries, writers who wanted to make satirical comments on the world's absurdities felt free to use a variety of other forms. The satirists have in fact from the beginning used a bewildering range of vehicles, some of which I shall describe in a later chapter. Apart from (1) formal satire, the following categories can be mentioned: (2) the fantastic narrative, which includes such forms as the beast-fable, utopian or anti-utopian fiction, and allegory; (3) already existing literary forms taken over and transformed into satirical comment, e.g. the aphorism and epitaph; (4) parts of literary works in any of the genres taken over for satirical purposes. Some of the best satire in literature occurs episodically or fragmentarily in works which are not intended to be wholly satirical, It would be absurd to leave out Dickens from this survey, yet his best satirical passages often occur sandwiched between sentimental and melo-dramatic passages, and in novels whose overall vision of the world is other than a satirical one. The usual genres in which satire appears episodically are comedy and the novel; but it may appear almost anywhere else, even in sermons and not least in Shake-spearian tragedy. Faced with even these varieties of form (and there are many more) critics have, not surprisingly, been unable to reach agreement on the strict definition of satire. The definition of tragedy by 'rules' of structure and style may be artificial, but it has seemed since Aristotle to be at least a possibility and it is still being attempted. Critics have never felt happy about applying these kind of criteria to the Protean body of satirical literature. Yet what is commonly called satire is a distinct part of our literary ex-perience: any two experienced readers will show a fair measure of agreement in applying the word to something they have read. In trying to define the term and to explain the special literary ex-perience that satire gives, it may be best to abandon the traditional methods of literary classification and instead to consider the satirist's attitude to life and the special strategies by which he communicates this attitude in literary form. One way of approaching this question is by looking at the oldest and simplest examples of satire available. The emergence of satire, if not as a formal genre, then at least as a distinct type of literature, is probably very ancient. It can apparently be found in the literature of the prim-itive peoples whose words have been recorded and who may be

Eskimo engraving of the nineteenth century, one of a series illustrating traditional tales. It shows creatures, half-human and half-dog, who, like the perfect satirist, can kill merely by pointing their bows.
From Riuk, *Tales and Traditions of the Eskimo*, a Danish work.

thought to have preserved the most ancient traditions of mankind. It is striking that two of these literary traditions appear in the special combination of realism and fantasy which, as I have suggested, is the keynote of true satire. One is the 'lampoon' or personal attack; the other is the 'travesty', or fantastic vision of the world transformed.

In the literature of primitive peoples both types can be seen clearly, sometimes separately and sometimes in combination. 'Literature' is not a very satisfactory word, since it implies letters, while the most primitive peoples are illiterate; but no one has found a better word for the art of verbal expression, so I shall use it without further apology. Nor shall I apologise for discussing primitive literature, since it is not essentially different from the more sophisticated literature of higher civilisations. The problems of living, the experiences of love and death, the delights and miseries of primitive men are not so very different from ours; and many men from a simpler world even than Homer's have found out how to express such things movingly in words. The anthropologist Paul Radin has pointed out that every primitive society has a highly developed literary culture, in which nearly all the genres of sophisticated literature appear more or less distinctly, sometimes presented with astonishing poetic or narrative skill, with satire conspicuous among them:

I know of no tribe where satires or formal narratives avowedly humorous have not attained a rich development. Examples of every conceivable form are found, from broad lampoon and crude invective to subtle innuendo and satire based on man's stupidity, his gluttony, and his lack of a sense of proportion[1].

The simplest example of the first type (lampoon, invective) is the Eskimo song of derision. Eskimo society was until recently on about the same level as that of the late Stone Age: it lacked any distinct system of law, let alone police or magistrates to enforce the law, or schoolmasters or preachers to warn against misconduct: its religion has no strong supernatural sanctions such as a hell where

evil-doers will be punished. The chief means of punishing bad social behaviour is by the satirical song, which makes the delinquent hang his head in shame. The Eskimo satirist has precisely the same aim as Alexander Pope, to make 'men not afraid of God afraid of me'. This is said to work in practice: the man who is worsted in a satirical song-contest will try to reform himself; in extreme cases one can picture him stumbling wretchedly out of the igloo, like Captain Oates on Scott's polar expedition, to rid the community of its obnoxious burden – which is more than Pope's victims ever did. I have not found any translations of great merit but as an illustration 'The Strife of Savadlak and Pulangitsissok' will serve:

There was a time when Savadlak wished that I would be a good

kayaker,

That I could take a good load on my kayak!
Many years ago one day he wanted to put a heavy load on my kayak,
When Savadlak had his kayak tied to mine (for fear of being capsized).
Then he could carry plenty upon his kayak,
But I had to tow him and he cried most pitifully.
And then he grew afraid,
And nearly got upset,
And he had to keep his hold by means of my kayak string[2].

Other songs insist that the victim's sexual desires are unlimited, his performance totally inadequate – much as Rochester and other Restoration wits used to write in their lampoons on Charles II, no less crudely. Satire-duels of this kind are also found among the Indians of the north-west coast of America and in Melanesia. They cannot all be described as moral in intention, since some consist of direct attacks on individuals for the purpose of revenge or the assertion of superiority; but insofar as literature is a public activity and thus preferable to private violence, they contain the germ of moral and also of political satire; that is, of literature as propaganda for right action, which 'heals with morals what it hurts with wit'.

This primitive kind of satire or lampoon keeps appearing throughout literature. When Dr Johnson was asked why Pope put a certain line in his *Dunciad*, he replied, no doubt correctly, 'Sir, he hoped it would vex somebody'. At the simplest there is Martial's epigram in its well-known adaptation:

> I do not love thee, Doctor Fell,
> The reason why I cannot tell;
> But this I know and know full well:
> I do not love thee, Doctor Fell.

At the most complex and elegant there are A.E.Housman's strictures on the incompetent scholars who had dared to edit the text of Manilius (one of whom had the misfortune to come from Strasbourg, 'a city famous for its geese').

The primitive lampoon is closely related to the curse, and the curse or imprecation is based on beliefs in the magical power of the word. By an effective combination of images and rhythms, and by the invocation of supernatural forces the curse is intended to exert a positive influence over its victim, to make him shrivel up or die, or a negative influence, to restrain his powers of doing evil. That, at least, is one way of putting it, as has been done brilliantly by R.C.Elliott in his book *The Power of Satire*, who traces satire back to magic spells and rituals. Just as one type of primitive ritual is designed to increase the fertility of the crops or to cast love-spells, so another is designed to cast out demons or to cause the tribe's enemies to perish in battle; both have been exhaustively discussed by Frazer in *The Golden Bough*. In this view, satire springs from primitive witchcraft; it is thus the verbal equivalent of pointing the death-bone and causing an Australian aborigine to die of sheer terror, or, perhaps better, of making a wax image of your victim and sticking pins in it. But this only raises the question: why is the word considered to be magical? The answer may be simply that the word is magical *because of* its satirical, that is, its literary power. A curse, like all other literary forms is effective just as far as it is well composed, in compelling rhythms, skilful rhetoric, relevant argument and true content – which are among the normal criteria for all good literature. Wizards, of course, may sometimes mumble a curse in a dead language or in nonsense words, but even then the literary qualities of sound and rhythm would seem to be important. Most primitive curses or lampoons, however, seem to be lucid and meant for effective communication, like this love-curse from the Ba-Ronga of south-eastern Africa:

> Refuse me as much as you wish, my dear!
> The corn you eat at home, it is made of human eyes!
> The goblets that you use, they are of human skulls!
> The manioc roots you eat, they are of human shin-bones!
> The potatoes you eat, they are of human hands!
> Refuse me as much as you wish!
> No one desires you![3]

That could hardly make its point more tellingly. Savages, as anthropologists tell us, are practical people, and they have very good practical reasons for believing in the power of the word. They have discovered empirically, by trial and error, just how much the word can do if it is properly employed, as the example of the Eskimos shows. The word used with literary art really can affect people in a striking way, even to the point of sickness and death. Poor Keats was not the only one to be 'snuffed out by an article'; every sensitive author knows the unpleasant psychosomatic effect of a clever and hostile review (and some reviewers know it too). Most people cannot bear to hear themselves abused in a true and witty manner, which excites the scorn of the audience. I am told that among certain primitive peoples, the tongues of condemned criminals were torn out before their execution, lest in their last minutes alive they should say something damaging to their judges and hangmen, or to the whole community[4]. In this view, written word *precedes* magic in history: the proven power of the word to cause acute shame and demoralisation led to the attribution of magic powers to the word. I presume therefore that primitive literature has a practical purpose and effect. Just as the purpose of a love-lyric is to win the beloved, so the purpose of primitive satire is to get the better of the enemy; and primitives try to achieve these ends, less by invoking magical sanctions than by normal literary means, by graphic style and telling content.

Satire of this kind has been traced by R.C.Elliott and others in the ancient literature of three peoples, the Irish, the Greeks and the Arabs. It is a persistent tradition in Irish, as referred to by Ben Jonson in his *Poetasters:*

> I could doe worse,
> Arm'd with ARCHILOCHVS fury, write Iambicks,
> Should make the desperate lashers hang themselves,
> Rime 'hem to death, as they do *Irish* rats
> In drumming tunes.

The ancient Irish bards were supposed to have quasi-magical powers: they could not only rhyme rats to death, they could cause serious injury ('the three blisters of contempt' in ancient saga) or death to stingy chiefs or patrons or others who got across them, simply by writing potent verse – or so tradition has it. There is a wealth of material in Vivien Mercier's excellent study *The Irish*

Comic Tradition, which shows that the habit of eloquent cursing in prose and verse lasted through the Middle Ages in Ireland and has continued to the present day. What landlady would not feel discomfited if she had refused a drink to James Stephens and then heard him hope that she might 'marry a ghost and bear him a kitten, And may the High King of Glory permit it to get the mange'? – which is an adaptation of two Middle Irish satires.

Archilochus, the Greek satirist mentioned by Jonson, is the earliest recorded poet after Homer. He was a soldier of experience, who won his bread and wine by his spear, but was expelled from militaristic Sparta for admitting that he had once thrown away his shield in battle – the first known piece of autobiography in verse. He was said to have invented the iambic metre, which at first was used exclusively for satire, and retained this association throughout classical times – hence Ben Jonson's 'Iambicks'. But he is chiefly famous for the legend that, when one Lycambes betrayed him he wrote such an effective piece of invective that Lycambes and his family went off and hanged themselves for shame. This legend may be taken as evidence for the power of straightforward literature rather than for the magical power of the word. We do not know for certain if the poem against Lycambes is among the few fragments of Archilochus that survive, but this one would seem to be a likely candidate:

May he be driven out of his course by the waves; and at Salmydessus may the top-knotted Thracians seize him, when he is stripped of his friends and family, and make him eat the bread of slavery and drink a full cup of evil; may they seize him when he is shivering with cold, with long strips of seaweed over his body, as he lies on his belly like a dog, helpless in the surf, spewing out the sea-water. And I'd like to be there to see him – because he wronged me and broke a solemn oath, he that was once my friend[5].

A third set of examples has been taken from ancient Arabic satire, which also seems to have had a perfectly practical purpose: the satirist would ride into battle at the head of his tribe, and before physical fighting began he would assail the enemy in witty and cutting verse. If this were well done, it is said, it would raise morale on one side and lower it on the other, sometimes to the extent that spears and swords were no longer necessary, as the losers slunk off the field.

That kind of primitive satire, connected both with the curse and with the personal lampoon, is one of the origins of modern political and moral satire, which calls for repentance and reform. But it is not the only origin. Complaint and moral teaching alone, even when expressed with wit and point, do not of themselves make satire. In all literary satire we can recognise another dimension, which also has primitive roots. Satire at all levels must entertain as well as try to influence conduct, and the entertainment comes, I think, chiefly from the joy of hearing a travesty, a fantastic inversion of the real world. The type figure of primitive travesty is the trickster, who is at the centre of many legends of the North American Indians, fully described by Radin; while a variant of the trickster, Eshu-Elegba, is well known in West African folktale and sculpture[6]. The Winnebago trickster is a semi-divine man, who breaks all the most sacred taboos and consequently is driven out of society and forced to go alone on a fantastic journey on which he has many absurd and often violent adventures. He is totally anarchic, especially in his sexual behaviour: he has a penis many yards long, which has literally to be cut down to size before he can return to normal social life; and yet part of his education is to change sex and bear children. The trickster is both sinned against and sinning, both fool and rogue, shark and gull, a Priapic buffoon – and among other things the probable ancestor of the amoral hero of the picaresque novel. Trickster stories belong to the religious mythology of the tribe, and are told on solemn occasions; yet they treat with levity everything that is most sacred in the tribe's religious life. For example, to the Winnebago two of the supremely important things in life are the sacred vision of the spirits. experienced by the braves after fasting, and going on the war-path, a highly ritualised process which involves the preparation of the holy medicine bundle and taboos against sexual intercourse. Yet it is precisely these institutions that are held up to ridicule in the trickster myths, by means of parody and travesty. According to Radin, in the Winnebago, unlike other North American versions, there is a strong secondary development of satire of a more literary nature: the implications of the original myth are worked up into a humorous attack on social and religious customs. But even without this literary overlay the function of trickster is profoundly subversive; it is, as Kerenyi says, 'to add disorder to order and so make a whole to render possible, within the fixed bounds of what is permitted, an experience of what is not permitted'.

The name of the Winnebago trickster (Wakdunkaga) means 'spider'; and his myths are related to the stories of cunning-foolish animals found all over the world; the best known to Europeans are those of Reynard the Fox. In West Africa in particular, stories are told about the clever spider; and among the Yoruba there is a special trickster, a divine creature in human form, whose adventures, sexual and criminal, are not unlike those of the African spider and the Winnebago trickster. He is described by Joan Westcott as 'a creature of instinct and great energy who serves a dual role; as a rule-breaker he is . . . a spanner in the social works, and beyond this he is a generating symbol who promotes change by offering opportunities for exploring what possibilities lie beyond the status quo'. He is represented both in wood sculpture and by a pillar symbol, like an ancient Greek herm; this is set up in the market place, where there are crowds and trouble may break out. Like Hermes, whom the herm symbolised, he is a cunning god and the special deity of all those who live by their wits.

His role is dual and paradoxical – both social and anti-social. He is not only the symbol but also the solution of man's conflict between instinctive desires and social demands. In accepting the blame he keeps the peace, while still offering escape from the rigidity of social laws.

Finally, Miss Westcott notes that satire is associated with Eshu-

The Polynesian god Tangaroa
in the act of creating
the other gods and man;
possibly an eighteenth-century
wood figure.
British Museum, London.

The comic slave, with large belly
and grotesque mask,
is a stock figure of the
classical stage, here represented
by a statuette of the
Hellenistic period.

Elegba and his cult (presumably, as with the Winnebago this is a secondary literary development), and as satirist he 'dramatises the dangers which face men and the follies to which they are prone'.

The reason for the widespread popularity of stories of the trickster type in primitive literature seems to be that every society has its laws, taboos and moral regulations which preserve or are felt to preserve the social structure, yet on occasions become intolerably restrictive. There is therefore a periodical, perhaps annual, breaking of taboos, which gives a cathartic release of social tension; and as a result the taboos will be taken all the more seriously once they are reimposed and normal life is taken up again. This is the origin of Carnival and Saturnalia, and the licentious festivals which F.M. Cornford[7] saw as lying behind the Old Comedy and Aristophanes. On such a special occasion the most scandalous things could be said about the laws and the political dealings of the state; socially depressed classes like slaves – and women – could be given freedom of speech, and even the gods themselves could be mocked, and this in the context of an avowedly religious festival. The Old Comedy was performed at the festival of the Dionysia, but the god in whose honour it was held could be a low character in the play: the cowardly and disgraceful Dionysos in Aristophanes's *Frogs* addresses bawdy remarks to his own priest, sitting in the front row of the theatre. As Jung points out in his commentary on the Winnebago trickster stories, many parallels can be found in the history of the church during the Middle Ages. There was the ceremony of electing a boy bishop from among the choristers: for a few days he sat enthroned in the cathedral (if he died during his office, he was buried with full episcopal honours). More startling was the Asses' Mass (*festum asinarium*) during which donkeys were led up to the high altar and the responses were brayed. The Feast of Fools was a similar upsetting of rank and propriety in the life of the court. All such festivals tended to involve blasphemy, obscenity and the temporary subversion of the social order. They presented in mime and song satirical parodies of the very things that church and state claimed to take most seriously – and this in the rigid

Lucas Cranach's 'Der Papstesel zu Rom' (the Pope-Ass in Rome) illustrates a pamphlet by Luther and Melanchthon of 1523. It was earlier published as a true picture of a monster allegedly found in Rome, but here receives an elaborate allegorical explanation. The Warburg Institute, London.

hierarchical background of medieval society, which in theory at least was extremely illiberal. The essence of the carnival and saturn-alia is the glorification of irresponsibility, even to the point of anarchy.

Not only is incidental literary satire found in association with such festivals, but there are strong elements of travesty and anarchistic parody in *all* good satire, from Aristophanes onwards. The great satirists not only attack people or customs they think are bad, but they also create a dream world in which the real world is fantastically inverted or travestied. This may take the form of the fabulous voyage, like the absurd visit to the complete world of men inside a whale's belly, as told by Lucian in his *True History* and imitated by Rabelais in his fourth book (Pantagruel's voyage in quest of the Holy Bottle) and by Swift in *Gulliver's Travels*. Or it may be an imaginary kingdom, a Cloudcuckooland, a utopia or anti-utopia, where women take over the government (*Lysistrata*) or where horses rule over men, like Swift's Houyhnhnms. Satire may draw on the beast-fable, which in turn draws on the magical world of the folk-tale; in the folk-tale or fairy tale animals sometimes talk and even help the hero to win the princess. (The fairy tale, because the victorious hero is nearly always the youngest son, and many marvels take place, is itself a fantastic inversion of the real world.) The animal folk-tale is associated with satire, as we have seen, in some of the trickster and spider stories. The beast-fable, a more sophisticated development, is often used for gentle irony or moral teaching, as in the versions of Aesop by Robert Henryson and La Fontaine; but often becomes a vehicle for sharper comment. It is manifestly used for social satire, as well as for picaresque farce, in the medieval *Roman de Renart*, from which the stories about Reynard the Fox descend; the most famous modern example is George Orwell's political fable *Animal Farm*. Again, the framework for satire is often a travesty or parody of the most serious forms of literature, and those most highly valued by the parodist himself, as for example the Bible in Dryden's *Absalom and Achitophel* or classical epic in Pope's *Dunciad*. This variety is known as 'mock-heroic': the dignified and heroic world of Homer and Virgil is

Der Bapſteſel zu Rom

The tedium of Academe.
A carving on the Bell Tower of New College, Oxford.

Zeus caught in the act of visiting Alcmene. The Greek vase-painting, of the fourth century BC, probably represents a farcical stage performance, in which the gods are cut down to size and ridiculed. The lecherous old father of gods and men has to use a ladder to reach his elegant love: the exaggeration of belly and bottom is a basic device for lowering dignity. Vatican Museum.

transformed into the grossness and triviality of modern life. The effect of mock-heroic is never simply the opposition of ancient and modern, the contrast of the good old with the bad new way that people live, although it usually includes such a contrast; it also gives the pleasure of seeing the traditional values, conventions and styles of epic turned on their heads: Pope, in *The Rape of the Lock* and in the *Dunciad*, invents new worlds which delight by their absurdity.

In these varieties of saturnalian travesty from the trickster stories to mock-heroic there is one fairly constant element, and that is obscenity. Because this is characteristic of satire in general (and of pictorial as well as literary satire), it demands some comment.

Obscenity in satire can nearly always be clearly distinguished from pornography, if one takes the latter to be the deliberate description of sexual topics with the purpose of increasing sexual desire in the audience, reader, or beholder. The usual form that pornography takes is the detailed and loving description of the sexual act, or of things associated with or substituted for the sexual act (that is, courtship, fetichism, perversion, etc.). That there may be a certain amount of this incidental to good satire is undeniable – no one would care to claim that Rabelais had a pure mind – but pornography is not the main point of the sexual references in satire. These are rather part of that systematic breaking down of taboos which marks the saturnalia; and because sexual taboos, even in unpuritanical societies, are among the strongest of taboos, their breaking down in saturnalian reversals is usually catastrophic and sometimes complete. Obscenity played an essential part in the ancient Greek and Roman festivals which, according to some classical scholars, preceded satire and comedy, with their phallic songs and rude 'fescennine' verses. It is also observable in the medieval travesty-festivals. The tradition of obscenity combined with literary fantasy begins with Aristophanes and is maintained by most of the great public satirists up to Swift and Pope. Thereafter changes in literary fashion and social mores tended to separate the two, but there is a notable revival of satirical obscenity in the greatest of James Joyce's fantastic travesties, the 'Circe' episode of *Ulysses*. Sexual obscenity in this tradition goes together with scatology, of which Rabelais is the undisputed master, and the two are akin; the free mention of sexual topics has much the same function as the comic or disgusting mention of excretion. Such things are discussed openly in saturnalian contexts just because they are not allowed to be mentioned on more formal occasions, and they have a natural place in satire. It is commonplace for Aristophanes's characters to break wind or relieve themselves with fright, like Dionysos in *The Frogs*, while Swift's Yahoos are remarkable for their urine and dung. Much learned comment, some of it psycho-analytical, has been written about Swift's 'cloacal

The masterly series of grotesque heads by Leonardo da Vinci
has been the inspiration of all subsequent caricature in Europe.
The heads are types, not portraits of individuals, and suggest
infinite depths of vice and folly.

obsession'; but it should also be remembered that Swift was following faithfully an ancient tradition. Obscenity, like the saturnalian festival itself, is reductive. It reduces men to equality, humbling the mighty. In the festivals, the fool changes place with the king, the chorister with the bishop, and the rigid social hierarchy is confounded for the occasion. So too the effect of obscenity in satire is to level all men, and to level them downwards, removing the distinctions of rank and wealth. The satirist's aim is to strip men bare, and apart from physique one naked man is much like another. 'Robes and furred gowns hide all', as King Lear says of the symbols of authority. By using obscenity, the satirist can go even further, reducing man from nakedness to the condition of an animal, in which any claim to social or even divine distinction must appear even more ridiculous. The simplest and most effective device of the Greek Phlyax vase painters was to show a hero like Odysseus or Oedipus, or Zeus himself, father of gods and men, going about his adventures with an erect phallus. When used like this obscenity means destruction to the heroic view of life, as enshrined in ancient myth, epic and tragedy. The heroic view of life insists that the hero is a special sort of man, a prince or a general, who by his birth and prowess is set apart, and demands respect, from the rest of society. The satirist's aim is often to deflate false heroes, imposters or charlatans, who claim a respect which is not their due, and the vehicle he chooses for this is usually the mock-heroic. But saturnalian travesty-satire, especially when it involves obscenity, goes much further than the mock-heroic: it is profoundly anti-heroic.

Travesty, in the sense I have used, is a requisite of satire. But the converse does not hold, since not all travesty is satire. There are pure travesties, like the *Virgile Travesti* by the seventeenth-century Paul Scarron, who was concerned only to cause mild fun by an ingenious parody of Virgil's style and of the artificial conventions of epic. There is a great deal of excellent literary parody of this nature, which insofar as it is too good-humoured to cause offence, cannot qualify as satire (malicious and destructive literary parody, which belongs to literary politics or warfare, is another matter, and will be discussed later). There are also many kinds of fantasy in literature, in which the real world is turned upside down, such as *Alice in Wonderland* but in which the satirical content may be very slight indeed. To qualify as satire, a travesty must contain the other element I have discussed, namely the direct attack on human vice or folly; it must contain lampoons on individuals or critical and hostile comments on political or social life. Satire is therefore not one of the traditional literary genres, like epic, tragedy, comedy, the lyric or the novel; it is a special category of literature which cuts across the ordinary genres, a 'mythos', to use the term employed by Northrop Frye in *The Anatomy of Criticism*[8]. In this chapter, called 'The Mythos of Winter: Irony and Satire', Frye has put in a few words the best distinction between satire and the other conditions of literature: satire demands (at least a token) fantasy, a content recognised as grotesque, moral judgments (at least implicit), and a 'militant attitude to experience'. Satire no longer works as such 'when its content is too oppressively real to permit the maintaining of the fantastic or hypothetical tone', and its final distinguishing mark is the 'double focus of morality and fantasy'.

Thus, a satirical play may draw its audience into an enchanted world of make-believe, but the dramatist's comments extend to the real world outside the theatre, to the political and moral problems that face the audience when they return to ordinary life. Hence in satire the subject-matter and the author's attitude to it is of primary importance. The satirist engages in the troubles of the world and expects his readers to do the same. He does so even though he is aware that he is incurring a double risk, of being unpopular in his own time and of being forgotten by later generations, to whom the day-to-day issues of his time may be of merely academic interest. The satirist appears in his noblest role when he accepts the challenge of oblivion, by taking on an ephemeral and unpleasant topic. For this reason I shall begin by discussing examples of the content of satire rather than its typical forms, and I shall take first the pre-eminent topic of satire, which is politics. This field offers the greatest risk and the greatest rewards: politics is traditionally considered a dirty business, yet the satirist is most a hero when he enters the forum and joins in the world's debate. To achieve his ends he *must* use some of the basic strategies of satire, but he *may* use almost any of the common forms (which I discuss in chapter 5). What is essential is that he should commit himself boldly to his 'impure' subject, yet retain a purity of attitude, in his aesthetic disengagement from the vulgarities and stupidities of the struggle. Here he demonstrates his mastery of the twin traditions of comic travesty and aggressive lampoon, which he has inherited from the distant past; and looking in two directions, keeps his vision sharp.

2 The topics of satire: politics

The most pressing of the problems that face us when we close the book or leave the theatre are ultimately political ones; and so politics is the pre-eminent topic of satire. 'Public affairs vex no man' said Samuel Johnson, but he could not have been more wrong: to some degree public affairs vex every man, if he pays taxes, does military service or even objects to the way his neighbour is behaving. There is no escape from politics where more than a dozen people are living together.

There is an essential connection between satire and politics in the widest sense: satire is not only the commonest form of political literature, but, insofar as it tries to influence public behaviour, it is the most political part of all literature. Both are felt to be rather discreditable: the word 'politician' has an unfavourable sense, and satirists keep apologising for their wicked tongues. But both are necessary, since all social and legal systems are in need of continuous reform, and politics is the only means of achieving reform; while only satire can release powerful enough acids to break down the attitudes of mind which hinder reform. Most of the great satirists have in fact been deeply interested in politics, and most have been against the established government of their countries. Those who have supported the government by writing satire against its critics, as Dryden did in *Absalom and Achitophel*, are usually attacking the alternative kind of government which they can conceive of the critics setting up: thus Dryden, who had lived through the Commonwealth, had a very clear idea of what Whig opposition could lead to, as well as a deep fear of civil war.

The enemies of satire are tyranny and provincialism, which often go together. Tyrants dislike any form of criticism, because they never know where it will lead to; and in provincial life free criticism is felt to be subversive of good order and decency. Satire did not flourish under Stalin, nor will it ever flourish in Little Rock or Alice Springs. Political satire needs a measure of freedom, the background of large cities and some sophistication: political sophistication (both the satirist and his public must understand some of the processes of politics) and aesthetic sophistication (the satirist must be able to contemplate the political scene with humour and detachment as well as with passion, or he will produce only crude polemic). In the great days of fifth-century Athens, these conditions obtained to perfection. Aristophanes commented with unparalleled freedom on the affairs of the day, combining the primitive traditions of satire, the lampoon and the saturnalian travesty, with an extraordinary inventiveness. He represented real citizens like Cleon and Socrates on the stage, and he created wonderful realms of fantasy in which the social and political order is crazily inverted. His earliest extant play *The Acharnians* was produced in 425 BC when he was barely twenty. It is a powerful plea for an armistice in the bitter war against Sparta, and a violent attack on the war-party led by the demagogue Cleon. Significantly, it begins with a picture of Athenian democracy in action: Dicaeopolis, the anti-war hero, comes to the assembly saying that he has 'decided to shout at, to interrupt and to satirise (*loidorein*) every orator who speaks about anything else but peace'. Aristophanic satire is here shown as closely linked with free speech and democratic decision, a link which is maintained throughout his work. Dicaeopolis has no success in the assembly, so he decides to make a separate peace with Sparta, as a private individual – he contracts out. He then earns the hatred of the Chorus of Acharnians, a rural clan who were famous for being warlike and anti-Spartan; but he wins over first half and then the whole of the Chorus by a series of comic arguments to show that the causes of the war are ridiculous. Now won over, the Chorus speak the *parabasis* of the author (traditionally known as the instructor or producer of the Chorus):

Since first to exhibit his plays he began,
                                          our chorus instructor has never
Come forth to confess in this public address
                                          how tactful he is and how clever.
But now that he knows he is slandered by foes
                                          before Athens so quick to assent,
Pretending he jeers at our City and sneers
                                          at the people with evil intent,

> He is ready and fain his cause to maintain
> > before Athens so quick to repent.
> Let honour and praise be the guerdon, he says,
> > of the poet whose satire has stayed you
> From believing the orators' novel conceits
> > wherewith they cajoled and betrayed you[9].

Dicaeopolis, thanks to his peace, is able to get the food and drink which have been in short supply during the war. At the end, his opponent, the general Lamachos, a real person in Athens, returns defeated and ingloriously wounded while the sensible Dicaeopolis is enjoying himself with feasting, music and women.

In his next play *The Knights* (424 BC) Aristophanes moves from an attack on Cleon's war-policy to an open attack on the democratic leader himself, who was virtually head of the state or the equivalent of prime minister. The most striking instance of Aristophanes's confidence and boldness is that he represents Cleon on the stage as a rascally Paphlagonian leather-seller. 'It is said', remarks Moses Hadas, 'that the mask-makers refused to provide a mask for Cleon and that Aristophanes played the part himself. But that the play could be presented at all, with Cleon himself in the audience, is another evidence of Athenian freedom of speech.' To defeat the Paphlagonian favourite of old man Demos (the people), his two slaves discover an even viler demagogue called the sausage-seller; finally Demos is brought to his senses, that is, moderate policy prevails. The slaves were masked to represent two generals of whom Aristophanes approved, and the chorus of knights represent the aristocratic and conservative class of Athenian society, with which he identified himself. Conscious of his daring, the poet defends himself and satire itself in the second parabasis:

Satire against the wicked has nothing odious about it – it is homage paid to the good, as will be seen by those who reason well. (*Knights*, 1274–5.)

The Clouds (423 BC) is Aristophanes's most delightful and subtle comedy: here the target is the new education provided by the sophists or professional philosophers of Athens. Socrates appears in person, perhaps unjustly ridiculed as representative of the sophists; the plot centres on the old farmer Strepsiades, who wants to learn from the new-fangled professors how to cheat his creditors. The most amusing passage is the debate between two allegorical characters called the Just and the Unjust Logos (literally 'word' but with the sense of 'logic' or 'argument'). This illustrates a general rule of Aristophanic satire, which is largely true of Rabelaisian and Swiftian satire: if the satirist is ridiculing something in favour of its opposite, which he sets up as an ideal, he will tend to ridicule the opposite as well. Satire often cannot help overflowing its bounds and making everything ludicrous. Thus, in *The Frogs* Aristophanes champions the old-fashioned Aeschylus against the 'modernist' Euripides, but he includes an absurd and accurate parody of Aeschylus's most turgid mannerisms. So in *The Clouds* the Unjust Logos or new education may be vicious but the old education, which was good enough for the heroes of Marathon and for the old days of plain living, is comically reduced to athletics, the singing of hymns and abstention from homosexuality – like a parody of the modern English public school system. *The Wasps* (422 BC) is first an attack on the litigiousness of old men; and secondly on the system of hiring paid jury-men. But by implication it satirises the political abuses of Cleon and his party, who control the legal system for their own ends. Unwilling to give up his feud, Aristophanes calls his law-crazy old man Philocleon or 'Cleon-lover' and his more sensible son 'Cleon-hater'. The next two plays turn away from political satire, perhaps because the war situation was now so desperate that free speech had become dangerous. Instead Aristophanes gives sophisticated versions of primitive saturnalian satire, seeking relief and escape from the horrors of war in creative fantasies. In *The Peace* (421 BC) a farmer climbs on a beetle to heaven, where the gods have washed their hands of men; there he builds a kind of New Jerusalem of peace, like the absurd and apocalyptic New Bloomusalem of Joyce's *Ulysses*. This theme is repeated with greater delicacy and charm in *The Birds* where the heroes, tired of Athens, build a Utopia called Nephelococcygia or 'Cloudcuckooborough'. He returns more openly to his pacifist propaganda in the *Lysistrata* (411 BC) which also illustrates the tradition of saturnalian satire very clearly. When the women of Athens gain control of the government by refusing to sleep with their husbands until they make peace, the fantastic reversal could not be more complete; for in reality women were disfranchised and had no more political influence than the slaves. In *Lysistrata*, with its happy and unashamed carnality, Aristophanes is also implying what other satirists from Chaucer to Henry Fielding have implied: that natural sexuality is better than violence, oppression and chicanery.

In the later plays the only major satirical theme is literature, and this is best treated in *The Frogs*. The god Dionysos, because he cannot find any good tragic poets alive, goes down to Hades to seek Euripides, who had died the year before this comedy was produced. The adventures of Dionysos and his slave Xanthias on their way through Hades are farcical and blasphemous: the gods, the gluttonous demigod Heracles, the myths of the Underworld and even the sacred Eleusinian mysteries themselves are handled with levity or grossness in this most outstanding of all travesties. The poetic competition of Euripides and Aeschylus is the first great example of literary satire, combining destructive literary criticism with accurate parodying of style.

Aristophanes is naive only in the construction of his plots. On a framework of primitive and folkloric ritual, which Cornford has discerned as underlying the Old Comedy, he presents a series of loosely connected episodes, with lyrical interludes by the Chorus: the result is more like a modern revue or burlesque show than a modern comedy. His lyricism is untranslatable, his topical allusions are often obscure, his parodies difficult to follow; but in every other respect Aristophanes is undated, as available to the modern reader as Ionesco or Brecht. It is a joyous criticism of life, made possible by the greatest audacity in claiming the right to free speech.

This freedom of speech, which is the essential condition of great satire, the Romans envied but dared not claim. Whatever may have been the situation under the Roman republic – and it is hard to judge that from the fragments of satire that remain – during the Civil War and under the Caesars open political satire was simply too dangerous. Satire is always a test of nerve, the nerve to get up in public and say something offensive about the powers that be. Faced with the risk of libel actions, exile, imprisonment or death, under an oppressive legal and political system, the Roman satirists lost their nerve. Persius (AD 34–62 under Nero) discusses this problem rather obliquely. In his First Satire he looks with admiration at the Greek Old Comedy and Aristophanes the 'Grand Old Man' (*praegrandi cum sene*), and he claims descent from the old republican satirist Lucilius 180–3 BC, who 'flayed our city' (*secuit urbem*, I, 114); but when he appears to be on the point of talking of politics he changes the subject to the corruption of literary taste, a far less dangerous topic. So in his Fifth Satire, which is on the subject of freedom: 'what we need is true liberty' (*libertate opus est*, V, 73), but this turns out to be the philosophic freedom of the stoic, the individual's escape from human bondage by freeing his mind from all passionate desires, and not political freedom; as one editor remarks, there is a remarkable 'avoidance of all reference to public life'[10]. Private folly and vice are far less dangerous topics, especially when the satirist avoids mentioning his bad examples by name and shifts his attacks to *types* of wicked or foolish men. When the topic of politics does come up, as it does in Juvenal's Tenth, 'The Vanity of Human Wishes', it is illustrated by safe examples out of past history, 'to point a moral or adorn a tale', like Hannibal or Sejanus. The reader could apply these examples to the contemporary scene if he wished; but the satirist could always plead that he was innocent of any subversive intent. Since the great days of classical Greece, the ideal conditions for political satire have not often obtained: but they did obtain in England from the late seventeenth century and in France in the sixteenth and from the early eighteenth century onwards, and favoured the genius of those masters of political criticism, Swift and Voltaire. This is not to say that democracy is a necessary condition: it will suffice if an autocratic regime is simply inefficient in suppressing its opponents, as the French *ancien régime* was in its last years. Even a censorship is no great handicap, provided that, as in Czarist Russia, there are ways of circumventing it. 'Satire which the censor understands deserves to be banned' wrote Karl Kraus: an author may even thrive on the ingenious labour of baffling the censor by means of irony, allegory or fable; witness *Gulliver's Travels*, Voltaire's *Lettres philosophiques* or the *Fairy Tales* of Saltykov-Shchedrin, the nineteenth-century Russian liberal. In the last centuries of the Roman empire, political satire was kept alive only by the 'mimes', the comic actors who improvised speeches in the middle of the plays. Because they were public favourites, they could get away with a good deal of free comment, as is described by the Roman historian Julius Capitolinus:

In the end, because of his strength in body and mind, he [the Emperor Maximinus, 235–8] came to regard himself as immortal. A certain mime is reported to have uttered these Greek verses in the theatre when he was present:

    He who cannot be killed by one is slain by many.
    The elephant is huge, but he can be killed;
    The lion is strong, but he can be killed;
    The tiger is strong, but he can be killed.
    Beware of many if you fear not individuals[11].

But when the Emperor asked his friends what the mimic fool had said they replied that he had sung only some ancient verses against harsh men; and the Emperor, being a Thracian and a barbarian, believed them.

Anti-clerical satire, which may appear to be merely social comment, is often a special type of political satire. It is to be distinguished from religious satire, the ridiculing of the gods or of supernatural beliefs, which appears in primitive trickster stories and saturnalia, and in many other irreverent parodies of things sacred. Anti-clericalism is political insofar as the clergy are in politics, as those of many religions have always been. As soon as a church emerges from the stage of being a small sect, it acquires

'Woman and Dominican Tilting' (late thirteenth century).
Both the woman and the friar are out of their proper sphere of life –
a common subject of medieval complaint – and the woman seems to be winning.
Probably anti-feminist and anti-clerical satire, but not intended too seriously.

wealth and power; and it tends to seek still more power, in order to
protect its property, suppress its enemies and further its good works.
The Catholic church in medieval Europe was a vast land-owning
corporation, which drew off the greater part of the continent's
wealth, largely for the building and maintenance of monasteries.
Even in seventeenth-century France the clergy had an income of
about half that of the entire nation, from rent tithes and fees; and
they had the monopoly not only of public worship but of marriage,
education and charities. The church tended to form a state within
the state, sometimes supporting the civil régime, if it guaranteed its
privileges, and sometimes engaged in more or less successful conflict
against it; and to a lesser degree this was true of England after the
Reformation. Toleration is not part of the traditional system of
Christianity. If you sincerely believe that the most important goal in
men's lives is the next world, and that only your own church can
guide the good to heaven and the wicked to hell, then you will not
easily concede any rights to other sects or churches, let alone other
religions. Hence the long history of persecution which is part of the

nightmare of European history, and has signalised the church's chief incursion into politics: the church's reliance on the civil power to carry out these persecutions has often led to its support of political tyranny. The church is not only a state within a state, it is a society within a society: and in the Catholic and Anglican churches this was a hierarchical society, with most of the wealth and power concentrated in the hands of the bishops and with a very large number of poor priests at the bottom of the pyramid. Because of the church's monopoly of education during the Middle Ages, most poets were either poor clerics themselves, or trained by poor clerics, and so the social tension within the church often found expression in literary satire.

The church was also the guardian of morality, and until recent centuries only a few sophisticated thinkers, with some knowledge of classical philosophy, have ever conceived of a system of ethics that could be at all independent of Christianity: these few included the thirteenth-century French satirist Jean de Meung, his disciple Geoffrey Chaucer, and the small body of free-thinkers who grew in strength only slowly from the Renaissance onwards. With these exceptions the ethical basis of all literature, including satire, was largely Christian until the Enlightenment. Now the official morality of the church was, and is, extremely austere; and has proved extremely difficult for the laity or the clergy to comply with in practice. The discrepancy between the ideal morality and the actual way of the world has always been greatest in the field of sexual morality; and as we shall see in the next chapter the tension caused by the church's extreme views on sex added a great deal to the vast tradition of anti-feminist satire. Yet the church's view on money and power are hardly less austere. The monastic orders, which made up a great part of the church, were vowed to poverty, yet obviously possessed great wealth, both corporately and among their individual members. And as for power, the church was committed to a wholly unworldly position, on the basis of the text 'My kingdom is not of this world'; yet it no less obviously had great power in the world, and was conspicuous in politics.

The political system of the Middle Ages, and of most other political systems in Europe up to the French Revolution were, judged by no very high standards, inefficient, autocratic and unjust. The vast mass of the population were miserably poor peasants; their rulers were usually oppressive and failed to provide the stability and peace of the Roman empire. Social discontent, manifested in peasants' revolts and in outbreaks of heresy, was endemic. Yet no one had any clear alternative to offer to the politics and economy of feudalism, and few had even any idea that it could ever be changed into anything more just or efficient. It is therefore not surprising that social discontent was often expressed indirectly through attacks on the church, which was the part of the system most open to attack, because its practice was most obviously at variance with its ideals. Political criticism, whether consciously or unconsciously, was often masked by anti-clerical polemic and satire. It has been noted that the same was broadly true even of early eighteenth-century France: the outbreak of attacks on the church's doctrines, wealth and intolerant practices, made by Voltaire and lesser Deists and freethinkers, preceded by many years the first open attacks on the political system made by conscious reformers and revolutionaries. Another factor was the need for discretion: anti-clerical criticism, though never wholly safe, tended to be a good deal less dangerous than open criticism of the civil powers.

The earliest political satire in the Middle Ages, which was also the first political satire in Europe since that of Lucilius under the Roman republic, was anti-clerical. It is to be found in a remarkable group of works in Latin, written in France, England and Germany during the twelfth century[12]. One the earliest is the *Ysengrimus* of Magister Nivardus. Written about 1150 in a learned and obscure style, it is a 'beast-epic', consisting of a number of beast-fables and stories about the wolf and the fox strung together with digressions on ecclesiastical affairs. Isengrim the wolf is made to speak like a monk, and is portrayed as endlessly grasping and also stupid: he is outwitted by Reynard the Fox, a trickster or picaresque character,

Russian china: one of a set of 'Bim and Bom' plates (1922).
The Czars granted to certain privileged aristocrats ('merry counsellors')
the right to make satirical political comment. This tradition of
free comment continued for some years after the Revolution of 1917:
'Bim and Bom' were two imaginary party members who did an
anti-government turn on the stage.

who is handled more sympathetically. Most of the Latin satires are much shorter and clearer than the *Ysengrimus:* they are songs in popular and rousing metres, probably intended for singing aloud. One of these metres and the songs themselves were known as Goliardic, after a mythical poet called 'Golias'. Most are anonymous, and have been attributed to the wandering scholars or 'vagantes', who moved across Europe from university to university, or took minor administrative posts in the service of the church. Their verse is truly international, using Latin, the medium common to educated Europeans; and it is the verse of bitter and disillusioned intellectuals, celebrating the forbidden pleasures of drunkenness, the dice and lechery. The medieval manuscript collections, of which the most famous is the *Carmina Burana* (found in the monastery of Benediktbeuern), have preserved many of these lyrics: some are straight love-songs, others are drinking-songs which parody religious texts, and still others are satires. The chief subjects of complaint are the papal curia, the bishops and the monks, who are accused of simony or the purchase of ecclesiastical positions, of avarice, gluttony and most of the other deadly sins. Particular targets were the cardinals and other officials of the papal court, who are accused of taking bribes to settle legal appeals. The chief satirical technique used in these works is parody or travesty of sacred texts from the liturgy and the Bible. A famous example is the *Evangelium secundum marcas argenti*, or 'The Gospel according to Saint Silver Mark', which says that in Rome only money talks. The *Apocalypsis Goliae* is a comic parody of the medieval dream-vision poem and of *Revelation:* Golias is carried off to heaven by an angel, where he reads in a book sealed with seven seals about the greed of the Pope and the vileness of the clergy. Many of the shorter poems are strewn with allusions, some blasphemous, to the gospels and to the offices. The splendidly cynical and sophisticated *Aestuans intrinsecus*, ascribed to 'the Arch-poet' (Archipoeta) is based throughout on the sacrament of confession; but instead of repenting of his sins, the author ironically rejoices in the pleasure of his sins, and hopes to make a good end:

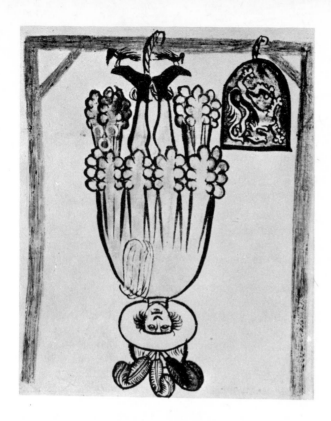

Mihi est propositum in taberna mori;
Vinum sit appositum morientis ori;
Ut dicant cum venerint angelorum chori,
'Deus sit propitius huic potatori'
(I propose to die in a tavern; may the wine be put to my dying mouth;
that the choruses of angels may say when they come for me,
'God be gracious to this drinker'–[for *peccatori*, sinner].

The satire in this candid and blasphemous poem is based on the
assumption that the world, and least of all the ecclesiastical world,
is no better than the poet; and he at least is no hypocrite. This is the
earliest example I know of satire written from the standpoint of
libertine shamelessness; and it is only excelled by Villon and Lord
Rochester. It can be inferred that the Archpoet was a German, but
almost nothing else is known about him or about the twelfth-

century Hugh (Hugo) of Orleans, known as 'Primas'. Primas's best satire is a macaronic poem, partly in French, about what happens when a monk becomes a bishop:

> *Or est venuz li moines* ad episcopium,
> pallidus et macer propter ieiunium ...

Now is the monk come to his bishopric, pale and thin after fasting; but his subsequent gluttony, avarice and lustfulness are described with crude relish. Some of the other poets are known by name, such as Philip the Chancellor (*c*. 1165–1236) and Walter of Chatillon (Gautier de Chatillon), who wrote in the late twelfth century. The latter's best-known work, which caused much indignation among orthodox churchmen, is his *Utar contra vitia carmine rebelli* – 'I shall use against vice a song of rebellion'. This is not only the most political of all the Latin satires, it is, after the Archpoet's Confession, the wittiest. In a string of elaborate word-plays, rhyme-patterns, and learned allusions, it attacks the hypo-crisy and avarice of the curia, with more cynicism than indignation.

As Raby and Jackson have pointed out, these men were not naive reformers, or indignant moralists: they were true literary satirists, treating the absurdity and hypocrisy of the church with detachment and humour: using their poetic imagination freely, they speak in literary terms for the amusement of their learned colleagues.

The earliest political satire which is both secular and written in a European language other than Latin dates from the same period as the Goliardic poems, that is, the late twelfth century. It is found among the songs of the Provençal troubadours, and is an outgrowth of the most advanced literature and the most sophisticated civilisa-tion that Europe had known since the fall of the Roman Empire. 'Provençal' then meant the whole southern half of France and the language spoken there, otherwise known as the 'langue d'oc' and by the troubadours themselves as 'latin'. This civilisation was based on the ancient Roman cities of Arles, Nîmes and Toulouse, and on several small feudal courts, where the nobility had learned more refinement in love and manners than their northern French

Reynard the Fox: 'Dropsical Fox cured by Weasel', from
Der Spiegel der Weisheit. The original story appears in a
thirteenth-century Latin composition attributed to
Bishop Cyrillus and for the most part is a monologue by
the weasel on the results of worldly excesses which
damage body and soul. British Museum, London.

neighbours. Nearly everything in the versification and the rhetoric of the European lyric and nearly everything in the cult of courtly love springs from twelfth-century Provençal song, perhaps even romantic love itself; the satirical literature, though less famous, is almost as original. The vehicle for courtly love was the 'canso' (French *chanson*) in elaborately rhymed stanzas, for satire the 'sirventés', written in similar verse-forms, and like the 'canso' meant to be sung in public. The 'sirventés' is not always satirical: according to the old Provençal authority on poetry, the *Leys d'Amors*, it is a form used 'for chastising the foolish and the bad, and in which one may, if one desires, speak of war'. The earliest master was Bertran de Born, a nobleman of Limousin who wrote his songs about 1180–94; they are not wholly satirical but they are passionately political; he speaks of war with enthusiasm, taking sides in the conflicts of Henry II of England and his sons. It is not surprising that Dante places him deep in the Inferno as a sower of discord: he evidently thought that De Born's songs, with their scathing references to cowardly princes and barons, had some real political influence. The best Provençal satire, however, appears somewhat later, in the last or Albigensian period, and is associated with the names of Peire Cardenal (1225 ?–72) and Guillem Figueira. These troubadours do not seem to have been Albigensian heretics, but like the heretics they were anti-clerical and bitterly anti-Roman. At this point in history politics and religion came together dramatically and tragically; the crusade encouraged by the Papacy and other violent persecutions not only extirpated the heresy but destroyed the whole of Provençal civilisation, including its literature, by the end of the thirteenth century. It was impossible for the later troubadours not to be involved in politics: and some responded with passion and eloquence, preserving in the heat of controversy the elegant techniques of their tradition. Guillem Figueira writes of Rome, the scourge of the world, criticising Papal politics at length. Other sirventés complain of the domination of the French, the cruelty of the Dominican Inquisitors who were suppressing the heretics, and the decline of their native land:

Cranach, 'Geburt des Papsttums' (Birth of the Papacy). The climax of
Lutheran propaganda was reached in 1545 with the album of broadsheets
known as the 'Representation of the Papacy' (Abbildung des Papsttums).
Here the Devil is giving birth to the whole Papacy, with the cardinals.
The Furies act as midwives, which means, according to Luther, that the child
is trained in wickedness and will curse and blaspheme like a madman.

A Catholic counter-attack to Protestant cartooning.
Schoen's print of the Devil playing Martin Luther
like a set of bagpipes (about 1535) shows a fine combination
of fantasy and precision. Gotha, Landesmuseum.

Der septen pfiff ich hin vnd her
Auß solchen Pfeiffen dicht vnd mer
Vil fabel Ceremn vnd Fantbasey
Ist verwundt auß vnd gar entzwey
Das ist mir leyd auch schwer vnd bang
Doch hoff ich es wer auch nit lang
Die weyl die welt so far trutz ist
Eintricklich durch sich vol arger list.

Ai! Toloza e Proensa
E la terra d'Argensa,
Bezers e Carcassey
Quo vos vi et quo'us vey!
(Alas! Toulouse, Provence, land of Argence, of Béziers and of
Carcassone, how I saw you once and how I see you now!)

Such themes receive their finest expression in the songs of Peire
Cardenal, a deeply religious man who attacked the greed of the
clergy, and especially of the monastic orders, with ferocity;

Li clerc si fan pastor
E son aucizedor
E semblan de sanctor;
(The clergy make themselves out as shepherds, but are nothing but
assassins, under cover of sanctity.)

The same themes and the same illustrations keep reappearing in
medieval poetry, for which originality was not considered necessary
or even desirable. But it is over two hundred years until we find
political and anti-clerical satire to equal the Provençal in boldness
and skill. The *Moral Fables* of Robert Henryson, a schoolmaster of
Dunfermline, Scotland, who wrote in the middle of the fifteenth
century, are remarkable for their humanity and their sympathy for
the oppressed peasantry. He takes beast-fables from the versions of
Aesop and stories of the trickster fox from the 'Renart' cycle,
retelling the traditional stories with delicate fantasy and naive
humour, and giving a delightful picture of the Scottish countryside;
but the 'moralitas' at the end of each fable makes it clear what his
real aim is. He represents the 'poor commons' or peasantry as
sheep, whom the unscrupulous lords, lawyers and higher clergy of
Scotland combine to fleece; and even gives allegorical accounts of
contemporary political scandals and abuses. Such courage and
independence of mind is rare in late medieval poetry, for the good
reason that most poets were attached to a court, like Chaucer and
William Dunbar, and were afraid to offend their royal patrons by
outspoken criticism.

Medieval political protest was necessarily indirect and inchoate, since the general level of political understanding was so low, and so few took part in the mysteries of state. Poets refrained from criticising the monarchical system, which was believed to be established with divine approval and support; and this conservative attitude, which is not conducive to political satire, persisted long after the Middle Ages – in England, for example, up to the middle of the seventeenth century, and in France until after the sun of Louis XIV had set. But before the rise of explicit and secularised political satire, there were two complicated movements in history which affected all literature, the Renaissance and the Reformation. I shall not try to sort out the tangled skeins of these vast events, considered singly or in their interconnections, but will mention only two aspects which were important for political satire: humanism and the wars of religion. By humanism is meant here the revival of classical studies in the fifteenth and early sixteenth centuries, and the consequent attempt to imitate Greek and Roman literature. This led to the rebirth of formal satire, the satire of morals, but had also an indirect effect on political satire, of the anti-clerical kind. The humanists had an educational programme, which included the writing of good Latin and the free pursuit of general knowledge, as opposed to the traditional education in scholasticism, churchman's Latin and obscure theological controversy. The early humanists had little sympathy with the Protestant reformers, but they were thrown into conflict with the established monopoly of education by the church and in particular by certain monastic orders; and this conflict sometimes led them into politics. That is the background of Rabelais' first book (1534): Gargantua receives two educations, the first a ridiculous course in medieval rubbish administered by Master Tubal Holofernes and the doctors of the Sorbonne, and then a proper humanist training in science, rhetoric and good manners. Humanist freedom of thought is, of course, the mainspring of two famous satires of this period, Erasmus's *Encomium Moriae* ('Praise of Folly,' 1511) and the *Utopia* of his friend Sir Thomas More (1516). But the effect of humanism on political satire is shown more clearly in a once-famous work that appeared in 1515, the *Epistolae Obscurorum Virorum* ('Letters of Obscure Men')[13]. In 1507 one Johann Pfefferkorn, a converted Jew who was backed by the Dominicans of Cologne, began to write anti-semitic propaganda, which helped to cause within two years a serious persecution of the Jews in Germany. Since this persecution meant a serious hindrance to the new study of Hebrew by the humanists, Pfefferkorn was opposed by the distinguished scholar Johann Reuchlin; a pamphlet war followed, in which the enemy sides were broadly the humanists and the Dominicans; Reuchlin found himself summoned by the Inquisition, his case taken to Rome, and finally one of his works condemned by the Sorbonne with the approval of Pope Leo x. In the next year the *Epistolae Obscurorum Virorum* was published in Reuchlin's defence; the authorship is unknown but has been attributed to members of a circle of enlightened humanists at Erfurt. It pretends to be a set of letters written to Ortwin Gratius (von Graes), who was suspected of being Pfefferkorn's ghost-writer and was a notorious opponent of the new learning, by a number of nonentities. The supposed authors are zealous in the case of Pfefferkorn and the Dominicans, but reveal themselves to be obscure in every sense, ignorant, gluttonous and lecherous; every kind of bad Latin is parodied, in prose and verse, while canon law and scholastic theology are ludicrously burlesqued. The humour is rather naive and brutal, but the work is imaginative enough to be considered true literary satire, as well as an effective instrument in ecclesiastical politics.

From the moment when Luther nailed a *printed* copy of his *Theses* to the door of Wittenberg church, the Reformation spread by means of the printed word, and it is doubtful if it could have spread otherwise. All the early reformers were vigorous pamphleteers, and masters of abuse, lampooning and crude satirical techniques. Their violence and lack of taste is sometimes remarkable: Théodore de Bèze, who was also a distinguished humanist, was not above writing verses on an enemy's losing his nose from syphilis:

> Messire Pierre, estonné
> De voir son nez boutonné
> Prest a tomber, par fortune,
> De la verole importune ...[14]

They supported the written word with satirical woodcuts printed on cheap broadsheets: thus Luther commissioned Cranach to make obscene drawings of the Pope. But out of the welter of pamphlets which poured out from Lutheran, Calvinist and Roman Catholic presses during the Reformation and the wars of religion that devastated Europe in the sixteenth and early seventeenth centuries, there are very few that deserve to be called literary satire. The same is true of the English Puritans, who carried on the spirit of the early reformers: even the pamphlets of 'Martin Marprelate' possess little more than historical interest. This illustrates the political satirist's dilemma: unless he is committed to a fairly extreme position, he will not write satire; but unless his outlook is given perspective and breadth by something outside his cause – by humanism, by a sense of history or by liberalism – he is unlikely to produce literature. The sectarian spirit is hostile to the freedom which creative satire requires. There are, however, three works that stand out of the confused and bloody history of late sixteenth-century France, Ronsard's *Remonstrance*, D'Aubigny's *Les Tragiques*, and *La Satire Ménippée*, all of which have added to the dignity of political satire. Ronsard was an orthodox Roman Catholic, and a sincere royalist: he warmly supported Catherine de Médicis and the young Charles IX against the Huguenot party. But his *Remonstrance au peuple de France*, a long poem published in 1562, contains besides sectarian polemic an eloquent appeal to the church and the nobility to put their own houses in order, a broad view of the miseries of France and of Christendom, and a deep concern for the peace of his country. Ronsard's graceful natural and forceful language is not equalled by any other satirist of his period, and *Les Tragiques* is clumsy and rough by comparison. Yet Agrippa d'Aubigny (1552–1630) has a more impressive political imagination. He was a humanist and a man of action, soldier and politician who fought for the Protestant cause; like other fighting Protestants he looked for inspiration in the Old Testament, which he read in Hebrew. *Les Tragiques*, written intermittently between 1577 and 1590, is in part an epic of the Huguenot warriors and martyrs, in the spirit of Milton's sonnet, 'Avenge, O Lord, thy slaughtered saints'; and indeed God is shown as preparing His vengeance on the persecutors. It combines detailed descriptions of recent history with a cosmic and biblical setting. The most moving passages describe the atrocities which D'Aubigny saw during his campaigns, like the murdered family in the section called 'Misères', and these are beyond satire. Yet embedded in this unclassifiable work there are passages of pure satire, which show a firm grasp of political realities and a passionate concern for justice. D'Aubigny contrasts the just king with the unjust tyrant, of which the most evil example is Catherine de Médicis, presented as a reincarnation of Jezebel; and with harsh realism and even grossness attacks the 'mignons' or homosexual favourites. It is an admirable recreation of the disgusted tone of Juvenal; but D'Aubigny will suddenly switch to the mood of an Old Testament prophet, from satire to apocalypse. It is the combination of realism, epic sweep and 'sombre lyrisme' that makes D'Aubigny one of the greatest of political satirists.

The third outstanding work of this period is *La Satire Ménippée*. Published in 1594, it is a parody of the 'Etats généraux' held in the previous year, and an attack on the 'Ligue' or ultra-Catholic party, Like the *Epistolae Obscurorum Virorum*, it was published anonymously, written by a group of authors (Leroy, Gillot, Pithou, Nicholas Rapin and others). It shows humanist inspiration, and takes a moderate point of view. Although it ridicules the fanaticism of the Ligueurs, the monks and the reactionary doctors of the Sorbonne, together with their Spanish and Roman allies, it is free from the asperities of Protestant sectarianism: it expresses the policy of the 'Politiques' or middle-of-the-road Catholics, who put the peace and prosperity of France above embattled religion – and who with the accession of Henri IV ultimately prevailed. What is remarkable is that wild fantasy is united with noble indignation, in the

Hieronymous Bosch, *The Ship of Fools*, c. 1500.
The painting may have been influenced by
Sebastian Brant's famous poem ('Narrenschiff') but
much of the satire and symbolism remains obscure.

nearest approach to Aristophanes that had appeared in European literature. The work has in fact a dramatic structure: the Ligueurs appear as charlatans selling their political quack-medicines, next in a ludicrous and farcical procession, and finally their leaders make speeches which travesty the policies of their party. The satirical technique is the simple and effective one of naive self-revelation: the characters cannot help exposing their true intentions, and passing judgment on themselves. So M. le Lieutenant:

Et, par notre bonne diligence, nous avons fait que ce Royaume, qui n'était qu'un volupteux jardin de tout plaisir et abondance, est devenu un grand et ample cimitière universel, plein de force belles croix peintes, bières, potences, et gibets.
(And by our fine activity we have brought it about that this Kingdom, which was once but a delicious garden of every pleasure and abundance, has become a spacious universal cemetery, full of painted crosses, biers, gallows and gibbets.)

The language is Rabelaisian, full of puns, plays on words and verbs of physical movement ('Ledit sieur Recteur suait, tempêtait, écumait, et frappait du pied'). And as in Rabelais, whom the authors admired, the language of the *Ménippée* suddenly shifts from gross absurdity to dignified classical rhetoric.

Like the best of satire, the *Ménippée* is at once very funny and very serious: it makes an uproarious saturnalian festival out of political crime and folly, without forgetting their bitter reality.

For all its sophistication of attitude and style, the *Satire Ménippée* still belongs to the pre-modern world of politics, in which the traditional structure of society, and especially kingship, was seen as part of a divinely established hierarchy; and in which politics, morality and religious belief were taken as inseparable. A new kind of political satire, which could make clearer distinctions between measures and men, between religious belief and practical matters of statecraft, required a considerable degree of secularisation in political thought. Such a revolution began with Machiavelli, and reached its first climax in the *Leviathan* of Thomas Hobbes (1651):

Thomas Hobbes is the most satirical of the
English philosophers. This detail from the frontispiece of his
Leviathan (1651), an allegory of the sovereign power,
catches something of his mocking wit.

it involved a realistic and quasi-scientific study of political and legal
systems, and of human nature. In particular it helped to discredit
the time-honoured view that kings were kings by divine right, and
encouraged the discussion of political reform on grounds of logic
and expediency. This was part of the rationalist, free-thinking
movement known as the Enlightenment, which supplied the background to literature for two centuries, and affected the outlook of
every satirist. Although Dryden and Rochester took much directly
from Hobbes, it must not be supposed that a change in the intellectual climate was enough to account for the new political satire. It
required other new conditions for its flourishing: a wide experience
of political change, the interest of a large public in home and
foreign policy, general discontent and disillusionment, and, most
important, some freedom of speech. These conditions were

Much political satire of the Restoration openly or explicitly attacked the extreme monarchist views of the period, such as those set out in Edward Gee's *Divine Right*. Other satire, including John Dryden's *Absalom and Achitophel*, defended the claims of the Stuart monarchy.

fulfilled, for the first time, since the peak of ancient Athens, in England of the Restoration period, and the golden age of English political satire began about 1665. It could not have begun much earlier, because of the relative lack of freedom under Charles I and Cromwell; although there was a first wave of satire from about 1640, the conditions of the Civil War and the Commonwealth were more favourable to controversial propaganda than to literary satire. Samuel Butler, it is true, deals with the politics and religion of this period in his *Hudibras*, a mock-heroic poem which burlesques the Cromwellian Puritans; published in part in 1663, this was the first Restoration satire which shows a true literary imagination. This, however, was satire after the event, rather than an active participation in the political struggle: Butler was safe in attacking a defeated enemy. The best seventeenth and early eighteenth-century

satires, on the other hand, were not only creative works of literature, but were written in immediate response to current political
situations, when something serious was at stake. From Marvell's
Instructions to a Painter through Dryden's *Absalom and Achitophel*
to Swift's *Drapier's Letters* and even to *The Candidate* of Charles
Churchill (1764), English Augustan satire gains its bite and urgency
from its immediate involvement in public affairs; and its high
quality from the fact that almost every writer of talent was engaged
in political strife. The sheer volume of this literature is astonishing:
from 1660 to 1714 alone more than 3,000 pieces of satirical verse
have survived, printed in various collections which were usually
called *Poems on Affairs of State*[15]: they run from major mock-
heroic narratives like Dryden's down to scurrilous broadside
ballads.

Immediately after the Restoration, the Roundheads were dis-
credited and Charles ii was generally popular at first. The change
began when the king's vacillation and the weakness of his government were exposed in the wars with the Dutch. The next stage was
marked by the revolt against Charles's subservience to France, and
by the movement to prevent his brother James, a Roman Catholic,
from succeeding to the throne. The opposition to his Catholicism
was based not so much on doctrinal grounds as on an anti-French
foreign policy. At this point the Whig and Tory groupings came
into being: they were not at first political parties in anything like
the modern sense, but loose coalitions of forces inside and outside
parliament. The Whigs consisted of an alliance between the great
territorial magnates and the bourgeoisie of London, and were in
favour of limiting the powers of the monarchy; the Tories were
based on the lesser gentry and the established church and tended to
be uncritically royalist. These words came to have rather different
meanings in the next generation, but until 1760 they represented a
real division in English public life and political literature. The third
stage was the opposition to James ii's authoritarian policies at home
as well as his pro-French foreign policy, an opposition which
culminated in the revolution of 1688. This revolution was not made

for the sake of 'democracy', but it did have the effect of ensuring certain civil liberties, among them freedom of publication. Under Charles II and James there had been in theory very little such freedom, and under the Licensing Act subversive writers were liable to and sometimes received severe penalties. The government, however, was rarely strong enough to enforce the law strictly, and although many satirists were forced to publish anonymously or to circulate their work in manuscript, they could still reach a wide public. It was a situation not unlike that which exists today in some Iron Curtain countries. After 1689 many of these surreptitious writings appeared in print, with their authors' names, for the first time. Thereafter there was always the risk of prosecution for sedition or libel, but open satire was able to take its place in public life.

The greatest satirist of the first period is Andrew Marvell, who had been a moderate Cromwellian and remained member of parliament for Hull. The occasion for his best work was the naval war with the Dutch 1665–7, which was the first event to damage the king's popularity. To celebrate an English victory off Lowestoft, Edmund Waller wrote in 1665 *Instructions to a Painter*, an inflated piece of panegyric, full of baroque heroics, in which the poet tells an imaginary painter how to paint the details of the naval action. This was soon parodied in *The Second Advice to a Painter*, probably by Marvell, which ridicules Waller's style and adds many details that Waller suppressed about the mismanagement of the campaign, and scathing comments on the admirals. This parody was highly popular and followed by a series of 'Advices' of which the most brilliant is *The Last Instructions to a Painter*, almost certainly by Marvell, describing the disaster of 1667, when the Dutch fleet sailed up the Thames, and the governmental scandals that caused it.

Most satires have tended to be written against the government, but the greatest of the second phase of the Restoration, John Dryden's *Absalom and Achitophel*, is a counter-attack. The Whigs, who had grown in strength in the 1670s, were trying to force through parliament a bill to exclude Roman Catholics from the throne; this was aimed at the legitimate heir, the future James II, whom they hoped to replace by Charles's illegitimate son, the Protestant Duke of Monmouth. The Earl of Shaftesbury, the Whig leader, was in 1681 charged with high treason; *Absalom* was written at the king's invitation and published just before Shaftesbury's arraignment, and was therefore intended to secure his conviction and possible execution. In fact it failed to do so, but we need to remember the grim realities behind Dryden's gay and witty couplets. The poem is also an expression of Dryden's sincere loyalty to his royal master, and of his desire for social peace and order, which he saw as seriously threatened. It is a triumph because of his choice of theme and his mastery of tone. He found a perfect parallel in the saga of the revolt against King David, which fitted beautifully in a dozen places — and is incidentally the best-written and shrewdest political narrative in the Bible. Dryden saw that it was no use writing fulsome panegyric of Charles at this stage: the king's private life was too well known to friend and enemy. He therefore portrays him as the great lover David, in a tolerant man-of-the-world spirit, which would bring the readers round to Charles's side, and make them feel that a few sexual misdemeanours were not to be weighed against the political crimes of the Whigs. This was his first masterstroke of propaganda:

> In pious times, 'ere Priest-craft did begin,
> Before *Polygamy* was made a Sin;
> When Man on many multipli'd his kind,
> Ere one to one was cursedly confin'd,
> When Nature prompted and no Law deni'd
> Promiscuous Use of Concubine and Bride;
> Then *Israel's* Monarch, after Heaven's own heart,
> His vigorous warmth did, variously, impart
> To Wives and Slaves; And, wide as his Command,
> Scatter'd his Maker's Image through the Land.

There is a secondary plot, besides the parallel with Absalom's revolt: the young Monmouth is tempted by the satanic Shaftesbury, an arch-rebel against authority. This is the theme of *Paradise Lost*, which Dryden deliberately parodies in his mock-heroic, even in places with mock-Miltonic language: 'Him staggering so when hell's dire agent found'. The style shifts throughout from the conversational to the high-flown rhetorical, from coarse idiomatic abuse to gentlemanly raillery. It seems to be an essential of good satire that it possess no single fixed style; it works by comparisons and contrasts, and these demand an ever-changing mimicry, like that of a comedian's monologue. Of this fluid style Dryden is the greatest master in verse, as Swift is in prose.

The greatest strength of *Absalom* lies in the portraits or 'characters' of the rebels, from the monstrous yet truly heroic Shaftesbury down to Shimei, the Whig Lord Mayor Bethel, who as Dryden notes with cold contempt

> Did wisely from expensive Sins refrain,
> And never broke the Sabbath, but for Gain.

In these portraits Dryden is at his most Juvenalian, it has been said; and it is true that he catches Juvenal's declamatory manner, and note of high indignation; it is also true that like Juvenal he works in an occasional gratuitous indecency, as when he writes of one who was both very thin and very lecherous:

> Can dry bones live? or skeletons produce
> The vital warmth of cuckoldizing juice?
> Slim Phaleg could, and at the table fed
> Return'd the grateful product to the bed.

But unlike Juvenal Dryden is never academic: he gives a sense of being near the heart of political affairs, engaged in public and responsible debate. He works up to a general statement of his philosophy, which is a rational and intelligent defence of conservatism, based on Hobbes's theory of the contract made between the sovereign and the people.

> If they may Give and Take when e'r they please,
> Not Kings alone (the Godhead's Images)
> But Government itself at length must fall
> To Natures state, where all have Right to all.

> Yet, grant our Lords the People, Kings can make,
> What prudent men a settled Throne would shake?
> For whatso'er their Sufferings were before,
> That Change they Covet makes them suffer more.
> All other Errors but disturb a State;
> But Innovation is the Blow of Fate.

The satire of the third phase, when the opposition to James II turned into open revolt, is best represented by the satirical ballads. Ballads of all kinds, printed cheaply on single sheets ('broadsides') and sung to old tunes, had a huge circulation in the seventeenth century. Before the first newspapers they were the main channel for mass journalism. Some came out of folklore, others were written by obscure hacks, but still others were written by distinguished poets for amusement – and for propaganda. Andrew Marvell in particular was a master of the satirical ballad, and the form was still being used brilliantly by Swift and Gay in the 1720s, and by others even later. The ballads were sung everywhere in streets and taverns, and could easily escape the censorship; there were also short ballad-like poems which would be nailed to the victims' doors: one such in *Poems on State-Affairs* is titled 'On Easter-Day 87, this was found fixt the King's Chappel-Door'. Some of the Restoration ballads are loyal and anti-Whig, but many contain crude lampoons on Charles, James and their least popular ministers, like the infamous Judge Jeffreys, who in a ballad of 1688 is made to boast to his wife:

> From an Ignorant Judge I was call'd by the King
> To the Chequer-Court, 'Tis a wonderful thing,
> Of which in short time the whole Nation did ring.

> CHORUS *This it is to be Learned and Witty*

> He had my Opinion, that 'twas in his Power
> To destroy all the Laws in less than an hour,
> For which I may chance to be sent to the *Tower*.

> CHORUS *This it is etc.*[16]

As royal prestige and authority began to disintegrate, the ballads became more effective in swinging popular opinion: the most famous song of the Glorious Revolution was perhaps the most influential ever written. *Lilliburlero* was said to have been written by the Earl of Wharton, who had 'sung a King out of three kingdoms'. One Irishman congratulates another on the coming triumph of Popery and the suppression of the Protestants: thus James's cause was identified with the barbarous enemies of England, as the Irish appeared in the eyes of nearly all Englishmen, and the Whig cause with constitutional freedom.

> But if Dispence do come from de Pope
> Lilli Burlero Bullen a-la,
> Weel hang *Magna Carta* and demselves in a Rope,
> Lili etc.

The immediate aftermath of the Revolution was a long and successful war with France, and a long period of Whig dominance in the Government. English politics became more mature, as the rudiments of Cabinet government and party groupings developed; and consequently political satire became more philosophical and responsible. The best comes from the opposition, from Swift, Pope, Gay and their circle, who are generally known as the Tory satirists – though some could more accurately be called dissident Whigs. Jonathan Swift, who had a wide experience of practical politics and had thought much on the theory of government, was the seminal mind of this group; his immense genius inspired two of the greatest satires in English, Pope's *Dunciad* and *The Beggar's Opera* by John Gay. Their main targets were first the war with France, and later the long-continued leadership of Sir Robert Walpole, who is directly lampooned as Flimnap in *Gulliver's Travels* and as Peachum in *The Beggar's Opera*. Pope is less openly political, but his self-appointed task was to provide philosophical support for his Tory friends, to state in poetic terms the general principles underlying their opposition to Whig 'corruption'. Paradoxically, just as political satire reached its greatest maturity in the hands of these

Hogarth: 'Some of the Principal Inhabitants of Y^e Moon as they Were Perfectly Discover'd by a Telescope brought to ye Greatest Perfection since ye last Eclipse, Exactly Engraved from the Objects, whereby y^e Curious may Guess at their Religion, Manners &c'. (About 1750). Royalty, episcopacy and law are satirised by being reduced to inanimate symbols. This kind of allegory has become a standard device of political cartoonists.

Some of the Principal Inhabitants of y^e MOON, as they Were Perfectly Discover'd by a Telescope brought to y^e Greatest Perfection since y^e last Eclipse; Exactly Engraved from the Objects, whereby y^e Curious may Guess at their Religion, Manners, &c.

Price Six Pence

great writers, it began to lose its practical effectiveness. Swift had been highly successful as a propagandist in his *Conduct of the Allies*, which more by persuasive argument than by satire had helped to win over the House of Commons to accepting the Tory Peace of Utrecht in 1713; and again in his *Drapier's Letters*, in which he took up the cause of the Irish. Single-handed he defeated the English government over a matter of currency reform, and became a hero of the dissident Dubliners: this was a reversion to the cruder methods of Restoration satire, including the satirical ballad, and worked very well in a revolutionary situation. But his masterpiece, *Gulliver's Travels*, had no perceptible influence on the political scene. Prime Minister Walpole was not in the slightest shaken, although readers ever since have been, as well as delighted and baffled, by this explosion of wit and misanthropy. *Gulliver* is the supreme example of a work of close and detailed political reference, which nevertheless failed as immediate political satire.

When the French translator apologised for omitting several passages not suitable for France, Swift replied:

If the volumes of Gulliver were designed only for the British Isles, that traveller ought to pass for a very contemptible writer. The same vices and the same follies reign everywhere; at least in the civilized countries of Europe: and the author who writes only for one city, one province, one kingdom or even one age, does not deserve to be read, let alone translated.

The phrase about vices and follies gives us a key to the structure. Book I (Lilliput) is about folly, shown in bad government: the Lilliputians have a few virtues, and are even Utopian at one point. Book II (Brobdingnag) is an exposition of good government: in contrast to the amiable and sensible giants, mankind is seen as petty and vicious. Book III returns to folly: the Laputans have almost entirely lost their wits in the pursuit of scientific speculation. The climax is reached in Book IV: the Houyhnhnms represent virtue, the Yahoos total depravity. They are the poles of behaviour that the human race is capable of attaining.

Into this framework Swift inserted many detailed references to the England of his day. Book I is a close allegory of the political events of the last years of Queen Anne's reign and the first years of George I's. This allegory is carefully disguised and with good reason. In the 1720s it was dangerous to attack prominent men and especially royalty in too open a manner; with the publication of the *Drapier's Letters* Swift had already risked losing his liberty. Swift sailed as close to the wind as he dared in depicting home politics as a struggle between High Heels and Low Heels, religious controversy as a dispute about the right end to break an egg. Blefuscu or France supports the Bigendian or Roman Catholic exiles; the heir to the throne has a tendency to High Heels, just as the Prince of Wales favoured the Opposition; Flimnap-Walpole capers along the tightrope of political jobbery. These identifications are obvious, but in the figure of Gulliver there is a deeper allegory. Except for the moment when he puts out the fire, Gulliver is not Swift but Swift's friend Bolingbroke, and sometimes an amalgam of Bolingbroke and Harley. The story is taken to 1714, when Bolingbroke was threatened with impeachment for treasonable correspondence with the Pretender and fled to France. The point of this interpretation is that Swift was not the complete egoist that some critics have seen in him: rather than expressing his many personal disappointments in a mood of self-pity, he is sending a message of loyalty to his friends in trouble. Brobdingnag is largely a political utopia – England as it might have been if the Tories had remained in power. Swift is being realistic here, implying that if Englishmen could not become Houyhnhnms they could at least be like the Brobdingnagians, who though rather repulsive when you look at them too closely are basically sound in their politics. Swift took politics to be an essential part of the good life, and venerated the memory of his patron Temple, who may be represented in the King of Brobdingnag. The king is also a Tory mouthpiece: among the things he denounces, a 'mercenary standing army in the midst of peace, and among a free people' and the national debt, were common objects of Tory attack. But the basis of the Brobdingnagian state is the humanist principle 'that whoever could make two Ears of Corn, or

Gulliver taking leave of his
Houyhnhnm master: the human
animal prostrates himself before
the godlike horse. From a
French translation published
in Paris in 1822.

two Blades of Grass grow upon a Spot of Ground where only one grew before, would deserve better of mankind and do more essential Service to his Country, than the whole Race of Politicians put together', which is still true today.

The third voyage was written last of the four, and is the least effective as satire or imaginative creation. Laputa, the Flying Island, is the court and government of George I, which keeps England and Ireland in subjection. The revolt of Lindalino (Dublin) was an incident so dangerously topical that it was suppressed in the early editions. The Laputans fail to crush this revolt because they are afraid of the combustible fuel directed at the island's adamantine bottom: a direct allegory of Swift's *Drapier's Letters*, by which he had just achieved a victory over the English government. The Laputans are typically English in their love of political intrigue (as Swift wrote to Stella from London, 'the rabble here are much more inquisitive in politics than (they are) in Ireland') and in their love of music, a reference to the keen dispute between the supporters of Italian opera and of Handel in the 1720s. The centre-piece of the satire is the Academy of Projectors, which is partly directed at the scientists of the Royal Society and of the Dublin Philosophical Society. It must not be assumed that Swift was completely philistine about science: as we have seen, he admired the practical inventor who could grow two ears of corn where one grew before, which is in accordance with the Baconian aims of the Royal Society. He certainly knew more about science than most literary men have done, as is shown by his close parody of scientific papers, based on careful reading of the *Transactions* of the Royal Society. But he considered scientific speculation as secondary to the main business of man upon earth, which is right conduct. There were less worthy reasons for his attitude: he saw the great Newton mainly as a Whig politician who had been called in by the Government for support over 'Wood's Halfpence', and he resented the lack of patronage now given to men of letters, as compared with the great days of Queen Anne. Finally 'projector' meant not so much a scientist, for which the usual eighteenth-century word was 'virtuoso' but a promoter of get-rich-quick schemes. Swift is also satirising the speculative financial projects which were floated in large numbers in the six years before 1720, when the greatest of them, the South Sea Bubble, burst.

Book IV, in which the rational horses appear, is still concerned with politics, although the argument has moved from the particular to the general. Whereas Book II contains a stock Tory attack on standing armies, Swift now offers a general indictment of war (chapter 5) in absolute terms. Against the complacent ideas about colonisation held in his time and optimistically expressed by Defoe, Swift opposes his perception of the naked truth (chapter 12) in his most startling reductive language:

For instance, a Crew of Pyrates are driven by a Storm they know not whither; at length a Boy discovers Land from the Top-mast; they go on Shore to rob and plunder; they see an harmless People, are entertained with Kindness, they give the Country a new Name, they take formal Possession of it for the King, they set up a rotten Plank or a Stone for a Memorial, they murder two or three Dozen of the Natives, bring away a Couple more by Force for a Sample, return home, and get their Pardon. Here commences a new Dominion acquired with a Title by *Divine Right*. Ships are sent out with the first Opportunity; the Natives driven out or destroyed, the Princes tortured to discover their Gold; a free Licence given to all Acts of Inhumanity and Lust; the Earth reeking with the Blood of its Inhabitants; and this execrable Crew of Butchers employed in so pious an Expedition, is a modern Colony sent to convert and civilize an idolatrous and barbarous People.

Swift has moved from opposition to particular Governments to the apparently total rejection of all governments; and that is the doctrine of anarchism. It is striking that the philosophical anarchist William Godwin quotes Book IV of *Gulliver's Travels* with approval, in support of his argument that all political institutions are totally corrupt; and it is paradoxical that the great Tory High-churchman should have reached so subversive a position. His vision was one which no one could take seriously in the eighteenth or nineteenth centuries, but one which finally came true in the concentration camps of thirty years ago. His mistake was to attack the wrong age.

The case of Swift has been considered in some detail because he was the last major English satirist to be in the political firing line. His immediate follower was John Gay, whom he inspired to write *The Beggar's Opera* (1728). This continued the attack of the Tory opposition on prime minister Walpole, who is represented as Peachum, the receiver of stolen goods and betrayer of members of his gang to the magistrates. The main satiric device of this astonishingly witty play is, as William Empson has pointed out, a variety of pastoral: just as the shepherds of traditional pastoral speak an elegant poetic diction, so Gay's criminals speak the polite language of the court and parliament. This has the effect of reducing Walpole and his associates to the level of the underworld, and Whig politics to that of bribery and corruption. But although Gay caricatured the sordid side of Walpole in Peachum, he could not help feeling some admiration for the dashing confident qualities of the great man; he portrayed these in the highwayman Captain Macheath, who was to become the romantic hero of the age. Walpole joined in the applause at the theatre and was himself cheered by the audience for his sportsmanship. The play had an immediate success and probably could not have been suppressed without causing so much popular discontent that the Government's prestige would have suffered. But Gay's sequel *Polly* (1729) was prohibited in the theatre by the Lord Chamberlain, supposedly on the command of Walpole, though its publication was allowed and was highly profitable. The appeal of *The Beggar's Opera* is permanent, and goes well beyond topical satire: the songs express to perfection the gallantry and freedom of the highwayman's way of life, and an anarchist and romantic spirit is held in control by ironic contempt. Its poetic vitality makes it far superior to the satiric novel *Jonathan Wild* (1743) in which Henry Fielding used the same satiric device of comparing the 'great men' of politics to a famous criminal. Fielding's irony is too long sustained, and the story is not redeemed from a certain monotony by his muscular style. He would have preferred to use the stage for his political satire, but his play *Pasquin* hastened the passing of the Licensing Act in 1735; this not only ended Fielding's dramatic career but effectively killed off the whole genre of English dramatic satire for the time being. In the quiet interval of the 1740s and 50s, when there were no serious controversies at home, political satire died down; but as soon as a new round of conflict began in the 1760s it had a brief and lively revival. It is difficult today to see what the real issues were behind the apparently trivial campaigns of the demagogue John Wilkes. It must be assumed that there was a serious crisis of social discontent, which found obscure and violent expression in Wilkes's attacks on the prime minister and in the rioting of his supporters. At once a satirist appeared to support Wilkes's cause, his dissolute friend the Reverend Charles Churchill, who wrote a number of coarse and vigorous poems in the last three years of his life, as well as most of Wilkes's periodical *The North Briton*. Churchill attacked the Scots in the *Prophecy of Famine*, and Wilkes's enemies in the House of Commons in *The Duellist*. When Hogarth published a famous caricature of 'that devil Wilkes', Churchill counter-attacked in *An Epistle to William Hogarth*. There is no finesse and no integrity of principle about Churchill; but there is a sense of immediacy and involvement in the battle of the day that makes him a worthy representative of a great English tradition.

This tradition was revived for the last time by the Radicals of the Romantic period. Byron looked back in admiration to Dryden and Pope, and used the medium perfected by these masters to pour aristocratic scorn on the reactionary politicians and poets of his day, first of all in *English Bards and Scotch Reviewers* (1809). When Byron writes as a satirist he shows a freedom of mind and energy which sweeps away his victims like a tempest. His political position was a simple one: a generous radicalism, as shown in his support for the Luddite weavers in their revolt and for the Greek revolutionary movement, and for what he called

> ... plain, sworn, downright detestation
> Of every despotism in every nation.

His most sustained and powerful satire is *A Vision of Judgment*

'The Lion and the Unicorn fighting for the Crown': the title
of George Cruikshank's cartoon is taken from a rhyme about the
Royal Arms: the subject is Napoleon and King George III
just before Waterloo. The most tense moments in British history
were relieved by a flood of such prints commenting with
irreverent patriotism on the affairs of the day.

(1822), where the spirit of George III stands for everything that is
callous and restrictive about the 'stupid old system'. But there is
even finer incidental satire scattered throughout *Don Juan* (left
incomplete at his death in 1824). With perfect confidence and good
humour he ridicules the pretensions of reactionary Europe of the
post-Napoleonic era, reducing the dead world of rank and wealth
to absurdity by the absurd juxtaposition of his rhymes. In this
unclassifiable story, half romance and half realistic autobiography,
Byron reaches the ultimate point of the satirist's freedom of
speech, the absolute ability to speak his mind on every topic. His
friend Shelley, a much greater lyric poet, was potentially a fine
satirist in the same cause. His political outlook was anarchistic, and
philosophical anarchism is too idealist a doctrine for a satirist's
involvement with the sordid world of politics; but he entered the
battle gaily and wittily in *Oedipus Tyrannus or Swellfoot the Tyrant*
(1820), an attack on George III, and wrote the most sombre
invective in English poetry in *Lines written during the Castlereagh
Administration* (1819). It was Shelley who voiced his doubts about
the genre itself in *Fragment of a Satire on Satire* (1820):

> If Satire's scourge could wake the slumbering hounds
> Of Conscience, or erase the deeper wounds,
> The leprous scars of callous Infamy.
> If it could make the present not to be,
> Or charm the dark past never to have been,
> Or turn regret to hope; who that has seen
> What Southey is and was, would not exclaim
> 'Lash on!' . . .

But these things political satire cannot do. Satire can survey the
world, in Dr Johnson's words, 'from China to Peru', – both of
which countries suffer at the moment from odious political evils –
but it cannot cure the world. At best it can sharpen our perceptions
and get rid of false values. Political satire is in part an entertainment
at the expense both of the rulers and the ruled, and sometimes

such an entertainment is in bad taste or at least inappropriate.

The disillusionment of the post-Napoleonic period produced some of the finest political satire in European literature. In Byron, in Stendhal's novel *The Red and the Black*, as in the cartoons of Daumier, one sees variants of the same attitude, amused disgust at the absurdities of reaction, disdain for the new bourgeois ethos, and attachment to a romantic ideal of liberty. The greatest German satire of the period is that of Heinrich Heine (1797–1856). A converted Jew, he shows the same ambiguity towards Judaism as he does towards Germany: a sentimental affection combined with a passionate desire to be free from the bonds of religion and patriotism. Heine is the epitome of the satirist's ideal of free comment: he never hesitates to press his shockingly frank judgments on politics, religion and literary dunces to the utmost limit. In trouble with the public censor throughout his career, and irritated by the scruffiness of German life, he chose the joys and pains of exile; he belonged to the revolutionary left wing of the democratic movement, yet preserved his independence of judgment. Heine shares the great satirist's ability to construct marvellous fantasies and to insert in them powerful images of the real world of political man, to combine imaginative vision with direct insult. It is perhaps surprising that with his immense gifts he did not write more pure satire in verse. In *Atta Troll*, the allegory of the death of a trained bear is too oblique, the references too obscure. But *Germany, a Winter's Tale* (Deutschland, ein Wintermärchen, 1844), his half-fictionalised account of a journey home, written in ballad metre and ballad style, is a sparkling denunciation of Prussian tyranny and provincial stupidity, combining rude comment in light verse with an intense lyrical invocation of the natural world. Apart from this great poem, Heine's best satire is scattered throughout his occasional prose, which is mostly occasional or polemical, and is crystallised in sharp images and aphorisms. No one has written with more irreverent wit and insight into the mysteries of religion than he did in *Zur Geschichte der Religion und Philosophie in Deutschland* (1834). Even more than Swift or Voltaire, Heine was a political prophet of power – the satirists who regard the absurdly horrible as always possible seem to be better prophets than the serious commentators – as when he foretold the coming of Nazi obscurantism and of Russian domination. But his sombre vision of the future is shot through with the gaiety of the authentic jester.

It is impossible in this space to trace the developments of political satire in the later nineteenth and twentieth centuries; some of its appearances in the novel, drama and other forms will be discussed later. To conclude, political satire requires special conditions for its appearance in strength: first, a degree of free speech, either through design as in Greece or England, or through inefficiency as in late eighteenth-century France and even in Czarist Russia. Secondly, there must be a general readiness of the educated classes to take part in political affairs; this need not imply the existence of a democracy, but it does mean the spread of democratic ideas. Thirdly, there must be some confidence on the part of writers that they can actually influence the conduct of affairs; and fourthly, there must be a wide audience that enjoys wit, imagination and the graces of literature, and that is sophisticated enough to enjoy their application to serious topics. These conditions existed to the full in England from about 1680 to 1820, and they have reappeared since in other parts of Europe, usually in pre-revolutionary rather than revolutionary situations; and as commonly associated with nationalistic as with social conflict. Whether these conditions will reappear in the future in the advanced countries seems doubtful, although they may do so in countries which have still to pass through the corresponding stages in their political evolution. The complexities of modern economic and social systems is now too great to be reduced to satiric formulae; and imaginative literature has declined from its leading position as the medium for spreading critical ideas. The cartoon and the revue sketch are always there to express political discontent and irreverent ribaldry; but an elaborate exposé of contemporary affairs of state, such as *Gulliver's Travels* was in its day, no longer seems an acceptable mode of criticism, and in any case would be outside the powers of even the greatest literary genius. Such are the demands of the world for knowledge and expertise that anything less than full documentation and careful analysis of a political situation is clearly felt to be unsatisfactory; and imaginative literature on public themes is perhaps already an archaic art. Literature remains for exploring the inner worlds of feeling and for recording human anguish and pleasure: but in the form of satire it will have less and less to contribute to 'the world's debate'.

3 The topics of satire: women

Since men enjoy the advantages of physical strength, intellectual energy, political power and wealth, and until recently also those of legal status and education, it seems unnecessary as well as un-chivalrous for them to have written as much satire on women as they have. A partial explanation has been offered by Dr Johnson: 'As the faculty of writing has been chiefly a masculine endowment, the reproach of making the world miserable has been always thrown upon the women'. He reminds us of the simple fact that nearly all satire, like the greater part of all literature, has been written by men. He also implies that since the world *is* miserable, the blame is always being thrown on some person or persons: if not on the political party currently in power, or the capitalists or the workers or the Jews, then on the scapegoat most conveniently to hand, which is the female sex. The fact that, unlike racial minorities or political régimes, women cannot be banished or abolished but are here for ever is therefore a deeper source of irritation to the male satirist as well as a more persistent stimulus to writing than those produced by any other subject. The correct analogy to be drawn, moreover, is with the Jews and the workers (or slaves), not with the rulers: women are among the ruled, or as the sociologists say, they form an under-privileged subculture in nearly all societies. The satirist who pursues this topic runs little risk, except at the hands of his own wife, who may like Chaucer's Wife of Bath, fling his odious book into the fire. Men perhaps feel some guilt about their exploitation of women's inferiority, but they also feel resentment, because with all their advantages their power over women is far from complete, and in some ways women may have power over them. This resentment lies behind much anti-feminist literature, as it does behind much that masters have written about servants. Here again Johnson is helpful, provided that we turn his aphorism upside down: 'nature has given women so much power that the law has wisely given them little' is a paradoxical way of saying 'although the law, and education, the economic system etc. have deprived women of so much power, they are still formidable opponents in the sex-war'. The traditional weapons of the sex, according to a saying quoted by the Wife of Bath, are deceit, weeping and spinning: 'Fallere, flere, nere, dedit Deus in muliere'. Deceit includes cuckoldry, a shaming blow to the male ego; weeping implies that feminine weakness and sensibility may have some inhibiting effect on masculine brutality; and for 'spinning' we should now read 'knitting', which is symbolic of the woman's withdrawal of her attention into household tasks or into exclusively female society – the man, his advances and complaints ignored, loses self-esteem. An even more potent weapon is the *Lysistrata* tactic or the refusal of sexual consent, by which the errant Greek husbands in the play were soon brought to heel – a fantasy, but near enough to the truth, since sexual pleasure without consent or co-operation is hardly pleasure at all. To resentment there must be added a certain fear which men have of women, even without admitting it: the ancient awe of prehistoric religions, most of which included the cult of the Great Mother; the worship of the White Goddess, who according to Robert Graves is the woman in her triple role as mother, lover, and layer-out of the corpse; the terror aroused by the witch.

The reality behind what men have written about women is an ambivalence of feeling, which includes deep antagonism. This reality has been elaborated and disguised by a variety of myths; in fact, as Simone de Beauvoir reminds us in *Le Deuxième Sexe*, almost everything written about women is myth and myth made by man. Taken seriously, sex antagonism is the stuff of several great tragic plays and novels, by Euripides, Strindberg, Richardson, Choderlos de Laclos and others; taken lightly, it is the basis of most comedies of manners, e.g. by Congreve or Shaw; but taken moralistically it has inspired satire. The opposite of satire is the encomium, the formal work 'in praise of women', which became a formal genre in the Middle Ages, like Chaucer's *Legend of Good Women*. The encomium embodies myth: it sets out to praise the ideal woman, but in fact prescribes how women, in men's opinion, ought to behave. The story of patient Griselda, whose incredible sufferings at the hands of her tyrannous husband were duly rewarded, is an extreme example, but it was recounted solemnly as a model of docility. The encomium also reflects the double standard of sexual morality which has prevailed until recently in civilised society: women have been expected to be more chaste than men, as well as more modest in dress and demeanour. The fuss made by the moralists about women's fashions, cosmetics and coiffure is based only partly on the very reasonable grounds of expense; it also voices the suspicion that such adornments are meant to allure men other than the husband. Satire on women is a comic recording of deviations from the ideal set up by the encomium, and traditionally it has been centred on the cardinals of docility, chastity and modesty.

Since its roots are in human nature, the 'praise-or-blame' of women must be as old as anything in literature. Traces can be found in the ancient civilisations of the Near East, as in the wise sayings attributed to the vizier Ptah-Hotep (2450 BC):

Thou shouldst not contend with her at law, and keep her from gaining control ... Her eye is her stormwind. Let her heart be soothed through what may accrue to thee; it means keeping her long in thy house ...

The theme appears in the Babylonian *Pessimistic Dialogue between Master and Servant:*

Servant, obey me.
Yes, my lord, yes.
A woman will I love.
Yes love, my lord, love. The man who loves a woman forgets pain and trouble.
No, servant, a woman I shall not love.
Do not love, my lord, do not love. Woman is a well, woman is an iron dagger – a sharp one! – which cuts a man's neck[17].

This ancient wisdom literature influenced the biblical Book of Proverbs, where the same ambivalence about women appears: on the one hand there is the encomium in chapter 31 ('her price is above rubies'), on the other, 'it is better to dwell in a corner of the house-top than with a brawling woman in a wide house', and 'as a jewel of gold in a swine's snout, so is a fair woman which is without discretion'. These picturesque remarks gave a good precedent in holy writ for the Christian anti-feminism of the Middle Ages. The first step in formalising such feelings about women into satire was apparently taken by the Greeks, and in particular by Semonides of Amorgos (seventh century BC). In a witty diatribe, offered as advice to a young man, he divides women into classes, each with the nature of an animal, whether sow, vixen or monkey.

> At the creation God made women's natures
> various. One he made from a bristly sow:
> and all her household welters in confusion,
> lying aground in miscellaneous muck,
> while she unwashen in unlaundered clothes
> reposes in her pigsty, fattening.

Only the bee-wife is worth marrying: happy the man who gets her, for she alone makes life flourish. But on the whole the greatest evil that Zeus has sent to men is women. 'For whoever lives with a woman he never passes a whole day in happiness,' and cannot even give a cordial welcome to a guest; a woman was the cause of the Trojan War.

> Her husband gawps and doesn't notice; neighbours do,
> and smile to see how still another man gets fooled.

> Each man will pick the faults in someone else's wife
> and boast of his own each time he speaks of her. And yet
> the same thing happens to us all. But we don't see,
> For women are the biggest single bad thing Zeus
> has made for us; a ball-and-chain; we can't get loose
> since that time when a fight about a wife began
> the Great War, and they volunteered, and went to hell[18].

Aristophanes, although he treats the subject of sex with unashamed indecency, is at heart sympathetic to women. The *Lysistrata* is aimed at the militarist party, not at the women who try to stop the war so intelligently and generously. Elsewhere he praises women for being more conservative than men (which is true) and therefore not so likely to be drawn into the new-fangled and wrong-headed schemes of the Athenian democracy. In the *Ecclesiazusae*, or 'Women in Parliament' as Jack Lindsay translates it, which is yet another play built around a saturnalian reversal of the social order, he praises as much as he satirises, expressing charmingly through Praxagora the ambivalence which the best writers on this subject seem to show.

> PRAXAGORA:
> You won't find *them* (the women) I warrant, in a hurry
> Trying new plans. And would it not have saved
> The Athenian city had she let alone
> Things that worked well, nor idly sought things new?
> They roast their barley, sitting, as of old:
> They on their heads bear burdens, as of old:
> They keep their Thesmophoria, as of old:
> They bake their honied cheesecakes, as of old:
> They victimize their husbands, as of old:
> They still secrete their lovers, as of old . . .

There is no ambivalence in Juvenal. His sixth satire is a scabrous diatribe against the vices and follies of contemporary Roman women. His class bias is noteworthy: all his examples are taken from the ladies of high society, whose wrongdoings are highly expensive ones. He has thus produced yet another tract against luxury and decadence, in contrast to the primitive simplicity of the Golden Age, and to the chastity and modesty of republican Rome. He describes with verve fashionable ladies who take a fancy to actors or run away with gladiators, the empress Messalina who took her turn in the brothel; then turning to folly, he ridicules women who beguile their time with athletics, music, gluttony, literature and fortune-telling. (I confess to finding his female athlete, flushed after her fencing exercises, rather attractive, but we are not supposed to think so.) He ends on a more sinister note, where his satire

This plate originally appeared in Mercurialis' *De Arte Gymnastica* 1573.
It was later used to illustrate the English translation of
Juvenal's Satires by B. Holyday, Oxford 1673, where its relevance
seems very slight: the ladies' gymnastics are presumably quite
innocent. An illustration of the way in which books are sometimes
illustrated – and that in itself could be the subject for satire.

puts on the buskin of Tragedy, with abortion and the poisoning of
husbands: there is a Clytemnestra in every street. All women are
potential tyrants who may have their slaves flogged or crucified on
a moment's whim, saying 'Hoc volo, sic iubeo, sit pro ratione
voluntas' (I wish it, I insist on it, let my will stand instead of
reason). And all are deceivers: lock your wife up, men say, but 'Quis
custodiet ipsos custodes' (Who will guard the guardians?). Juvenal
employs so much violent obscenity and comic exaggeration that,
although we can believe his account of *la dolce vita* as it was lived in
second-century Italy, we cannot take him seriously as a moralist.
There is throughout his sixth satire a note of mock-rage and self-
parody, which Dryden caught perfectly in his masterly translation.

> In Saturn's Reign, at Nature's Early Birth,
> There was that Thing called Chastity on Earth …
> Those first unpolisht Matrons, Big and Bold,
> Gave Suck to Infants of Gygantick Mold;
> Rough as their Savage Lords who Rang'd the Wood,
> And fat with Akorns belcht their windy Food.

It is doubtful whether the coming of Christianity made much
difference to the real situation of women. Their legal and economic
position did not improve; and their moral position, as advisers to
their men-folk, did not worsen. Whereas the Roman matron had
been traditionally an important figure in the household, so women
began to play an active role in the growing church, on balance
neither gaining nor losing authority. What Christianity did was to
emphasise the peculiar virtues of celibacy and virginity, and to
dramatise sexual morality around the cardinal figures of Eve and
the Virgin Mary, both with far-reaching effects on literature. The
Old Testament is not particularly puritanical about sex, and
emphatically in favour of marriage, as is orthodox Judaism to this
day; the gospels are somewhat ambiguous about sex and marriage.
The first real change begins with the Pauline Epistles. St Paul was
pro-feminist, in that he evidently had a high regard for the women
members of his church, but he held any form of sexuality in horror.

'Better to marry than to burn' he wrote, implying that it was even better not to marry at all. Since the early Christians held apocalyptic views, they saw no good in getting entangled in marriage, when the end of the world could come at any moment. Again, they wished to set themselves apart from the pagan world, where sexuality played such a large part in everyday life; and austerity is the most conspicuous way of doing so. By abstaining from the brothel and the sadistic gladiatorial show they possibly saved a good deal of energy, which became available for the purpose of building up the church. Again monasticism, which involved the setting up of austere and celibate communities cut off from the wicked world, became in the early centuries an essential part of the church's structure: by the Middle Ages 'religio' had come to mean exclusively monastic religion. As the celibate members of the clergy came to acquire a near-monopoly of education and literacy, they communicated their anti-feminine bias to all Christian literature. This had curious and unexpected results for the art of satire. The learned St Jerome was extremely well read in pagan classical literature, which he piously tried to forget but in vain. When he came to write polemic on the subject of virginity and marriage, he could not help drawing on the traditional satire on women, and in particular on Theophrastus. What should have been a serious homily became uproariously comic satire, and the saint unwittingly provided the medieval humorists with a mine of pagan and quite unedifying jokes about women.

There is a golden book current under the name of the philosopher Theophrastus; it is entitled *On Marriage*, and the question is whether a wise man would take a wife. The author concludeth that a wise man would sometimes do so if the lady were fair to see, well bred, and of honourable parentage, and if he himself were healthy and wealthy; but unto this he addeth: 'These things are seldom all concurrent in a marriage; the wise man, therefore should not wed'.

First, it impedeth the study of philosophy; no man can serve his books and his wife with equal zeal. A married woman hath many needs; precious robes, gold and gems, great expenses, handmaidens, furniture of all kinds, litters and a gilded car. Then he must listen, all night long, to her wordy complaints. 'This woman goes abroad better clad than I; that other hath universal honour; I, poor wretch, must hang my head down among my fellows. Wherefore hast thou made eyes at that woman over the way? What hadst thou to say to the maidservant? What didst thou bring home from the market?' We do not have a friend or a companion, the wife suspects our love to others, our hate to herself. However learned a teacher there may be in any city, we may not leave our wife, nor can be burden ourselves with her at his lectures ... A horse or an ass, an ox or a dog, or even the commonest slaves, are tried before we choose to buy them; so also with clothes and kettles, chairs and cups and earthen pipkins; a wife alone is not to be had on approval, lest she be found wanting before we marry her....

Such, then, briefly, are the reasons of (the heathen) Theophrastus; do they not put us Christians to shame, who have our conversation in heaven, and whose desire is to depart and to be with Christ?[19]

A major development in Christian mythology and iconography also affected all subsequent satire on women. This was the dramatisation of man's ambivalent feelings about women around the polar antitheses of Eve and the Virgin Mary. Sin came into the world through a woman; redemption became possible because a woman was God's Mother on earth. The taking of the apple and the Annunciation are often pictured side by side, as in medieval windows. The Genesis story was not given much importance in the Old Testament or in the gospels, but it became all-important in the Epistles, with the Pauline emphasis on Christ as the second Adam. There grew up the view that of our first parents the woman was the more culpable of the two in yielding to temptation, and even that carnal desire was an unfortunate consequence of the Fall. Eve-baiting became the sport of the moralists, and was not seriously counteracted by the cult of the Virgin Mary, which began in the early centuries and reached its peak in the twelfth. The more devotion was paid to the sinless Mother of God, the more execration was heaped on Eve, who became the symbol of everything that was wrong with women. Her chief faults were her forwardness, and her domination of her husband, whom she persuaded to eat the fatal fruit; so she is shown in the medieval drama, and in the

The Temptation of Eve and the
Annunciation, matching pictures
from the *Speculum Humanae Salvationis*,
(1470), a frequent source for
medieval stained glass and carvings.

ludicrous account given by Chaucer's Chaunticlere (where Chaucer is ironically ridiculing the whole tradition: the picture of Adam 'merry and well at ease' is deliberately naive).

> Wommenes conseiles been ful ofte colde;
> Wommanes counseiles broghte us first to wo,
> And made Adam fro Paradys to go,
> There as he was ful myrie and wel at ese.　　　(*Nun's Priest's Tale*)

The tradition lingered on well after the Reformation, affecting even the greatest of English epics. Milton often makes oblique hits at the heroine of *Paradise Lost*, comparing her in passing to Pandora, whose box brought all human ills, and after the great event breaks into open satirical comedy. Eve even blames Adam for allowing her to persuade him to the apple – a highly feminine reproach – Adam makes a furious generalisation:

> Thus it shall befall
> Him who to worth in Woman overtrusting
> Lets her Will rule; restraint she will not brook,
> And left to herself, if evil thence ensue
> Shee first his weak indulgence will accuse.　　　(*Paradise Lost*, IX, 1182)

Later Adam elaborates ingeniously and in doubtful taste on the story of Eve's creation from one of his ribs: it must have been a crooked rib, from the left or unlucky side, he must have had too many and he is well rid of it:

> all was but a show
> Rather than solid virtue, all but a Rib
> Crooked by nature, bent, as now appears
> More to the part sinister from me drawn,
> Well, if thrown out, as supernumerary
> To my just number found.　　　(X, 883)

It must be added that Adam, moved by Eve's generosity, later apologises for his pedantic bad temper; Milton makes both parties to the first of all conjugal quarrels recover their dignity and nobility.

The virulence of the fathers of the church and their medieval followers can scarcely be exaggerated. In particular they emphasised the physiological fact – which seems to fill some people with an irrational horror – that the organs of parturition, excretion and sex are situated close together. 'Inter faeces et urinam nascimur' wrote St Augustine, and he was echoed even less elegantly by the medieval preacher's 'Mulier est sterci saccum' ('Woman is a sack of dung'). But he might have reflected, so is man and so are all animals; it is merely one of the penalties one pays for not being a vegetable. This neurotic disgust with the body and especially with excretion keeps reappearing in later satirical tradition, most notably with Swift. The Dean's most scatological inventions, like the filthy female Yahoos, or the nymph going to bed ('Celia, Celia, Celia shits') are in an old and established vein of clerical homily, which makes a surprising reappearance in the rational and humane eighteenth century. The preachers also inveighed against women's vanity and immodest dress, while a third topic was the unnatural and sinful domination of women over men. When the Calvinist John Knox thundered against the monstrous regiment (i.e. rule) of women, he was repeating a medieval commonplace. Still, sermons are not satires; and the transformation of homiletics into literary satire, begun unwittingly by St Jerome, was a slow process, which began to accelerate in the twelfth century. This century saw the birth of courtly love, a set of ideals which offered the aristocracy a complete reversal of clerical values. The courtly poets glorified carnality, adultery and the humility of the male before his haughty mistress; and through the concept of 'courtoisie' they stressed the civilising effect of the well-conducted love affair. It is doubtful whether courtly love, which was a literary fantasy or at most a half-serious game, did much to improve the real status of women, except possibly in increasing the respect paid to them in polite society. It became itself an absurd system which attracted the

Jean de Meung in the thirteenth century wrote the second part
of *Le Roman de la Rose*, including vigorous diatribes
against celibacy and the hypocrisy of the clergy. This scene from an
illuminated manuscript (Flemish, about 1500) shows the painter
Zeuxis and five models: nature is De Meung's goddess.

ridicule of satirists from Chaucer to Cervantes. A second event of
note in the twelfth century was the revival of the classics: Ovid was
the favourite reading of the secular poets, who learned from him
how to treat the comedy of seduction with grace; but Juvenal's
satire on women was also widely read. Next appeared the oriental
stories about the wiles of women which came into European folklore and popular literature from Arab civilisation, as a result of the
crusades and of increased trade. These tales were spread by the
preachers, who used them for their *exempla*, that is, picturesque
tales to illustrate moral teaching. The frame-tale of the *Seven Sages*
is a competition in telling the most striking examples of deceitful
and treacherous women; the ingenious stories of this sequence
spread widely throughout Europe. Another such compilation is the
Disciplina Clericalis, of Petrus Alphonsus, a Spanish Jew of the
twelfth century. The most famous of oriental anti-feminist stories
is the frame-tale of the *Thousand and One Nights:* a husband is so
jealous that he carries his wife everywhere locked up in a box;
nevertheless she manages to deceive him with other men. This
found its way into the fourteenth-century collection of tales by
Sercambi, centuries before the first translation of the *Nights* by
Galland.

The thirteenth century was the age of the *fabliaux*, rhymed
stories in verse, written for the entertainment of popular audiences
in the small towns and cities of north-eastern France. The fabliau
grew up in a secular and bourgeois environment but it is pre-
dominantly anti-bourgeois in tone. The time-honoured stories of
deception and the wiles of women are told in a new way: the main
target is usually the newly-rich, the 'riche vilain', the miser or the
thievish miller; or it is the greedy upstart priest who is too keen on
the money that was beginning to flow in the towns. The hero of a
fabliau, and, we may suspect, the author, is often a poor 'clerk',
who has to defend himself against merchant and priest by using his
wits. The fabliau, like the formal and dramatic satire of Elizabethan
England, reflects the over-production and under-employment of
university wits, or 'povres escolliers'; it deserves a place in the

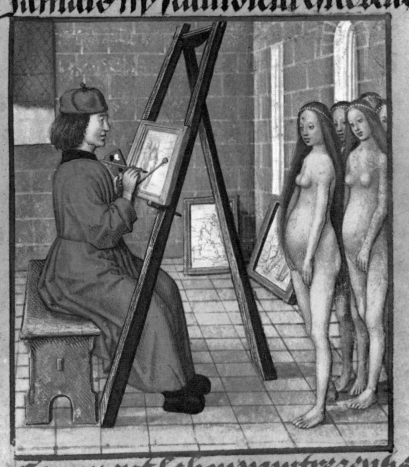

Comment le bon paintre zensis
fut de contrefaire pensis
La tresgrant beaulte de nature
Et de la paindre mit grant cure
enly ... nchez par son

history of satire for its realistic, bawdy and violent picture of contemporary life. Sexual relations are the main theme: the bourgeoise of Orleans turns the tables on her husband when he appears disguised as her lover; another heroine persuades her husband that he is dead, so that she can receive her gallant in peace. But the married couple usually unite when it comes to dealing with the voluptuous and avaricious priest: it is the priest who has to hide in the tub of lard, is smothered in feathers or forced to restore his ill-gotten gains. The fabliau thus combines, with rude force, the two great satirical themes of anti-feminism and anti-clericalism.

One of the best-written of the fabliaux, which shows a courtly elegance of description, provided the most famous example of the theme of female domination. The *Lai d'Aristote*, better known as *Aristotle and Phyllis*, tells how the philosopher warned his distinguished pupil Alexander the Great against the dangers of sex, and reproved him for being distracted from his duties by a favourite courtesan; irritated by this good advice, Alexander set the courtesan to tempt the philosopher. She persuaded him that to gain her favours he must allow himself to be saddled and bridled and let her ride on his back; when Aristotle did so, Alexander appeared from hiding to draw the moral that love is stronger than philosophy. The main scene of this story found its way into medieval art, and is represented several times on French and English misericords.

Already in the fabliaux the old themes of women's wiles are being transformed into literary satire. Meanwhile a huge literature concerning marriage and its problems was growing cumulatively, each author repeating and adding to the material of his predecessors, and this too became gradually transformed from moral homily into imaginative narrative. Around the kernel of Theophrastus, Juvenal and St Jerome there grew successively the *De Nugis Curialium* of the twelfth-century Walter Map, the *Lamentations* of the thirteenth-century Matheolus (a cleric who lost his benefice because of his marriage), the second part of the *Roman de la Rose* by Jean de Meung, the fourteenth-century *Miroir de Mariage* by Chaucer's friend Eustache Deschamps and finally Chaucer's triumphant use of this material in the *Canterbury Tales*. Jean de Meung, who has been called the Voltaire of the Middle Ages, wrote a long and diffuse sequel to Guillaume de Lorris's courtly allegory of the rose, which offers a kind of encyclopedia of learned subjects: his object was to take such learning away from the church's monopoly and offer it to the laity in clear vernacular French verse. His satire ranges widely, but anti-clericalism is his main theme: his brutal portrait of the hypocritical friar Faux-Semblant, who exposes his tricks in a cynical monologue, is the model for Chaucer's Friar and Pardoner. When he turns to the subject of women, his drift is two-fold: first, to repeat the traditional slanders, not as an awful warning, but as realistic comedy; and secondly to attack the church's doctrines of celibacy. There are long speeches by Nature and Genius, who attack virginity and ask every man to do his duty in propagating the species. De Meung makes a spirited defence of the flesh and of natural sexuality, in anticipation of the spirit of Boccaccio's *Decameron* and *The Wife of Bath's Prologue*. The model for Chaucer's Wife of Bath is De Meung's *La Vieille*, or the Duenna, the experienced woman who passes on her amorous secrets to the younger generation, telling the truth about her scandalous life without shame or repentance:

> Par Deu! si me plaist il encores
> Quant je m'i sui bien pourpensee:
> Mout me delite en ma pensee
> E me resbaudissent li membre
> Quant de mon bon tens me remembre
> Et de la joliete vie
> Don mes cueurs a si grant envie:
> Tout me rejovenist le cors
> Quant j'i pens e quant jou recors
> (By God! it pleases me still, when I think over my past life: it delights me much in my thought and my limbs feel their vigour return, when I remember the good time I had and the gay life, which my heart now so longs for; my whole body grows young again, when I recall it to mind.)

Coloured woodcuts illustrating the German translation of Boccaccio's *Decameron* (Augsburg 1490). (*left*) Masetto, by pretending to be dumb, is welcomed into a convent, where he seduces all the nuns (Day 3, story 1); (*right*) a monk finds his abbot guilty of the sin for which he has just been punished (Day 1, story 4). The satire in Boccaccio's polished and licentious stories is aimed at the clergy rather than the frailty of women.

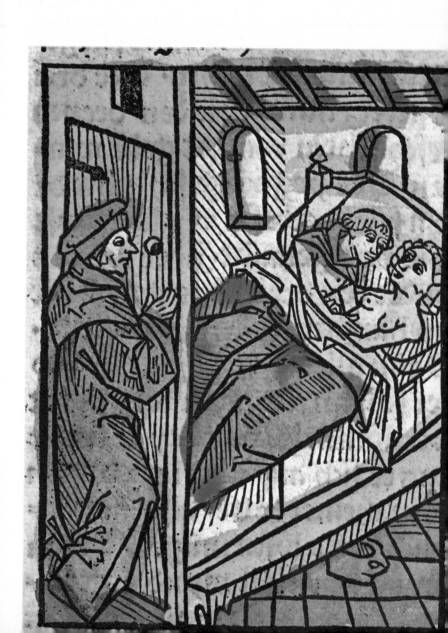

Or as the Wife of Bath puts it:

> But, Lord Christ! whan that it remembreth me
> Upon my yowthe, and on my jolitee,
> It tikleth me aboute myn herte roote,
> Unto this day it dooth myn herte boote
> That I have had my world as in my tyme.

Chaucer surpasses de Meung in richness of invention and complexity of irony. The Wife of Bath rehearses the preachers' views on virginity, only to refute them: the body was made for love and fertility or 'engendrure' she says, quoting scripture gaily, for 'God bad us for to wexe and multiplye', while Solomon and the Patriarchs had many wives. Virginity may be the ideal state, but there is a place for everything: Christ did not tell every man to sell all he hath:

> He spak to them that wolde lyve parfitly
> And lordynges, by your leve, that am nat I.

She tells her life-story with zest, describing racily how she dealt with her five husbands, 'How piteously a-nyght I made them swynke' (work). She repeats the traditional satires, from the Book of Proverbs, St Jerome and the rest – her fifth husband used to read them out aloud until she burnt his book – only to brush them aside:

> Thou sayest that dropping houses, and eke smoke
> And chiding wyves maken men to flee
> Out of hir owen hous – a benedicitee!

She produces her horoscope; since she was born under Venus but with the evil influence of Mars, she has been driven by the planets into a life of carnality: so

> Alas, alas, that ever love was sin!

The Wife of Bath is an independent bourgeoise, who by her skill in weaving could make enough money to do as she liked: hence her confident feminism when she comes to the central issue of the satirical tradition, which is women's domination or as Chaucer calls it 'maistrie' (mastery). Her solution for marital happiness is for the husband to hand over all authority to the wife; and this is the moral of the witty and graceful tale which she then tells to the pilgrims. This subject is explored at length in the group of Canterbury Tales that follow, until what one feels is Chaucer's personal view, a humanist one, is put forward with modest irony in the Franklin's Tale: neither husband nor wife is to have the 'mastery' but marriage is to be a partnership of equals. Chaucer has turned satire against the satirists: he accepts the absurdities and grossnesses of sexuality and marriage with ironic good humour, as the richest part of life's comedy. Neither defending nor blaming the Wife of Bath he presents her as triumphant in her animal vitality. As James Joyce wrote of his own Molly Bloom, who is an even richer character, she is 'sane full amoral fertilisable untrustworthy engaging limited prudent indifferent Weib. "Ich bin das Fleisch das stets bejaht!" '

On this topic, as on others, the Middle Ages are repetitive. As the tradition goes on, only a few works of the fifteenth century show anything to equal Chaucer's genius: one may cite the Scottish William Dunbar's *Twa Mariit Women and the Wedo*, the *Celestina* of Fernando de Rojas, a Catalan Jew, and *Les Quinze Joies de Mariage*. The medieval material is worked up, together with much classical learning and medical lore, into the elaborate burlesque of Rabelais' Third Book, which tells how Panurge took thought about getting married. In chapter 30 there is an eloquent parody of the orthodox theological view of marriage; in the next chapter the physician Rondibilis instructs Panurge how to quell his carnal concupiscence, namely by wine, antaphrodisiac drugs, hard work, study, and 'Fifthly and last, you may assuage the sexual stimuli by performing the act of copulation'. 'Ha!' said Panurge, 'I was waiting for that. Let any one who likes use numbers one to four inclusive: I'm for number five.' Rabelais thus reduces this, like every other subject, to total absurdity. On a lower level, the old themes of women's deception, vanity and domination ('who shall wear the breeches?') had a long life in the sixteenth century, appearing *ad nauseam* in drama, jest-books and cheap woodcuts, and of course even much later in popular literature, folklore, satirical ballads, etc. The street songs of London and the stories of the European peasantry show what a long and vigorous life the medieval motifs enjoyed.

The poems of François Villon (born 1431) open a new chapter in the literature of prostitution, a satirical topic somewhat distinct from the ones already discussed. Comparatively little that has been written about prostitution can be called satire in any strict sense: it usually varies between pornography and the Awful Warning. It is perhaps also rather loose to call Villon's *Grand Testament* satire; but he has more of the tough-mindedness of the great satirists than any other medieval poet except Dante; in Villon satire is transmuted into lyric: the old woman of the *Roman de la Rose* becomes the powerful moving prostitute of *La Belle Heaulmière*, regretting her past beauty and gaiety. Villon refuses to condemn, even to condemn himself: he is the first pimp to describe his profession without shame, just as he is the first poet to express a dead-beat philosophy of life. In places he uses the traditional satiric themes with perfect economy and force. There is, for example, no finer conjunction of sex and religion than his picture of the fat canon in the brothel, in *Les Contredis Franc Gontier*':

> Sur mol duvet assis, un gras chanoine,
> Lès un brasier, en chambre bien nattee,
> A son costé gisant dame Sidoine,
> Blanche, tendre, polie et attintee,
> Boire ypocras, à jour et à nuitee,
> Rire, jouer, mignonner et baisier,
> Et nu à nu, pour mieux des corps s'aisier,
> Les vi tous deux, par un troup de mortaise :
> Lors je connus que, pour dueil appaisier,
> Il n'est tresor que de vivre a son aise.

> (Sitting on soft down, a fat canon, near a bright fire, in a room with good rush matting, and lying at his side lady Sidoine, white, tender, glossy and bedizened, drinking good wine by day and night, laughing,

playing, petting and kissing, and naked body to body, the better to take their pleasure – I saw them both, through a hole in the mortice: then I knew that to calm all sorrow there's no sovereign remedy like taking things easy.)

It was this that attracted one of the finest modern satirists, Bertold Brecht, who took Villon's lyrics as the starting-point for the songs in the *Threepenny Opera*. *The Balade de la Grosse Margot*, with its refrain 'En ce bordeau ou tenons nostre estat' becomes Mackie Messer's song:

> In einer Zeit, die längst vergangen ist
> Lebten wir schön zusammen, sie und ich
> Und zwar von meinem Kopf und ihrem Bauch.
> Ich schützte sie and sie ernährte mich.
> Es geht auch anders, doch so geht es auch.
> Und wenn ein Freier kam, kroch ich aus unserm Bett
> Und drückte mich zu'n Kirsch und war sehr nett
> Und wenn er blechte, sprach ich zu ihm: Herr
> Wenn sie mal wieder wollen – bitte sehr.
> So hielten wir's ein volles halbes Jahr
> In dem Bordell, wo unser Haushalt war.
>
> (Once on a time – who knows how long ago? –
> We shared a home together, I and she.
> My head and her abdomen turned the trick.
> I protected her and she supported me.
> (Some say it's different, but I say it's slick.)
> And when a wooer came I crept out of her bed
> And got myself a schnapps and showed myself well bred.
> When he shelled out, I said: Auf Wiedersehn
> If any time you'd care to, come again!
> For half a year we had no cause to roam
> For that bordello was our home from home.)
> (translated by Desmond I. Vesey and Eric Bentley)

In the sixteenth century the spread of syphilis took on alarming proportions, causing a marked change in the literature of prostitution and indeed in all writers' attitude to sexuality. The horror of the aching bones and of the missing nose spread across Europe: if men made jokes about such things they were cruel or 'sick' jokes, like Falstaff's 'A pox of this gout or a gout of this pox'. Syphilis is the hideous reality behind Shakespeare's most satirical comedy, *Troilus and Cressida*, where he has changed the faithless Cressida from Chaucer's pathetic widow into a brazen 'daughter of the game'. The diseased Thersites appears on the stage as the satirist – or rather, a parody of the typical satirist figure of the age – reducing everything to 'wars and lechery'. The Trojan war becomes a senseless and ludicrous brawl fought over an adulterous wife; while Cressida's treachery brings all romantic love down to the level of lechery. At the end we are left with Pandarus jesting bitterly about the 'Neapolitan boneache'. Images of disease run through this play, as they do through Hamlet, also dated just before 1600. When Hamlet speaks of the 'film'd-o'er ulcer', he means venereal disease, with which the state or 'body politic' is rotten; while the nunnery he tells Ophelia to go to is a brothel, in Elizabethan slang:

I have heard of your paintings too, well enough: God hath given you one face and you make yourselves another: you jig, you amble, and you lisp, and nickname God's creatures, and make your wantonness your ignorance. Go to, I'll no more on't; it hath made me mad. I say, we shall have no more marriages; those that are married already, all but one, shall live; the rest shall keep as they are. To a nunnery, go.

Hamlet, whose descriptions of sexuality are among the most disgusting ever written (like 'The rank sweat of an enseamed bed') is the ultimate satirist on women. The lesser Jacobean tragedians, however, show the same obsession. John Webster (about whom one of the few things that we know was that he wore a 'satirical hat', whatever that was) interrupts his savage melodramas, *The Duchess of Malfi* and *The White Devil*, with a series of satirical witticisms; notably in the speech beginning 'What are whores? Cold, Russian winters. . . .'

The medieval attitude lingers in English literature of the early

ALPHABET
DE L'IMPERFECTION
ET MALICE
des Femmes.

*De mil hommes i'en ay trouué vn bon, & de
toutes les femmes pas vne, Ecclef. 7.*

Reueu, corrigé & augmenté d'vn friant Deſſert, &
de pluſieurs Hiſtoires en cette cinquieſme Edition pour les Courtizans & partizans de la Fem-
me Mondaine.

Par IACQVES OLIVIER *Licencier aux
Loix, & en droict Canon.*

Dedié à la plus mauuaiſe du monde.

A PARIS,

Chez IEAN PETIT-PAS, ruë S Iacques, à
l'Eſcu de Veniſe, pres les Mathurins.
_____

M. DC. XXVI.

Auec Priuilege du Roy.

A nineteenth-century view of a timeless classic:
Madelon and Cathos, Les Précieuses Ridicules themselves,
are ravished by the fantastic manners of their bogus visitor.

seventeenth century: not only in Webster but in the tirades of Cyril Tourneur and outside drama in Jacques Olivier's *Alphabet de l'Imperfection et Malice des Femmes* (1617) and in Burton's *Anatomy of Melancholy*. In the section of that infinitely rich encyclopedia of archaic learning called *Love Melancholy* Burton illustrates in racy and energetic style the whole range of satiric attitudes to the topic. But thereafter the subject is handled in a new way: the relation of the sexes is treated as part of the wider subject of social refinement and manners, as in the formal satire of Régnier and Boileau, and in Molière's *Les Précieuses Ridicules*.

The gentle raillery of Addison and Steele in the *Tatler* and the *Spectator* was more appropriate to the partial emancipation of women that began in the eighteenth century. The last time in English that the note of medieval preacher's horror of the flesh was sounded was in the most disgusting poems of Swift and in his description of the female Yahoo; but here we are moving from satire to the borders of the psychopathic grotesque. Pope is the best of the verse satirists to comment on women with the right blend of malice and sympathy. The moral of his *Rape of the Lock* (1714) is ostensibly 'Vanity, vanity, all is vanity', and this delicious mock-Homeric epic sees women as the exemplars of vanity. Just as the plot of the poem is the exaltation of a trivial event into a great action, so the basic rhetorical device is zeugma, the absurd linking together of the trifling and the serious: 'When husbands or when lapdogs breathe their last', 'To stain her honour or the new brocade', 'Puffs, powders, patches, bibles, billets-doux': to Pope's heroine and to women in general these things are equally important. The poem states simultaneously that women are responsible for the minor vanities of civilised life, and that it is precisely these trifles, whether silverware or porcelain, that give life its grace; it is a triumphant celebration of these minor arts as well as a courteous mockery of those who give them exaggerated value. Women are both absurd and vulnerable, the symbols both of vanity and of ideal beauty:

> Oh if to dance all night and dress all day
> Charm'd but old age and the smallpox away

> Who would not scorn what housewife's care produce,
> Or who would learn one earthly thing of use.

Some years later Pope returned to the subject in *Moral Essays*, Epistle II to Mrs M. Blount, also known as *On the Character of Women* ('Most women have no characters at all'). This poem rehearses much of the traditional material, from Juvenal onwards, with great polish and verve. Some of it is powerful invective, like

> Chaste to her husband, frank to all beside,
> A teeming mistress but a barren bride.
> Men, some to business, some to pleasure take;
> But every woman is at heart a rake.

But in the end Pope returns to his old theme of the pathos of beauty: satire is subsumed into a lament for the passing of youth:

> See how the world its veterans rewards:
> A youth of frolics, an old age of cards. ...
> See, round and round the ghosts of beauty glide,
> And haunt the places where their honour died.

The literal meaning is that old dowagers revisit the ballrooms where they were first seduced; but the effect of the music and imagery is one of infinite sadness. It is impossible in the space of this book to pursue the subject of anti-feminist satire through the late eighteenth to the twentieth century. The radicals of the Enlightenment and most of the Romantics were pro-feminist, enough for the topic to decline in significance. The consequences of tension between the sexes is explored in the nineteenth century, mainly in regions lying well outside satire. But a later revival of the genre took place in early twentieth-century America, though perhaps that too is now a closed chapter. The special status of women and the special power of the matriarch in the United States have been commented on by sociologists; we need not discuss the causes but must note the literary consequences. If Philip Wylie's invective on 'Mom' in his *Generation of Vipers* deals heavy-handedly with the all-powerful White Goddess figure, the theme receives a classic realistic treatment in the short stories of Ring Lardner, and achieves mythical status in the cartoons and essays of James Thurber, who transforms the Strindbergian sex war into an absurd and touching mock-epic. More recently, there is an exquisitely acid account of the New England wife and mother in one chapter of John Cheever's otherwise undistinguished novel *The Wapshot Chronicle*. Finally there is *Lolita* (1955). A dozen years after the stormy appearance of this book few would still be willing to acclaim Vladimir Nabokov as a great romantic novelist: but of the anti-feminist satire he is certainly a minor master. He attacks the topic of sexuality with the agility and venom of a featherweight boxer: Humbert Humbert's obsession is the starting point for a poetic evocation of an America (who knows whether it is real or not) where the mother, the educationalist and the nymphet reign with the triple majesty of Hecate, goddess of crossroads. For a moment he recaptures the primeval awe out of which this kind of satire arose.

4 Techniques of satire

If the most important aspect of satire is its subject-matter – whether politics, sexual relations, bad manners, personal absurdity or literary stupidity – what sets it apart from other kinds of literature is its approach to the subject. The satirist can use a wide variety of literary forms, but he is bound to use a fairly limited range of techniques. Satire, although its content is often the harshest realities of human existence, is meant to make us laugh or smile. The smile, one assumes, is a sub-laugh, a laugh inhibited by good manners, or not fully called out by the situation. But what is laughter? The subject, it seems, is still wrapped in obscurity, and literary critics cannot get much help from the psychologists. Laughter is a set of physical symptoms – spasmodic guffaws, shaking abdominal muscles, even weeping or in extreme cases loss of bladder control – but what causes these symptoms is obscure and complex. The primary cause is probably relief from tension: here I should like to follow the zoologist Konrad Lorenz. He pictures, in *Man Meets Dog* a band of Old Stone Age hunters crossing the bush, shaken by a recent encounter with a sabre-toothed tiger; they are suddenly scared by a sound but it turns out to be an antelope: 'their fear gives place to relieved but excited chatter and finally to hilarious laughter'. That would be the most primitive version of the strange sounds of hilarity that the human race has been letting out intermittently ever since: a moment's respite from the remorseless claims of doom. One can imagine the band of hunters, safe in the evening round the camp fire and well-fed, going over the traumatic experiences and escapes of the day and miming them out to the accompaniment of the same guffaws: this could be one origin of comic literature. It seems likely that the sequence of tension and relief lies behind many of the manifestations of the comic whether seen or in words. Slapstick or clowning makes us worried because of the possibility of violence and injury – we laugh when it turns out to be harmless. A verbal joke puzzles the listener at first because it is unfamiliar, even if only momentarily – relief comes with understanding. The sudden solution to a riddle or a problem produces the same effect. But although this is an essential part of verbal wit, it cannot be the only cause of laughter, since laughter appears in too many different situations. Another explanation is that laughter is one of the body's ways of getting rid of superfluous energy. The spasm is a substitute for movement, or rather a 'displacement' of the urge to attack or to run away: like the 'displacement' activities of birds, which will interrupt a combat to peck the grass. Freud notes that much of the comedy of movement (clowning or slapstick) invokes unnecessary expenditure of energy; the spectator responds to such miming sympathetically by expending his own energy in laughter. Thus laughter is part of the process of play, which is apparently essential to young mammals.

If the first explanation assumes that man is a timid animal and the second that he is a playing animal (*homo ludens*), there is an assumption, equally true, to explain laughter: namely that man is an aggressive animal. This is to take the pessimistic view of human kind, put forward urgently by Thomas Hobbes: the life of primitive man is 'nasty, brutish and short' because he is perpetually in combat with his fellow creatures, his competitive and violent instincts only restrained by the fear of violent death. Hobbes on the basis of this view gives a famous definition of laughter (*On Human Nature*, 1650): it 'is nothing else but sudden glory arising from a sudden conception of some eminency in ourselves, by comparison with the infirmity of others, or with our own formerly'. This partly squares with the 'relief' theory: a laugh means 'there but for the grace of God go I', but it also implies that we usually laugh at someone else's misfortunes, or at our success in deliberately overcoming competition or opposition, and getting ahead in the rat race. If this is a pessimistic view, it is consistent with human history and experience, and takes us closer to an understanding of the mocking laugh of the satirist. This is an aggressive gesture, a means of waging war on his fellow creatures, albeit in a good cause. The Hobbesian view has been given a full exposition in Freud's *Der Witz und seine Beziehung zum Unbewussten* (1905); in the English translation 'The Joke' would be preferable to 'Wit and its relation to the Unconscious'. Whatever its value as scientific psychology, this book is about the best *literary* introduction to the nature of the comic and laughter. Freud does not try to give one exclusive explanation: he makes allowance both for the expenditure of energy and for the element of play in laughter. Part of his discussion centres on the aggressive joke, whether obscene or 'tendentious' (i.e. satirical). 'A whole class of dirty jokes allows one to infer the presence of a concealed inclination to exhibitionism in their inventors' – while to repeat such a joke is a mild form of sexual assault, either in reality (when telling it to someone of the opposite sex) or in fantasy. On the other hand 'aggressive tendentious jokes succeed best' when they are made by 'people in whose sexuality a powerful sadistic component is demonstrable, which is more or less inhibited in real life'. In the scope of this book it is not possible to discuss the lives of the satirists, but there is some biographical evidence to support Freud's view of the joker as possessing 'a disunited personality, disposed to neurotic disorders', whose witty attacks on the world are a consequence of and a relief from his sufferings: this is obviously true of the greatest of English satirists, Swift. But we are here concerned with the mechanism of the joke rather than with the joker. It is impossible not to agree with Freud that behind even the harmless jokes we make there is some desire to score off someone else, to humiliate by ridicule and, in other words, to satirise. The basic devices of the simple aggressive jokes are those of developed literary satire and of caricature: unmasking, degradation of *erhaben* (exalted) persons or objects by *Herabsetzung* (degradation), parody and travesty which 'destroy the unity that exists between people's characters as we know them, and their speeches and actions, by replacing either the exalted figures or their utterances by inferior ones'.

To illustrate both the aggressive nature of joking and the quality of unexpectedness in wit, Freud quotes a story about 'a witty and pugnacious journalist in Vienna' whose invective often led to his being assaulted by his opponents. When one of these had just committed a new outrage, someone remarked: 'If X hears of this, he'll get his ears boxed again'. X, incidentally, was the great satirist and aphorist Karl Kraus, who made one of the best jokes about the Freudians: 'Psychoanalysis is that disease of which it pretends to be the cure'.

The essence of the joke and of literary satire is *wit*, which it is usual to distinguish from humour. The word in English originally meant 'mind' or 'understanding', later 'cleverness': a 'witty child' to Shakespeare means just a clever child. But already in Shakespeare's time it was gaining its modern sense, 'the power of giving pleasure by combining or contrasting ideas', the quality of speech or writing which can 'surprise and delight by its unexpectedness'. In the seventeenth century wit, 'a just mixture of Reason and Extravagance', was the essential component of all poetry; and in its modern sense wit remains close to poetry. Like poetry it rests on the ability to discover and reveal the power hidden in language: e.g. similarities in sound (puns or rhymes), or unsuspected parallels in grammar and syntax. But whereas a great deal of poetry is untranslatable, because it depends so closely on the rhythms and associations of words in a particular language, some of the essentials of wit can be translated, provided that the essential ideas can be put across. Thus, Voltaire's comment on the unjust execution of Admiral Byng can probably be rendered in any language: 'Dans ce pays-ci, il est bon de tuer de temps en temps un amiral pour encourager les autres'. ('In this country it is considered good from time to time to kill an admiral to encourage the others.') The translator need only use any literal translation of 'tuer' to convey the idea of murder against judicial execution, and find the right equivalent for 'encourager', which coming in the place of the expected 'terrify' is the point of satire. Oscar Wilde's wit is nearer to poetry: 'The English country gentleman galloping after a fox – the unspeakable in pursuit of the uneatable' can be translated only if there is an equivalent to 'unspeakable' which gives the proper parallelism.

These examples show the essential features of verbal wit: ingenious compression, a sudden revelation of hidden implications, and the linking together of two incongruous ideas. The last of these points has recently been elaborated by Arthur Koestler in his

In Doré's drawing, the phantasms of chivalric
romance, knights, maidens, giants and dragons,
swirl round Don Quixote's head as he reads.
Even the mice are jousting.

theory of 'bisociation' (double association). In ordinary discourse
and logical thinking we follow a fixed set of rules, laid down by
logic and grammar, which he calls 'frames of reference'. To adapt
Koestler's terms slightly, wit 'is the effect of perceiving an idea or
event, simultaneously or in quick alternation, in two habitually
incompatible frames of reference. Instead of being associated with
a single context, the event is bisociated.' Thus, in the Voltaire
quotation, the two expected contents are (i) rewarding an admiral
to encourage others, and (ii) judicial punishment to deter the others;
and in fact there is a second bisociation between judicial punishment and simple murder. Koestler's analysis is useful for the
understanding of all forms of verbal wit, even of the outrageous or
surrealist joke – of which the classic example is Groucho Marx's 'I
would horsewhip you if I had a horse.' But it need not be confined
to verbal wit, since it can equally well be applied to the visual wit of
caricature and cartoon, which yoke together two different frames of
reference, usually the exalted (a public figure) and the humble
(e.g. an animal).

Many attempts have been made to distinguish between humour
and wit, without much success. The difficulty is that in the English
language *humour* is an imprecise word, with a far wider range of
meanings than wit. The original meaning of the word was the
physical one of 'moisture' (Latin, *humorem*); hence one of the four
chief fluids of the body (blood, phlegm, bile and melancholy – or
black bile) which are present in every man in various combinations
and determine his physical and mental temperament, or as we
should say now, his psychosomatic type. The division of humanity
into types according to humours was important in the history of
comedy and satire, as we shall see. But the word took on other
senses in the sixteenth century, i.e. 'mood, temper, inclination' and
later 'quality of action or speech which excites amusement' and the
faculty of perceiving this. Some authorities now take it to stand for
all forms of the laughable other than verbal ones, and thus we
speak of the humour of events or situations. In this sense the word
is applied to the amusing effect of an anecdote, short story or novel.

Mark Twain (S. L. Clemens) drew his own illustrations for
The Innocents Abroad (1869). 'They took out one of my ablest jokes
and read it over twice … They said they believed it was
an incendiary document, levelled at the government'.

Much depends on the context, which may be taken for granted, as in an anecdote told about a mutual acquaintance, or fully explained in the course of the narrative. The humour of *Don Quixote* or *Pickwick Papers* cannot be summarised or conveyed in short quotations: nor does it depend on verbal wit, although Cervantes and Dickens are sometimes very witty.

The other chief meaning of humour, as in 'the English sense of humour', is even harder to define. Here humour is distinguished from the malicious quality of wit; it implies the ability to see the joke against oneself, and to look on the world with gentle irony. This mild self-mockery is a homoeopathic remedy against the cruel mockery of the human race and indeed of the universe; it antici- pates attack and cushions the blows of fate. At its best, as in the fine American tradition from Mark Twain to the *New Yorker*, it leads to genuine humility and curiosity about the oddities of life; at its worst, as in *Punch*, it is the father of spiritual complacency, insulating the English middle class, by mild jokes about foreigners and the lower orders, in their smugness and snobbishness. Humour in this sense has nothing in common with satire; it is, in fact, the enemy of satire. 'The humorist runs with the hare: the satirist hunts with the hounds', according to Father Ronald Knox, himself no mean satirist.

The technique of reduction

The basic technique of the satirist is reduction: the degradation or devaluation of the victim by reducing his stature and dignity. This may be done on the level of plot and will almost always be continued to the level of style and language. The classic example of a reductive plot is that of *Gulliver's Travels:* the changes of scale in Books I and II first present the political scene in England as the absurdly trifling antics of the Lilliputians, and then the narrator's country- man appears to the giant king of Brobdingnag as 'the most contemptible race of little odious vermin that nature ever suffered to crawl on the face of the earth'. This device for belittling or

The great Bernini, master of Baroque architecture and sculpture,
was one of the first to draw true portrait caricatures.
His idiotic 'captain of the company' and the owl-like faces
of two clerics (*opposite*) are wholly modern in conception.

Il Capitano della Compagnia de Romaneschi fagaioli nella guer
di Vrbano VIII.

(*Bottom*) Grotesque and ribald sketches by
Annibale Carracci (1560–1609), one of the
famous family of Italian painters,
are among the earliest European caricatures.

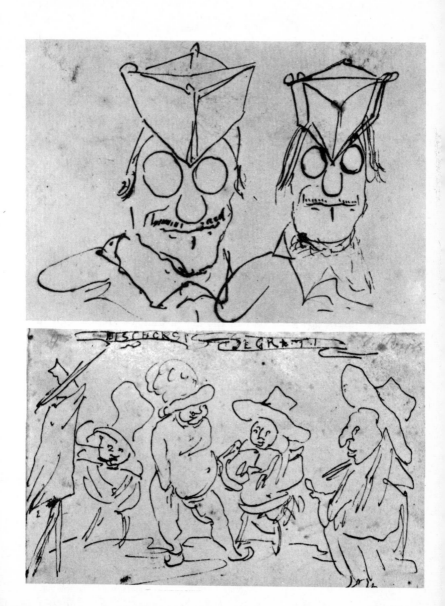

cutting down to size has been so perfectly done by Swift that no one has dared to imitate him. But size is not the only factor: the satirist tries to reduce his victim by removing from him all the supports of rank and status, of which clothes are the simplest example; there is nothing underneath all the gorgeous robes except an ordinary mortal. In developing the theme of clothes, Swift was again a pioneer. In his early work *A Tale of a Tub*, he shows the three main forms of Christianity – Catholic, Anglican and Puritan – as brothers contesting for the suit of clothes left them by their father. Swift was supposed to be defending Martin (Luther) against Jack (Calvin) and Peter, but the effect of his brilliant burlesque is to discredit all forms of dogmatic Christianity. Satire often deals with the idea of *nakedness*, though never with *nudity*. The nude is the idealised human body, both erotic and heroic in the noble tradition begun by the Greeks: the nude is appropriate to the context of Eros (undressing for bed) or for the athletic-heroic (stripping for the games); it is the apotheosis of human anatomy. The naked, on the other hand, means undressing in a wholly inappropriate context: the naked man is caught with his trousers down, caught in the act of guilt or shame. Our first parents, Adam and Eve, were in the pre-fallen state glorious nudes: after eating the apple they became aware that they were simply naked, and in their embarrassment tried to conceal their parts with fig-leaves – the first victims of divine satire. The Greeks who invented the godlike nude also used nakedness for the purposes of degradation: the Phlyax vases show gods and heroes, Zeus and Oedipus, ludicrously undressed, with erect phalluses. Nakedness thus reduces man from the godlike to the animal.

The animal world is continually drawn on by the satirist: he reminds us that homo sapiens despite his vast spiritual aspirations is only a mammal that feeds, defecates, menstruates, ruts, gives birth and catches unpleasant diseases. And dies? No, in satire mortality is usually kept just round the corner: the theme of death is best left to the literature of tragedy, lyric or stoic meditation, or even jesting. But apart from mortality, satire uses all the other attributes of the animal world. The animal image is an essential device in the visual counterpart, caricature and cartoon: it reduces man's purposeful actions, the ambitious aims of which he is proud and his lusts of which he is ashamed, all to the level of brute instinct: hog in sloth, fox in stealth.

Satire sometimes goes below the level of the animal world to the vegetable and the mineral. The literary satirist is more concerned in the realm of the automatic. *l'homme machine*, the robot. W. H. Auden points out how commonly the referent of satire is the monomaniac; the object of satirical attack is usually a rational man, who is aware of what he is doing, neither a madman nor a totally wicked man. At the moment of yielding to temptation, the normal human being has to exercise self-deception and rationalisation, for in order to yield he requires the illusion of acting with a good conscience; after he has committed the immoral act, the normal human being realises the nature of his act and feels guilty. He who is incapable of realising the nature of his act is mad, and he who, before, while and after committing it, is exactly conscious of what he is doing, is wicked. Auden points out that the satirical strategy consists in breaking down these categories, and presenting the object of satire either 'as if he or she were mad and unaware of what he is doing', or 'as if he or she were wicked and completely conscious of what he is doing without feeling any guilt'. Only the first of these devices concerns us here: to be told that our casual foolish actions are criminally wicked may be uncomfortable, but it may be even obscurely flattering, since it implies that we knew what we were up to or had some grand design. But to be told that our follies are compulsive, that we could no more help committing them than a madman can (or a machine can) is highly damaging to our self-esteem. Whatever their philosophical views, all men believe that they are to some extent free agents; and also that they have unique personalities. When the satirist deprives us of our freedom and uniqueness, he strikes a blow at our basic life-illusion – and it is a blow we half expect, because we are never sure that we are really free or unique or quite sane. The satirist shows his

G.B. Porta, the physiognomist, tried to show that men's characters
could be read in their faces by their resemblance to animals.
This theory was meant seriously, but only the satirists have exploited it.

enemy as condemned to repeat the same meaningless movements
over and over again, like the damned in Dante's hell. The most
convincing version of hell we can imagine is one of compulsive
repetition, a condition in which we would be unable to perform one
free act of our own volition, but are doomed to the endless produc-
tion-belt of our own obsessions as in Sartre's *Huis Clos*.

'L'enfer, c'est les autres', and the pain of being handed over to
the others lies in the fact that they have us typed. To be reduced to a
type is a less fearful circumstance than to be reduced to an animal,
madman or machine, but it is unpleasant enough. It implies, if less
rigorously, that the type-figure can never step out of the role
imposed on him, or act in freedom. Although satire uses it too,
typing is the essential device in stage comedy and ironic humour.
Chaucer in the *Canterbury Tales* classifies his pilgrims according to
the humours and by physiognomy, an ancient lore which combined

the humours with astrology and medicine. The Wife of Bath looks and believes as she does because of her horoscope: the planets at her birth imposed a pattern of character on it, which explains her dress, boldness, erotic adventurousness and love of travel. It does not matter whether Chaucer believed in this kind of explanation: he used it to extract exquisite comedy out of the types he created. Humour-types persisted in Renaissance comedy, and were given a new life by Ben Jonson (as in *Everyman in his Humour*). They are transformed into the satirical 'characters', English and French, of the seventeenth century. The Theophrastian 'character' is partly an attempt to explain the sorts and conditions of men on quasi-scientific or quasi-sociological lines, and partly a satirical placing of fools and knaves in their fixed categories. Dickens's characters descend indirectly from the humour-types of Jonsonian comedy, through the tradition of English stage comedy. Dickens is the master of the comedy of obsession and compulsive repetition: Mr Micawber, who is always waiting for something to turn up, Mrs Micawber who will never desert Mr Micawber – these and similar characters have been called 'caricatures', but the description is not exact; although they are not stock types and are highly individualised, they are still close to the monomaniacs of the comedy of humours.

This stage tradition is in turn related to the *mime*, and the mime depends upon *mimicry;* and some form of mimicry is an essential satirical technique. The mimic's power – and it can be a malicious even deadly power – comes from his ability to spot the compulsive unconscious gestures in his victim, and then reproduce them. He thus reduces his victim to a lower order of being, by insisting on his repeatability. Mimicry is an invasion of privacy, in that it destroys every man's private conviction that he is unique and inimitable: even though it may be affectionate in its malice, it is another weapon against human pride. The mimic must create a likeness, so that his audience shall recognise it; but he must not stop at a mere impersonation, he must go on to produce a ludicrous distortion in which the compulsive gestures and tics of the victim are exaggerated: a newly-created character is built out of them and superimposed on the original likeness. The visual equivalent of mimicry is caricature, which often fastens on unconscious gesture; and the literary equivalent is 'low' realism. 'High' realism in the novel and drama is better called 'naturalism': it arose with the determination of Flaubert and Ibsen to tell the whole truth about society. Naturalism has usually been linked with reforming purposes, with the getting rid of illusion for serious ends. But this is a comparatively recent development: it was preceded, for reasons given by Erich Auerbach in his classic study *Mimesis*, by many centuries of 'low' realism. Comedy and satire were the only vehicles for this kind of realism; they dealt with low life, that is, all social life below the ruling class, taking as characters slaves, whores, pimps, small merchants and the 'mob' of the ancient city. The language of this literature is also 'low', that is, colloquial, slangy, often obscene, far removed from the rhetorical and dignified high style put into the mouths of the heroes and heroines of epic and tragedy. It is thus based on mimicry of the speech of the market place.

Another form of mimicry is *parody*, which is the basis of all literary satire of literature. This involves the taking over and mastering of another writer's style and the reproducing of it with ludicrous distortions. The earliest extant literary parodies are those in Aristophanes's *The Frogs*, where he burlesques the style of Aeschylus and Euripides. In English the genre begins with Chaucer's 'Sir Thopas' which ridicules the popular 'romance' of the fourteenth century. There is a huge literature of parody up to the present day, skilfully anthologised by Dwight Macdonald (1960): much of it is gently humorous, but some of it, like Max Beerbohm's greatest efforts, highly destructive of inflated literary reputations. Joyce uses parody for satiric purposes in the 'Cyclops' chapter of *Ulysses* to explode the inflated pretensions of nationalism; and in the 'Nausicaa' chapter to take off the vulgarity of women's magazine journalism. Rabelais and Swift, Joyce's masters, were also great parodists. Parody is not always used with malicious intent, for it may spring from the sheer joy of travesty; but where it is so used, it is yet another example of reduction. The parodist reduces the individual style of another, of which he is particularly proud, as a carefully-wrought instrument for expressing his personality, to a handful of rhetorical formulae and verbal tics.

The last example of reduction I shall consider is the destruction of the symbol. This is related to techniques of 'undressing' but it goes even further and it is fundamental to satire. Men live by symbols, religious or political: the cross and the crescent, the tricolour and the red star are symbolic representations of group solidarity and group aspirations, standing for a way of life or a militant programme. The satirist who wishes to show that an emblem is being used for unjust ends or is being manipulated by tyrants and demagogues, pretends not to understand its symbolic connotations, and presents with as much realism as possible the thing in itself: the flag is just a piece of cloth. Religions, because they use a highly complex set of symbols are peculiarly vulnerable to this kind of attack. Protestant and free-thinking polemic against Roman Catholic doctrine has always made free (and usually highly offensive) use of desymbolisation, as in Swift's *A Tale of a Tub*. But militarism is also vulnerable, since all armies use a variety of symbols in order to maintain morale. The *locus classicus* for this satirical device is Voltaire's *Lettres Philosophiques* (I) where he describes an English Quaker. Voltaire begins by making gentle fun of this eccentric sectarian, who refuses to comply with the fashion of dress or formal manners: but he ends by using his Quaker as a mouthpiece to attack various aspects of orthodox religion and in particular the sanctification of war; finally war itself with its traditional panoply:

Notre Dieu, qui nous a ordonné d'aimer nos ennemis et de souffrir sans murmure, ne veut pas sans doute que nous passions la mer pour aller égorger nos frères, parceque des meurtriers vêtus de rouge, avec un bonnet haut de deux pieds, enrôlent les citoyens en faisant du bruit avec deux petits bâtons sur une peau d'âne bien tendue . . . .

(Our God who has commanded us to love our enemies and to suffer without complaint, certainly does not wish us to cross the seas in order to cut our brothers' throats, just because some murderers in red clothes with hats two feet high enlist citizens by making a noise with two little sticks on a stretched ass skin ...)

The final stroke is the literal description of the drum: that's all it is, and that's why Christians kill each other by the million.

In his capacity as symbol-destroyer the satirist either invents a mouthpiece or assumes a *persona* or mask. The difference between the two is slight: Voltaire for the moment speaks through the Quaker, just as Swift speaks through Gulliver. In formal satire the satirist appears in person and engages in a monologue: but his 'I' is partly a fictional character. This is a difficult role to sustain; and it has usually proved more effective to invent a persona distinct from the satirist in age or social position. This may be a child or a savage who does not understand the rules of adult and civilised society, and who refuses to see the symbolic values which such a society attaches to apparently trivial objects and actions; thus the absurdity of social institutions is exposed when they are reduced to childish or primitive terms.

'Primitivism', the cult of the noble savage, is the underlying philosophical outlook of much eighteenth-century satire. One of the earliest is Addison's *Spectator* essay of 1711, which presents London life through the eyes of a Red Indian chief; the classic attack on sexual morality is Diderot's *Supplement to Bougainville's Voyage* (1772), when a South Sea islander fails to see the point of Christian restrictions on free love. The child's-eye view of the nonsensical adult world is rarer in satire, probably because it has been felt wrong to expose even a fictional child to the corruptions of society; but parts at least of Lewis Carroll's *Alice* are satirical protests against the mad behaviour of grown-ups, as William Empson has shown in a brilliant essay; and Raymond Queneau in *Zazie dans le Métro* (1959) describes present-day France from the standpoint of a precocious little girl. Voltaire's Quaker is a child in the Christian sense ('except ye become as little children ...'). The child and the primitive are not 'educated', in that they have not learned how to attach symbolic importance to the right things; but like Alice,

they may be highly intelligent and logical in their approach to the complexities of the world, and will certainly be emotionally more honest than the worldly. If not a savage, then a naive intelligent outsider may be used, an observer from a different culture, as in Montesquieu's *Lettres Persanes* (1721) or Goldsmith's *A Citizen of the World* (1760–2). A society can be revalued only by such an outsider, who is interested and amused, but not impressed by what he sees. Sophistication and knowingness imply complicity with this wicked world; hence it is usual for the satirist's mouthpiece, if not actually a child, a savage or a Chinese, at least to be more naive than the reader knows the author to be. Gulliver, like the Drapier and indeed all Swift's other personae, is deliberately made more simple-minded than his fiendishly clever creator: the King of Brobdingnag who fails to understand what Gulliver tells him about European institutions, is even more of an honest John. When the satirist appears as an 'I' he always assumes the role of a plain-dealer (to use the title of Wycherley's satiric comedy), who cannot and will not grasp the subtleties of courtly or intellectual life, but knows a fool or a knave when he smells one. This pose is of course hard to maintain, since the protagonist of formal satire easily degenerates into an anti-social ranter, lashing himself into a fury of non-comprehension.

The general drift of satire is to reduce everything to simple terms: the appeal is always to common sense, plain reason and simple logic. The patron saint of this aspect of satire is Dr Johnson in his deflatory mood: he dealt with the idealist philosophy of Bishop Berkeley by kicking a stone and saying 'I refute it thus'. On the level of style, the counterpart to this philosophical reduction is clarity and simplicity. The satirist puts elaborate and bombastic language in the mouth of his victims: they express their paranoic delusions of grandeur and their monomaniac greed by inflated rhetoric, like Sir Epicure Mammon in Ben Jonson's *The Alchemist* ('I will have all my beds blown up, not stuffed'), or like Pope's Dunces. The satirist's enemies, to borrow the terminology of Orwell's *1984*, use the equivalent of 'Newspeak' jargon because they

'double-think': the satirist and his personae use the plainest of language, 'clear, masculine and smooth', following the ideal prescription of the King of Brobdingnag. Gulliver speaks plainly when he discusses the perverted science of the Laputans: when he becomes the apologist of European society he tends to relapse into bombast. He is put to shame by the total clarity of the noble horses who cannot understand 'the thing that is not'.

The satirist puts on a mask for the purpose of unmasking others. He strips off his victims' symbols of rank and their clothes to reveal the corrupt nakedness beneath. Unmasking is a version of reduction, but it goes much further than the other versions. The satirist refuses to allow the satirised to remain with any personae of their own, or with any secrets. He is not content with nakedness: he sees the skull beneath the skin, the hideous and shameful disease beneath the smooth envelope of skin. 'Yesterday I ordered the carcass of a beau to be stript in my presence;' writes Swift in the matter-of-fact tone of an experimental scientist, 'when we were all amazed to find so many unexpected faults under one suit of clothes. Then I laid open his brain, his heart and his spleen; but I plainly perceived at every operation, that the further we proceeded, we found the defects increase upon us in number and bulk.'

Some early satires were called 'Anatomies'; the word was coined in the sixteenth century to mean first 'the dissection of a body', later 'a body anatomised' and 'a skeleton'. The satirist uses wit and analytical power as instruments of dissection, claiming the privileges of a surgeon 'to heal with morals what he hurts with wit'. This is a difficult claim to maintain, since even the most disinterested satire walks on the borderline between the art of medicine (dissection and surgery) and sadistic vivisection. The writer may pretend to be a detective or a spy in the service of truth, but he may be received as a voyeur, who takes a psychopathic delight in discovering the secret lives of other men. It is from this point, I think that the world's resentment of satire springs; and it is often justified. The satirist may see himself as Dr Stockman in *An Enemy of the People*, the courageous doctor who insists, against official hushing-up, that the town's water supply is infected. But as Ibsen himself implies in a mood of ironic self-criticism, the satirist may find that he has unwittingly cast himself as Gregers Werle, in *The Wild Duck*, whose revelation of the secrets of the Ekdal family is motivated by neurotic Paul-Prying and causes nothing but disaster. The distinction between attacking pride and robbing another of his human dignity is a very delicate one.

The satirist's attack on pride, whether justified or not, takes other forms. As Kernan points out in *The Cankered Muse*, a common device is to present a crowded canvas. The victim appears in the midst of a sweaty and turbulent mob; he is only one of many representations of vice and folly, and with his fellow-culprits he forms the many-headed hydra, the stinking multitude. The device of the crowded canvas is found almost everywhere from Juvenal's *Rome* through Pope's *Dunciad* to the horrible collective canteens of *1984*. The reasons for its prevalence are that satire is an urban art, and that city crowds, mindless and faceless, *are* unpleasant to most people. But there is a deeper reason for the effectiveness of this device. The opposite of the satirist's butt is the heroic individual who in tragedy or epic is pictured as standing alone in his moment of triumph or defeat. The tragic hero loses in his conflict with society, but is allowed to die in glorious isolation. And so the great leader is depicted in painting or sculpture. When grotesque or comic realist art shows a seething mass, whether of devils in hell or of Flemish peasants, dignity is impossible. Thus the literary satirist will not permit his victim the psychic space to assert himself as an individual; when he sins, he sins with the mob.

Invective and irony

Any of these devices may backfire and injure the satirist as well as his victims. He is permanently vulnerable, not only because he tells unpleasant truths, but also because he faces the temptations of spiritual pride and vulgarity; he is always in danger of catching an infection from his enemies. This danger becomes the greater, the more the writer is committed to invective and abuse. Invective is of course one of his most useful weapons, and it is an art of its own: it requires elegance of form to set off grossness of content, and learned allusiveness to set off open insult. This combination is found to perfection in Swinburne's onslaught against Emerson, whom he describes as 'Coryphaens or choreagus of his Bulgarian tribe of autocoprophagous baboons, making the filth they feed on'. On a simpler level the Hebrew prophets were no less effective in their denunciations, e.g. Jeremiah (5:8). 'They were as well-fed lusty stallions, each neighing after his neighbour's wife.' This kind of invective is occasionally found in the New Testament, e.g. Matthew (23:23): 'Woe to you, scribes and Pharisees, hypocrites! You blind guides, straining at a gnat and swallowing a camel!'

But although invective has the sanction of holy writ, the best satirists use it only occasionally, for shock effect. Their standard device, which helps to avoid backlash, is irony: irony, which means literally dissimulation, is the systematic use of double meaning. It also assumes a double audience, one that is deceived by the surface meaning of the words, and another that catches the hidden sense and laughs with the deceiver at the expense of the deceived. This usually involves a *persona* (literally, a mask), or fictional character assumed by the satirist; and a narrative form which will allow a double flow of meaning to be maintained, such as a parody, imaginary voyage, utopia or mock-heroic. Irony of style is the rhetorical counterpart to the fictional narrative by which the satirist advocates cannibalism as a cure for the economic ills of Ireland: the children of the poor are to be fattened for the table. He adopts the mask of an economist who is gravely suggesting a serious measure of improvement, and parodies the calm and matter-of-fact tone of the pamphlets of his day, as he pretends to put forward this monstrous suggestion. The reader is temporarily carried away by the logic and smooth style, until the trap is sprung: Swift turns on him, saying in effect, 'You, hypocrite reader, who look on the starving Irish with indifference, are no better than a cannibal.' The art of the satirist lies in timing: as Swift does to perfection. He must choose the moment to drop his mask and make his intention perfectly clear. If too little irony leads to coarse abuse and lampoon, too much irony tends to be self-defeating, especially if it is directed against the satirist himself. Irony is the normal device for exposing the comedy of human pretensions, and as such has often been used by the great masters of comedy (Shakespeare, Molière, Jane Austen) with very little satiric purpose. Satire, as Frye has said, is militant irony: the satirist uses irony to make the reader uncomfortable, to shake him out of his complacency and to make him an ally in the battle against the world's stupidity.

5 Forms of satire

If satire is marked by its predilection for certain subjects, and by its special approach to these subjects, it is not limited to any special forms. Almost any literary form will serve, provided that it permits the characteristic combination of aggressive attack and fantastic travesty, and gives the satirist freedom to use some or all of the essential techniques that I have described. Most if not all of the existing literary genres have in fact been taken over for satiric purposes by means of parody, and, as we shall see, satire may be inserted to make self-contained episodes in plays and novels. Nevertheless there are certain forms that have been favoured by the satirists over many centuries, sometimes merely because of the conservativeness of literary tradition (such as formal satire), and sometimes because they offer particularly good possibilities for imaginative invention (such as utopian and anti-utopian story). What follows is not meant to be an exhaustive list of the possible forms, but it will show some of the commoner and more interesting formal structures that have supported the satirist's vision.

Formal satire: the classical tradition

Formal satire is a miscellany in verse: in a loosely constructed monologue the poet denounces various kinds of vice and folly, and puts up against them his moral ideals. The subject matter is daily life, not heroic life, and this is treated realistically. The style is 'low', using not the elevated diction of epic and tragedy, but words and phrases from ordinary speech; and the tone tends to be conversational, rather than declamatory. Vice and folly are delineated in 'characters' which may be individual (as in the primitive lampoon) or representative; and the poet himself sometimes appears as a character, describing some event autobiographically or speaking through a mask or 'persona' which he assumes for the occasion. 'All the doings of mankind, their vows, their fears, their angers, their lusts, their pleasures, and their goings to and fro, these shall form the motley subject of my page' is Juvenal's description of his own work (I, 85–6). The Romans claimed to have invented this genre: 'Satura tota nostra est' (satire is all our own) said Quintilian; the word has etymologically nothing to do with 'Satyr', a hairy god with goat feet[20]; although as we shall see it was often confused with this by classical and modern writers. It comes instead from the root *satur* meaning 'full' (as in 'saturated' and connected with *satis*, 'enough'). A *satura lanx* was a full dish, and in particular a dish filled with the first fruits of the harvest and offered to Ceres and Bacchus; a kind of cornucopia, it came to mean a medley, farrago or hotch-potch. The Romans believed their earliest satires to have been dramatic medleys in rude 'fescennine' verse, full of coarse raillery and ridicule. According to one Roman tradition, the early Roman poets, Ennius and Pacuvius, removed satire from its dramatic setting, and used the term to describe the more sophisticated verses they wrote on a variety of topics: 'satura', also spelt 'satira', now came to mean a poetical miscellany. Lucilius in the days of the Scipios (late second century BC), developed the form still further, turning it into a moral and political miscellany: his satires were open letters to the public, on matters of politics, morals and literary criticism. He was followed by Horace, who perforce abandoned politics, but kept the form of a moral miscellany. But in fact, Roman satire may be derived more directly from the parabasis or author's monologue of Aristophanic comedy, as Horace himself admits.

With Horace we are beyond the hazy ground of conjecture, since his work has survived to stamp its mark on formal satire ever since. His earlier works in the genre are called 'satires', his later ones 'epistles', but there is not very much difference between them; both are also called 'sermones' or 'conversations'. That is the essential point about Horatian satire: it is colloquial, dealing with a variety of not too serious moral, social and literary topics in the easy-going familiar style of a man talking to his intimate friends. The kind of topics he discusses are the folly of running to extremes, the defence of plain living and moderation in all things; the superiority of country to town life, and the simple pleasures of his Sabine farm (illustrated by the fable of the town mouse and the country mouse);

another poem is centred on the Stoic maxim *nil admirari:* don't get excited about anything; others on literary criticism and the defence of satire itself from its critics. Only a part of these works is satiric in the modern sense. There are several lively pieces such as 'The Bore' (Satire I. vi); Horace's account, in racy dialogue, of his meeting with the self-important snob, full of useless advice, whom he cannot shake off, was much imitated, notably by Donne. Horace was admired by later satirists for his ability to write about his own life without affectation (continuing the autobiographical tradition of Archilochus); and, secondly, to describe scenes from ordinary life straightforwardly. But a third quality was even more impressive to poets like Pope: Horace's urbanity, which comes from his poise, sustained tone and gentlemanly style. Just as the Sabine farm foreshadowed the English country house, so Horace's image of himself foreshadowed and helped to mould the English idea of the gentleman: learned without pedantry, countrified without boorishness, courteous without obsequiousness. The notion of the literary friendship, the confraternity of noble souls, dedicated to stoicism and poetry and set apart from the vulgarity of the market-place, is part of this ideal. Horace's style, conversational yet polished, concealing its art with art, is the perfect vehicle for conveying this complex of ideals, which belongs as much to the history of manners and taste as to literary history, and which helped to set the standards of behaviour for two or more centuries of upper-class culture in Europe. When Horace was forced out of the central field of Aristophanic satire, which is politics, he developed these secondary qualities as if in compensation for his loss of freedom; and thus paradoxically assured his fame as a satirist.

Juvenal, born more than a century after Horace, is his complete antithesis. Where Horace is conversational, Juvenal is rhetorical and declamatory; where Horace presents the comedy of life with amused detachment, Juvenal heightens his examples of vice into melodrama; where Horace preaches moderation with tact and humour, Juvenal thunders his denunciations with the heat of a prophet, in a spirit of pessimism which goes almost as far as Swift's;

where Horace is the comfortable philosopher. Juvenal is the severe moral teacher. Such, at least, is the accepted version in literary history; but in several ways it needs to be challenged. Juvenal's greatest asset is his realism, his ability to convey physical and social reality. He was also a master of rhetorical technique and of wit; while the moral and tragic power of his work remains an open question. His realism is supreme in the Third Satire. A friend of the poet explains why he is leaving Rome, where a poor man with any self respect cannot go on living: the horrors of city life are vividly detailed, the careerist Greeks, perverts and flatterers (in eighteenth-century English versions these are replaced usually by the French), the nouveaux-riches who ridicule the poor, the collapsing houses, the fires, the crowded streets where you get your toes trodden on by the brutal soldiery, the young hooligans and the burglars. The physical presence of Rome is wonderfully evoked, from the bullocks drawing marble blocks through the streets to the pigeons nesting under the roof tiles as they do in Rome today. This is the first great urban poem, the first to do justice to the complexities of city life, and that has been its fascination for writers ever since. Most writers, after all, have lived in cities for part of their lives: even if they prefer to live in the country, their patrons and public are in the capital cities, which are the centres of political and cultural life, and where most interesting events take place. At the same time cities are always unpleasant places to live in: if the plague gets better, the traffic gets worse. Thus writers are bound to their cities in a powerful love-hate relationship. Because the traditional genres of poetry take as their subject matter either pastoral life, or heroic-tragic life, which is on a plane above the mud and noise of the streets, poets have only been able to express their feelings about cities through formal satire; and this modelled directly or indirectly on Juvenal's 'Rome'. This can be seen in the translations and adaptations of 'Rome' which abound in the late seventeenth and early eighteenth centuries, beginning with Boileau's Satire VI (1660), the lively 'Les Embarras de Paris'. John Oldham (1682), John Dryden (1693) and Samuel Johnson (*London*, 1730)

An illustration to Satire 5, from Dryden's translation of Juvenal, 1697.   137
'The poet dissuades a Parasite from frequenting the tables
of great men where he is certain to be treated with the highest
scorn and contempt; and, at the same time, inveighs against
the luxury and insolence of the Roman nobility.'

with great energy translate Juvenal in terms of contemporary life in
London, the Great Wen; John Gay (*Trivia*, 1716) drew on him for
his charming burlesque Georgics about how to walk the streets;
and Juvenal left his mark on Swift's 'City Shower' and Pope's
Dunciad. Take his passage about the drunken bully, a young blood
who cannot sleep until he has beaten somebody up; yet he avoids
the rich man with scarlet cloak, with his long train of attendants
carrying torches, and fastens on the poet's poor friend going home
by candle-light. The finest English imitation is Johnson's. It brings
out the realistic force of Juvenal, by giving a brilliant picture of
Augustan London. Secondly, it shows where the moral centre of
Juvenal's satire really lies. This is not in the preference of the
country over the town: Johnson, who believed that the man who is
tired of London is tired of life, was patently insincere in saying that
he wished to escape, and we may assume that Juvenal was too: he
would have found the country even less tolerable than Rome. Nor
is it in politics, although Johnson is more political than Juvenal and
inserts some oblique criticism of Walpole's government. Instead
Johnson concentrates with weighty sincerity on one of Juvenal's
main points: that there is one law for the rich and another for the
poor, who must bear 'oppression's wrong': 'Slow rises worth by
poverty depressed'. Juvenal, forced to desist from political comment by an authoritarian régime, has succeeded in making a
powerful protest against social injustice. He cannot like Horace
write as a country gentleman; instead he identifies himself with his
wretched poet and with the poorer freemen of Rome. Uprooted
and powerless, Juvenal writes with true desperation – but with a
gaiety born of desperation.

Johnson noticed the element of exaggeration, of 'talking for
victory', in 'Rome' and follows it in his deliberately absurd
collocations:

> Here falling houses thunder on your head,
> And there a female atheist talks you dead.

Juvenal is a great comic writer; he cannot help making the miseries of life more absurdly unfair than they really are, and thus he reminds us that satire must entertain as well as denounce. Juvenal's other great satire is the Tenth, which since Johnson's version has been known as 'The Vanity of Human Wishes'; a pessimistic harangue on the folly of ambition, whether in politics, war or learning, and on the absurdity of praying to the gods for wealth or long life. The theme is an old one – 'Vanity, vanity, all is vanity' – and was first treated quasi-satirically in the archaic Greek poem of Semonides. Juvenal's satire is all related to the *declamatio*, or rhetorical public speech on a set theme: and particularly in his Sixth he dramatises his characters, like an orator. But the effect is not, as has often been said, tragic; it is at most tragi-comic, since he reduces his great men to figures of absurdity, employing a reductive technique which robs them of heroism; as when the huge bronze statue of Sejanus is melted down into basins and frying-pans. There is a wittily epigrammatic but somewhat perfunctory moral at the end; 'Pray to the gods only for the strength to endure the blows of Fortune' – *orandum est ut sit mens sana in corpore sano* – but the poem as a whole has no clear moral direction. It is as if Juvenal were returning to the saturnalian mood of primitive satire, over-turning the ranks and hierarchies of a society he found detestably restrictive, and exulting in the chaos he has produced by his demonic energy.

The main lines of formal satire were thus laid down in Latin literature, and were followed closely by three centuries of poets after the Renaissance. Some chose to imitate Horace, others Juvenal; still others borrowed eclectically from both and from Persius. The unoriginality of minor European satirists, as they pillage the classics and each other for ideas, could itself be a subject for satire. But the originality of the first modern formal satirist seems to be beyond doubt. Ludovico Ariosto (1474–1533) left seven *Satires*, which though slight as compared with his *Orlando Furioso*, that great ironic parody of romance and epic, possess an authentic charm. Written as epistles to his brothers and to friends like Pietro Bembo, they aim at the intimacy of the *sermones* and are the first to catch Horace's tone successfully. Most of them describe his life as an agent for the rulers of Ferrara, where he spent fourteen years in the service of Cardinal Ippolito d'Este. He was sent on uncomfortable missions, and the Cardinal, a hard master, was stingy about pay. There is a delightfully comic visit to Rome, where he describes the avarice of the curia with sophisticated contempt.

In France, formal satire began a little later than in Italy, but a considerable amount was written before the end of the sixteenth century, some of more than historical interest[21]. Du Bellay in his classicist manifesto, *La défence et illustration de la langue française* (1549 and 1568) showed his dislike of the medieval French tradition, and insisted that satirists should write like Horace, Persius and Juvenal. Formal satire came into its own when the religious and political struggles became less acute, in the reign of and with the encouragement of Henri IV. The first good writer since Ronsard and Du Bellay to try serious imitation of Horace and Juvenal was Jean Vauquelin de la Fresnaye (*Satyres Françaises*, 1604) but he was soon surpassed by Mathurin Régnier (1573–1613). With Régnier and still more clearly with Nicolas Boileau (1636–1711) the drift of French formal satire of the seventeenth century becomes clear. It is satire of manners, and is part of the education in right conduct and good taste demanded by the court of its members. Manners included not only courtesy, politeness, and freedom from eccentricity, but elegance of writing and speech, which went to form the idea of the *honnête homme*. At the beginning of the century manners at court, as a result of the civil wars and political confusion, had declined into barbarism; and a highly self-conscious effort was made by a small circle to improve standards of speech and behaviour. This was the purpose of the *précieuses*, a group of learned ladies who tried to create an artificially elegant way of living and writing; their endeavours helped to produce the civilisation of Louis XIV, and the glories of Racine. In this movement satire played an important part, and especially the gentlemanly tradition of Horatian satire. In his Satire VIII (1606) Régnier imitates Horace's Bore, and in X Horace's ridiculous supper: these are examples of how the *honnête homme* ought not to live, illustrated with the inventiveness and grotesque detail which appear in his famous character of Macette (Satire XIII). This has a delicious gaiety and absurdity which is not found in later French formal satire. Like Rabelais, it rambles on through a catalogue of pious jargon; the lady's easy switch from earthly to heavenly love is presented with a crude but disarming irony. Régnier still possesses the creative *naiveté* of the French Middle Ages.

Even Régnier, however, was not refined enough for Boileau and his royal master. Boileau, who won a pension and Louis' friendship by a eulogy of his victories, was in a real sense the king's voice, and had his full encouragement in his campaign to improve taste and manners. Cartesian and rationalist in the spirit of the age, Boileau pruned his satire of extravagant detail, tightened up the form, and soon achieved a classic purity of diction. After his lively imitation of Juvenal in his Sixth Satire (1660), 'Les Embarras de Paris' becomes more and more Horatian, and this results in an impoverishment of both form and content. Boileau's satire is partly a stylistic exercise of astonishing grace and poise – the style is itself the embodiment of his ideals – and partly a species of moral preaching, persuasive and good-humoured but confined to the narrow field of moral comment. Although a great deal of formal satire continued to be written in France in the eighteenth century, Boileau was the last master of the genre, and perhaps the last who is still readable. Voltaire praised Boileau but as a stylist and a teacher rather than a satirist: 'he saw that finally the art of instructing, when it is perfect, succeeds better than the art of slandering, because satire dies with those who are its victims, and reason and virtue are eternal'[22]. Coming from the greatest satirist of the eighteenth century, that is disingenuous; and it is significant that Voltaire, when he came to attack the real evils of his age, left formal satire for more potent mediums.

In England, formal satire began later than in France and Italy, and had a curious if not very distinguished history for its first century. With only a few scattered experiments in the earlier sixteenth century, it begins with a rush in the mid-1590s. *A Fig for Momus* by Thomas Lodge published in 1595 is the earliest of the late-Elizabethan formal satires of which the date is known, but the first two *Satyres* by John Donne may have been written earlier. Bishop Joseph Hall claimed wrongly in his *Virgidemiarum* 1597–8:

> I first adventure, follow me who list
> And be the second English satirist.

He was followed by John Marston, *The Metamorphosis of Pygmalion's Image* and *The Scourge of Villanie*, both of 1598. There was such a flood of satirical writing in that year and the following that in 1599 a prohibition known as the 'Bishop's Ban' was enacted against the publication of 'Satyres or Epigrams' and other scandalous and controversial books. This ban was not wholly effective but it certainly caused a marked decrease in the publication of satirical literature in the early seventeenth century. Elizabethan formal satire is largely the work of young literary men, who were determined moralists: they were voicing the discontent of a whole generation of over-educated and under-employed writers, and were rightly held to be subversive. But with the exception of Donne, this literature is sadly disappointing as poetry, and this is partly because of a wrong-headed theory. The classical rule of style-division had been accepted by the Italians and French; tragedy and epic were to concern exalted and heroic people and therefore to be written in 'high' style, while satire and comedy had to be in a 'low' colloquial style which decorum demanded should match the scenes of everyday 'low' life which were their subject-matter. But most of the Elizabethans went further than this: they pushed the doctrine so far that they made their satirical style as rough as possible, to match the violence of their feelings and the grotesqueness of their subjects. The critical doctrine that satire should be harsh and rough, because it attacks vicious men, had been found in Puttenham's *Arte of English Poesie* (1588), and is repeated in Hall's lines:

> The Satyre should be like the *Porcupine*,
> That shoots sharpe quils out in each angry line,
> And wounds the blushing cheeke, and fiery eye,
> Of him that heares, and readeth guiltily.

It was the pedantic application of this doctrine that made Ben Jonson say: 'John Donne for not keeping of accent deserved hanging'. Donne's satires are packed with brilliant ideas and images, but they are very hard to read aloud, and suffer from obscurity of thought. Yet Donne is by far the best of the Elizabethan satirists: Hall is frigid and mechanical, Marston turgid and chaotic, the others are mere bunglers. All these men quote and adapt Horace and Juvenal throughout, some favouring Persius because of his crabbed style; their self-conscious classicism is tedious. Donne alone escapes from it, by boldly discussing topics outside the normal field of formal satire. His greatest satire is his third, on religion; a weighty examination of the problem that vexed most thinking men of his age, namely, which is the true Christian church. This is satirical only insofar as he writes frankly and rudely of Calvinists, Anglicans and Romans; but it turns into a noble and anguished search for theological truth:

> On a huge hill,
> Cragged and steep, Truth stands, and he that will
> Reach her, about must, and about must go,
> And what the hill's suddenness resists, win so;
> Yet strive so, that before age, death's twilight,
> Thy soul rest, for none can work in that night.

The greatest achievements of the seventeenth-century satirists lie outside the field of formal satire, in Butler's *Hudibras*, Marvell's *Instructions to a Painter*, and Dryden's mock-heroic *Absalom and Achitophel*. But the debate on the style and purpose of formal satire went on with vigour in England, particularly in the freer air of the Restoration. The old notion that style should be rough died hard, appearing even in Dryden's elegy on his friend John Oldham, who died young in 1683:

> What could advancing age have added more?
> It might (what Nature never gives the Young)
> Have taught the Numbers of thy Native Tongue.
> But Satire needs not those, and wit will shine
> Through the harsh cadence of a rugged line.

By 'numbers' Dryden meant the musical effect of the balanced, antithetical heroic couplet, with a marked pause in the middle and at the end of each line; an effect invented by Denham and Waller, which was to charm English ears for more than a century. Inspired by Boileau and by the literature of the French court, Dryden tried to give to his satirical verse a refined cadence, and to make his diction polished and correct. For this he earned Pope's tribute:

> Wit grew polite, and numbers learn'd to flow.
> Waller was smooth; but Dryden taught to join
> The long majestic march and energy divine.

Paradoxically, apart from translating Juvenal, Dryden did not write formal satire or satire of manners like Boileau's: his best work is boisterous mock-heroic and hard-hitting lampoon. But his principles and techniques were taken over by Alexander Pope for his *Imitations of Horace* and *Moral Essays*, the apotheosis of English formal satire.

This meant a shift of allegiance from Juvenal to Horace. Dryden, in sincere admiration inserted passages of Juvenalian satire into many of his poems, imitating Juvenal's declamatory and dramatic style, and giving his victims the heroic grandeur of 'The Vanity of Human Wishes', as in the noble description of Shaftesbury in *Absalom and Achitophel:*

> A fiery soul, which working out its way
> Fretted the pigmy body to decay,
> And o'er-informed the tenement of clay.

As J.A.K. Thompson says, 'Dryden has got the invective force of Juvenal, his inexhaustible variety and resource, his moral superiority, real or assumed, to the men he assails'. Pope, however, did not whole-heartedly admire Juvenal's high-flown manner, although he occasionally catches it brilliantly; as in the picture of Buckingham's sordid end, in the third *Moral Essay* ('Of the Use of Riches') which reaches the right intensity of horror and disgust:

> In the worst inn's worst room, with mat half-hung,
> The floors of plaster and the walls of dung;
> On once a flock-bed but repaired with straw
> With tape-tied curtains never meant to draw,
> The George and Garter dangling from that bed
> Where tawdry yellow strove with dirty red
> Great Villiers lies....

Such is the miserable fate of ambition. Pope presents the scene with a painter's eye; Aldous Huxley notes that nothing could be more horrible than the walls of dung – floors we could stand, but walls, no. But such Juvenalian moments are rare in Pope, after the fury and murk of the first *Dunciad* (1728). At the height of his poetic career he devoted himself to adapting Horace, with remarkable success. Some of the reasons for this devotion and this success must be looked for outside literature. First, Pope like Boileau wanted to write the satire of manners; he felt himself to be a teacher, and manners were now to include what he was admirably qualified to teach, namely good taste in architecture and the fine arts. Secondly, Pope's own position in good society was much like Horace's: Boileau and Dryden had been servants of the court, but Pope was no man's servant. He was an independent gentleman, who lived on equal terms with the great men of England – with the Tory ministers Harley and Bolingbroke, and with Lords Bathurst and Cobham, and with the arbiter of good taste, Lord Burlington. The parallel with Horace's aims and social position was close enough for Pope to feel a spiritual kinship, which can be seen in his poetic style. Horace is colloquial and Pope tries to catch in his verse the tone of conversation, of the best conversation among the best people, refined yet man-to-man. For this purpose Juvenal and his followers must have seemed too rhetorical, pedantic and even too

The alternative title of Hogarth's *Calais Gate* was
O The Roast Beef of Old England, a patriotic song by Henry Fielding.
The French, who eat vegetables, are slaves: the English,
to whom the substantial sirloin belongs by right, are free men.
The Sublime Society of Beefsteaks, to whom Hogarth belonged,
had as its motto 'Beef and Liberty'.

'literary' for good taste. The right note of gentlemanly disdain he learned from Horace's casual dialogues:

> Shut, shut the door, good John! fatigued, I said;
> Tie up the knocker, say I'm sick, I'm dead.

Pope, who is capable of the most delicate effects of rococo decoration usually clinches a passage of Horatian satire with forceful and monosyllabic words of the simplest Anglo-Saxon origin, as in one of his finest lines, where he says he will not hesitate to attack vice even in those who wear orders of nobility, to 'Bare the mean heart that lurks beneath a star'. This combination of elegance and directness needs such technical mastery and social self-confidence as is hardly ever found in literature: many tried to follow him but there is no 'school of Pope'.

The centre of Pope's moral teaching is the notion of good taste, which implies not merely the ability to enjoy the arts but a whole way of living. Pope believed that it was immoral to have bad taste in architecture or gardening, and conversely that vice and folly are hopelessly vulgar. Flashiness, showiness and hardness of heart all go together. Pope learned these not very profound ideas from the philosopher Shaftesbury; and by the exquisite texture and rhythm of his verse, which is itself the perfection of taste, he brings the doctrine to imaginative life. This is most beautifully illustrated in the fourth Moral Essay, otherwise known as the Epistle to Lord Burlington, 'Of the Use of Riches'. He begins by giving instances of 'the vanity of expense in people of wealth and quality', and goes on to compliment Burlington as the founder of the new Palladian architecture, which was to replace the baroque splendour with restraint and harmony with nature:

> You show us Rome was glorious, not profuse,
> And pompous buildings once were things of use.

He continues by giving a little lesson in landscape gardening, which was listened to seriously in the mid eighteenth century. Gardens were not to be formal backgrounds for courtiers, but landscapes in which a country gentleman could walk in harmony with nature:

> Consult the genius of the place in all:
> That tells the waters or to rise or fall,
> Or helps th'ambitious hill the heav'ns to scale,
> Or scoops in circling theatres the vale.

This may seem to be moving a long way from the morality of money, but Pope gradually makes the connection between vice and taste more plain to see, as he turns his aesthetic discourse into satire. The man who violates the rules of taste is the millionaire 'Timon', a character probably based on the Duke of Chandos, a war profiteer. Pope ridicules the works of art with which Timon seeks to glorify himself: his villa is Brobdingnagian, 'His pond an ocean, his parterre a down.' In his vast private chapel, 'where sprawl the saints of Verrio and Laguerre' (fashionable and expensive mural painters), all the religion you will find is fashionable self-advertisement:

> [where] To rest, the cushion and soft dean invite,
> Who never mentions hell to ears polite.

Against this huge baroque background, the proud owner suddenly shrinks to insignificance, becoming

> A puny insect, shivering in the breeze.

This is a perfect example of the satirical technique of reduction: Timon is cut down to size, and he shivers in the breeze of human mortality. The theme is now pride, which makes men into violators of the laws of Nature; and Nature will take her revenge. Bad taste, vanity and greed are shown to be linked together, nemesis will follow hubris. The stoic maxim of 'living according to nature' comes to life in the wonderful passage which prophesies that Timon's villa will be demolished and return to farmland; which is the perfect expression of the saturnalian spirit of satire, the imaginative reversal of the wicked world:

Apart from the major works of Gillray, thousands of popular
prints, like W. Elmes's 'General Frost shaving little Boney',
were sold to the British public during the Napoleonic wars.
Shaving, as a symbol of defeat, was often used by the cartoonists.

The uses of Swift's masterpiece have been endless:
thus, in one of his more patriotic prints (1803),
James Gillray depicts George III of England
and Napoleon Bonaparte.

> Another age shall see the golden Ear
> Imbrown the slope and nod on the Parterre,
> Deep Harvests bury all his pride has planned,
> And laughing Ceres re-assume the land.

In these lines Pope gives us a perfect vision of paradise regained, of the good life as it could be lived on this earth.

Satire miniaturised: aphorism and epigram

The two shortest literary forms of satire, though by no means the simplest, are the aphorism and the epigram. The first is associated with wisdom and prose, the second with wit and verse. Neither confines itself to satire, but it is striking how many examples of each have a satirical flavour and how many of the best epigrammatists and aphorists have also been successful practitioners of the longer forms of satire; in English, for example, Swift, Johnson and Butler, and, in French, Voltaire, are masters of both micro- and macro-satire. There would seem to be some essential connection between the two. The only good satirist of eighteenth-century Germany – and still one of the few satirists of all German literature – is the great master of the aphorism, Lichtenberg: his most notable successor in the twentieth century is Karl Kraus. The aphorism is defined in the Oxford Dictionary as 'any principle or precept expressed shortly and pithily'; but an earlier meaning is 'a definition or concise statement of a principle in any science'. The earliest aphorisms were in fact the scientific ones of Hippocrates, a collection of medical facts and teachings couched in an unsystematic and crisp form. His first is the most famous of all aphorisms: 'Life is short, and art is long; the occasion fleeting; experience fallacious and judgment difficult'. The scientific aphorism was revived at the Renaissance, especially by Francis Bacon, who admired the form as a means of conveying experimental truth. Bacon's observations of the world of men, as in his *Essays*, were equally to him an accumulation of scientific knowledge. The Baconian aphorism was taken over by Lichtenberg, who was both physicist and satirist; as a

Newtonian empiricist he also disliked elaborate philosophical systems, and he also applied his scientific method to the study of human nature, trying to catch the essence of a moment's revelation in a witty form. In all good aphorisms there is something of the scientist's disinterested pursuit of truth. But it is truth of a special kind, usually the painful truth about human nature. The best satirists have the same passion for objectivity, and for the revelation of truth: they are, as we have seen, anatomists, and use the aphorism as a surgical instrument.

The more usual meaning of the aphorism, however, is not a scientific but a moral generalisation. It offers ethical teaching or 'wisdom' in a condensed and unsystematic form. There is a long tradition of wisdom literature which starts from ancient Egypt and Mesopotamia, continues in the biblical *Book of Proverbs* and such classical moralists as Marcus Aurelius and Epictetus, and reaches its peak with the great French aphorists of the seventeenth century, Pascal and La Rochefoucauld. It is striking how many of the early aphorisms have a satirical flavour: they often spring from a disillusioned and ironical view of life, from a bitter experience of human folly, and they use the cutting edge of metaphor and para-dox. Thus among the Akkadian aphorisms based on Sumerian originals (apparently before 2000 BC) we find a satirical situation in miniature: 'My knees keep walking, my feet are lifeless, yet a man devoid of understanding pursues me with sorrow.' The device of animal analogues appears in 'The dog understands "take it"; he does not understand "put it down" '.

The satirical note appears very clearly in that sophisticated compilation of oriental wisdom, the *Book of Proverbs*. Take for example the aphorisms which have served as texts for generations of anti-feminists: 'As a jewel of gold in a swine's snout, so is a fair woman which is without discretion.' Elsewhere a quarrelling wife (or contentious woman) is like a continual dropping of rain – the Proverbs use poetic metaphor tellingly to make their points, as in 'the dog returns to his vomit', or 'the thorns crackle under the pot; so is the laughter of a fool'. The best aphorisms of Johnson have this poetic quality: compare *his* anti-feminist dictum 'Sir, a woman preaching is like a dog walking on his hind legs. It is not done well, but you are surprised to find it done at all.'

The satirical note is less marked in the late Roman stoic aphorists, Marcus Aurelius and Epictetus, though they will prick the bubble of self-conceit by appealing to experience of the world: 'It has often surprised me that while each man loves himself more than anyone else, he sets less value on his own estimate than on the opinions of others.' In the seventeenth century Pascal, it is true, kept his powerful satirical gifts away from his *Pensées*, reserving them for the polemic of his *Lettres Provinciales;* but the less exalted of the *Pensées* have the same deflationary approach: 'Quand on voit le style naturel, on est tout étonné et ravi, car on s'attendait de voir un auteur et on trouve un homme' ('When we encounter a natural style we are always astonished and delighted, for we expected to see an author and find a man') – a gravely witty rebuke which must make every author abashed. The great masters of the satirical aphorism are his French contemporaries and successors, and above all the Duc de la Rochefoucauld (1613–80), whose *Maximes* devastatingly reveal the forces of egoism in every human being:

Nous avons tous assez de force pour supporter les maux d'autres (We have all enough strength to bear the misfortunes of others)

or

La reconnaissance de la plupart des hommes n'est qu'une secrète envie de recevoir de plus grands bienfaits (In most of mankind gratitude is merely a secret hope of further favours).

The cynicism is alarming but made tolerable by the elegant logic of the formulae. La Rochefoucauld is perhaps too Machiavellian and too much of the grand seigneur to have a universal appeal: but he sets the standards for the classic French tradition which continues to Joubert and Chamfort. The English aphorists are more empirical and humorous, more interested in the comedy of everyday life. The more disturbing and pungent is of course Swift, in his *Thoughts on Various Subjects* 'We have just enough religion to make us hate, but not enough to make us love one another'; 'The most positive men are the most credulous'; or his contribution to anti-feminism: 'What they do in heaven we are ignorant of; but what they do not we are told expressly, that they neither marry nor are given in marriage.' The basic idea of the Struldbrug episode in *Gulliver* Book III is found compressed in one sentence: 'Every man desires to live long; but no man would be old.'

Alexander Pope is the greatest master of the aphorism in verse. All Pope's satires, and in particular his *Essay on Man* are studded with terse summaries of his philosophical and political views in the tradition of the Stoics and ancient wisdom:

> For forms of government let fools contest;
> What e'er is best administered is best:
> For modes of faith let graceless zealots fight;
> His can't be wrong whose life is in the right.

The best aphorisms of Johnson are drawn from his conversation as recorded by Boswell; they not only have the poetic ring of the biblical proverbs, but they have an unequalled spontaneity and dramatic sense as they are drawn out by the heat of the moment. You can see the aphorism forming in his mind, as he reaches the climax of a crushing retort. To the Scot who defended his country as possessing 'a great many noble wild prospects' (i.e. scenery), he replies:

> I believe Sir, you have a great many. Norway, too, has noble wild prospects; and Lapland is remarkable for prodigious noble wild prospects. But, Sir, let me tell you, the noblest prospect which a Scotchman ever sees is the high road that leads him to England!

Lichtenberg[23], in many critics' view the master of the genre, developed the English rather than the French tradition. He is an observer of the minute trivialities of everyday life, which he elevates into sharp generalisations about human folly:

Geſchmack
Gout.

Geſchmack
Gout

Es wird in England des Jahres noch einmal so viel Portwein getrunken, als in Portugal wächst.

Twice as much port is drunk in England in a year as is grown in Portugal – true of port in the eighteenth century and true of Burgundy today, this is a beautifully neat simultaneous attack on credulity and chicanery. Lichtenberg is an ironist of Enlightenment freethinking:

Dass in den Kirchen gepredigt wird macht deswegen die Blitzableiter auf ihnen nicht unnöthig (That there is preaching in the church doesn't make lightning conductors unnecessary).

Much of the force of Lichtenberg's sentences comes from his subtle exploration of the possibilities of word-order in German, and of syntactical devices and puns; some of the best are therefore almost untranslatable. What comes through the filter of language is an unsentimental but humane criticism of life.

Lichtenberg wrote comments on the engravings of Chodowiecki,   155
as he did on Hogarth's. Thus, on 'Taste' from the series
'Natural and Affected Behaviour' (1780): 'One would divine
the lady's modishness from the free fluttering of the topsail alone,
were it not also evident from the position of the right arm which
... carries the fan as if it weighed a hundred pounds'.

From the end of the eighteenth century the aphorism takes a new
direction in European literature. The French tradition, based on
good conversation, verbal wit and worldly shrewdness, has survived
in France almost alone, presumably because these things are still
cultivated in French society; so that the *Carnets* of Henri de
Montherlant are in the direct line from La Rochefoucauld. But the
most brilliant aphorisms of the last century and a half have been
of the 'oracular' or 'vatic' kind; attempting not to comment on
social reality or to regulate behaviour but to penetrate the depths
of the human soul or to reach a metaphysical level. The forerunner
of the modern aphorism is William Blake, who scorned Bacon's
dicta as 'good advice from Satan's kingdom'. Such flashes of
perception as 'The tigers of wrath are wiser than the horses of
instruction' or 'The road of excess leads to the palace of wisdom'
have a wild intuitive power: they seem to tell us something profound about the hidden energies in every human being, but they
simply cannot be interpreted as comment on the world as we know
it. Such 'transfinite' aphorisms abound in the journals of Kierkegaard and Kafka, in the novels of Dostoevsky and in the quasi-
philosophy of Nietzsche: they are characteristic of the best
imaginative writing in the modern 'existentialist' mode, which
expresses a theology of crisis or a desperate conviction of the
absurdity of the universe. Although there is much shrewd comment
on the world in the aphorisms of Kierkegaard, Nietzsche and
Kafka, on the whole they take us far beyond satire and irony in
their traditional senses. This is one of the reasons for suspecting
that satire, as defined here, is itself a somewhat archaic survival
which is being abandoned by the avant-garde of literature.

It seems to be a common experience that reading a mass of this
literature consecutively causes a feeling of satiety and even revul-
sion, especially in the young and hopeful. The aphorists know too
much about the wickedness of human nature, about hypocrisy and
egoism. Johnson himself expresses this feeling in a moment of self-
criticism: 'That observation which is called knowledge of the world
will be found much more frequently to make men cunning

than good.' The aphorists take, as most satirists do, a low view of human nature: man is an irrational and dangerous creature, guided by his ruling passion, to use Pope's term, but he is an explicable creature and if he can be understood he can be manipulated and controlled. This is a Hobbesian view of man (and Hobbes was a notable aphorist), and it is also Hobbesian to suppose that prudence is the most important of the virtues and indeed, that the wisdom of the ages is only prudence; and that is 'but experience, which equal time equally bestows on all men, in those things which they equally apply themselves unto'. In other words, the problems of mankind are soluble by means of rational understanding. There is then an underlying rationalism in most of the aphorists, and this rationalism is shared by most of the classic satirists. It is a pessimistic view in that it does not suppose that man is naturally benevolent or wholly rational, but it is optimistic in assuming that man can learn from his errors if only he will get rid of his illusions about his nature. This accords with the outlook of scientific humanism, which we have seen as influencing the aphorists from Bacon to Lichtenberg.

The aphorism is the philosophic core of satire. If this philosophy is called cynicism, its exponents can reply that the Cynics were a respectable philosophical school who sought virtue through disenchantment. The cynic way of life invented by Diogenes comprised simplicity, unconventionality and denunciation of the follies and vices of the world. Menippus, the cynic who owns nothing and despises the accepted values of gods and men is the hero of Lucian's satire *Dialogues of the Dead*. But in fact the cynics were too unworldly to be the official philosophers of the ironic aphorism: a better patron saint might be Democritus of Abdera (*c.* 460–370 BC), scientist and freethinker, said to be a man of singular simplicity and disinterestedness and known as the Laughing Philosopher for his amusement at the foibles of mankind. Democritus left one aphorism of stunning simplicity: 'Happy is the man who has both money and sense; for he knows how to use his wealth aright.' – which is the kind of thing that enrages sentimental idealists who cannot bear the notion that ethics should be associated with money. Yet the underlying attitude is shared by that great Christian moralist and realist Johnson when he said 'There are few ways in which a man can be more innocently employed than in getting money', and 'No man but a blockhead ever wrote except for money.'

The aphorist uses the basic strategy of the satirist, namely reduction. He is bound to reduce in one sense, because he aims at brevity, which is the soul of wit. He has to simplify in order to generalise and he must refuse to discuss special cases or admit exceptions. But he also reduces his subject in stature and prestige, by cutting out time-honoured conventional and sentimental associations, which are always flattering, and getting to the root of the matter, which seldom is. Thus when Gibbon, following Voltaire, wrote that history 'is, indeed, little more than the register of the crimes, follies and misfortunes of mankind' he is not telling the whole truth; but he is protesting effectively against time-serving or biassed historians who gloss over the miseries of the past. This formula 'X is little better than Y' or 'X is nothing but Y' is often used by the aphorist; it is like a mathematical equation that reduces complexity to simplicity. Thus Rémy de Gourmont, 'L'homme est un animal arrivé, voila tout' (Man is an animal that has arrived, that's all – not a very good translation, since 'arrivé' has the over-tones of success in a derogatory sense.). Other definitions of man as 'the ungrateful biped' (Dostoevsky), 'a mixture of horse-nervousness, ass-stubborness and camel-malice' (T.H.Huxley), or definitions of love or the other vast subjects which aphorists like to pin down, have usually the same triumphant 'that's all', 'ce n'est que ça' at the end. The aphorist, like Hamlet, would wish to count himself a king of infinite space and yet be bounded in a nutshell. He usually succeeds in producing a caricature, in which a part stands for the whole, a nose or a pipe for a politician.

'I fancy mankind may come, in time, to write all aphoristically, except narrative' was Johnson's hope. The exception is crucial for satire: the aphorism is the kernel of satire, the centre of moral instruction, but without the imaginative expansion of narrative, which carries the element of travesty and play, satire is indigestible. To adapt another saying of Johnson's 'Claret for boys, port for men, but he who aspires to the condition of hero must drink brandy', we may say that the aphorism is the distillation of philosophic satire, but undiluted is fit only for heroes.

'Our live experiences, fixed in aphorism, stiffen into cold epigram' (F.H.Bradley). The essential quality of the best aphorisms is their ability to convey at once wisdom and the re-enactment of a moment's deep experience: the sudden and passionate insight of a man who has thought for long on the problem. The epigram, by contrast, is usually taken to mean the verbal shell of the aphorism – at best a memorable witticism without memorable content or a mere joke which Nietzsche calls 'the epitaph of an emotion'. As a term of literary criticism, the epigram must be defined more precisely than a witticism. G.Rostrevor Hamilton calls it 'any writing ... which achieves point and completion in very brief space, particularly in strict verse pattern but also in prose'. 'Point' and 'completion', we may agree, are essential; but what of the question of verse or prose? I would like to assume that the literary epigram is a genre that depends almost entirely on formal structure, which must make itself felt immediately, on something more obviously organised than ordinary verbal wit, and therefore will normally be in verse. If it is in prose, the prose must have some of the formal qualities of verse, such as symmetry or the equivalent to the finality of rhyme. This is very rare – I find it in only a few epigrammatists like Wilde, whose definition of a cynic as 'a man who knows the price of everything and the value of nothing' is practically verse. I shall therefore assume that the literary epigram, as used for satirical purposes, means a very short piece of verse, that makes a single point as efficiently as possible.

To understand the satirical epigram it is helpful to go back to the original meaning of the word: something lapidary and permanent, like an inscription carved on stone. The epigram is distantly related to the *graffito*, the drawing or writing scratched on a wall.

Room should be found for a study of graffiti in a longer history of satire than this; after all, one of the first references to Christianity is a Roman scrawl of a crucified donkey. The wittiest example of this vulgar and fugitive genre that I can remember is one written in a urinal: 'The future of the human race is in your hands.' But graffiti are meant to be fugitive, whereas the epigram is meant to be permanent; it is more closely related to the epitaph, the proclamation to posterity of the virtues of the deceased. This is in fact what the satiric epigram seems to be: a mock-epitaph, fixing permanently the vices and follies of one guilty man. The satirist mimes the killing of his victim, and then fixes him in the rigidity of death like a butterfly hunter. The sinner cannot struggle free to protest 'no, I wasn't like that at all'. The epigram is written on an imaginary tombstone to be everlastingly mocked by the passer-by. Thus Byron on his political enemy:

> Posterity will ne'er survey
> A nobler grave than this;
> Here lie the bones of Castlereagh:
> Stop, traveller – –

Many of the best satirical epigrams used this device – as, for example, Verdier, on an egoist:

> Ci-gît Paul, qui, vivant sans faire bien ni mal,
> N'aime rien que lui seul, et n'eut point de rival.
> (Here lies Paul, who living without doing good or evil, loved nothing but himself, and there had no rivals.)

Voltaire was a master of this form and is even better on the same theme in

> Ci-gît dont la suprème loi
> Fut de ne vivre que pour soi.
> Passant, garde-toi de le suivre;
> Car on pourrait dire de toi:
> 'Ci-gît qui ne dut jamais vivre'.
> (Here lies one whose supreme law was to live only for himself.

Traveller, mind you don't follow him; for then it could be said of you,
'Here lies one who should never have lived.')

The most famous example of political satire in mock-epitaph is
Rochester's poem which he is said to have pinned to the bedroom
door of Charles II:

Here lies our Sovereign Lord the King,
Whose word no man relies on.
Who never said a foolish thing
Nor ever did a wise one.

The act of pinning up and advertising to the world immediately is
an essential part of the production of epigrams. The epigram is a
civilised form of the primitive lampoon-satire, which aims magic-
ally at the destruction of the victim: it is civilised in so far as it
uses the elegant forms of sophisticated verse – and even brevity is
a sign of politeness – but remains cruel at heart. If the aphorism
is the condensation of moral satire, the epigram is the lampoon
miniaturised.

The serious epigram and the verse epitaph, like most other
literary forms, were invented by the Greeks: and so was the
satirical epigram, in this case probably by Archilochus himself.
This is his best:

Not for me the general renowned as the well-groomed dandy
Nor he who is proud of his curls or is shaven in part;
But give me a man that is small and whose legs are bandy,
Provided he's firm on his feet and is valiant in heart.

A famous epigram which is near to the mock-epitaph dates from a
century later:

A viper stung a Cappadocian guide
And poisoned by his blood that instant died.

(Democritus, translated by J.H.Merivale)

It is even better in Voltaire's adaptation:

> L'autre jour, au fond d'un vallon,
> Un serpent pique Jean Freron.
> Que pensez-vous qu'il arriva?
> Ce fut le serpent qui creva.

'The dog it was that died' – an emblematic warning, by the way, to every satirist against his being poisoned by his victim.

The best Roman epigrams are a handful by Catullus, which combined Greek elegance with a blacker tone of hatred and self-hatred than any Greek would produce; it has been suggested that this note came from his Celtic blood. The splendidly athletic attack on Equatius of the white teeth (XXXIX) is perhaps too long to qualify as an epigram, but there is nothing more compressed, final and anguished than these five lines (LVIII). After the lamenting cadences of the first three lines the obscenity appears with hideous immediacy:

> Caeli, Lesbia nostra, Lesbia illa,
> illa Lesbia, quam Catullus unam
> plus quam se atque suos amavit omnes,
> nunc in quadriviis et angiportis
> glubit magnanimi Remi nepotes.

> (O Caelius, my Lesbia, that Lesbia, Lesbia whom Catullus loved more than himself or his own family, now at crossroads and in alleys prostitutes herself to [but the word is more obscene] the descendants of nobleminded Remus [i.e. the Romans])

Martial seems to me grossly overrated as an occasional poet, and his good satirical epigrams are few and far between. He deserves his fame, however, for producing the archetype of the lampoon:

> Non amo te, Solidi, nec possum dicere quare:
> Hoc tantum possum dicere, non amo te. (I xxxii)

Martial's grammatical and metrical skill was much admired by the pedants and university wits of the Renaissance, who imitated him copiously. Indeed, in most European languages there was almost as much good epigram produced as formal satire. The genre was highly fashionable in Elizabethan England, and highly perishable. The faults of the Renaissance epigrams are pedantic boorishness and in technique, at least, a contorted style of wit. The epigram began to improve with the refinement of manners in the seventeenth century and became a vehicle for elegant irony and disdainful wit. There is a long line of French epigrammatists from the sixteenth to the eighteenth century, from Malherbe to La Monnoye, Rousseau, Lebrun and Voltaire. In England the first master of the playful-serious epigram is Herrick; the most brilliant of the Augustans is Matthew Prior.

Pope's couplets, each a triumph of balance and compression, form a treasury of epigram as well as of aphorism. After the Augustan age, however, the epigram declines from the level of serious poetry to that of occasional verse. Almost every major poet wrote a few good ones: I would single out Burns, Kipling and Ezra Pound, and from among the writers of light verse, Hilaire Belloc:

> The Devil, having nothing else to do,
> Went off to tempt my Lady Poltagrue.
> My Lady, tempted by a private whim,
> To his extreme annoyance, tempted him.

The satiric epigram is a kind of anti-lyric; it uses the lyric form and metre, usually associated with romantic love and exaltation, to convey a gross and unromantic message; the ironic tension between form and content produces an effect of surprise. The Japanese have since the eighteenth century used this shock effect in the *Senryu*, which is written in the strict form of the *Haiku* (with seventeen syllables in three lines), but uses colloquial diction to give realistic pictures of ordinary life. Their economy is a lesson to wordy Europeans, and the satiric comment on life is so exquisite that comment on the poems would be superfluous:

> Zen priests
> Meditation finished,
> Looking for fleas.

In the whole village
The husband alone
Does not know of it.

Waiting for his turn
For the European trip
The D.Litt., ageing.   (from *The Penguin Book of Japanese Verse*)

The epigram in the strict classical tradition has disappeared almost entirely from contemporary European poetry, but its spirit survived in the experimental, free-form anti-lyric of e.e.cummings and Jacques Prévert. Cummings, a sentimentalist in his love-poetry, used colloquial American with precision in anarchistic comments on public stupidity and stuffiness. Prévert is another master of popular idiom and anti-bourgeois scorn, who attacks the world of official shams with surrealistic violence. In their work, as in the best traditions of the epigram, the pretensions of the world are cut down to human proportions. Against the clichés of civilisation the epigram asserts common sense and the dignity of individual man.

The character

The 'character' is the literary form most closely connected with the satirical device of 'typing', which as we have seen is partly a scientific attempt to understand the variety of human personality, and partly a normative description of errors in social behaviour. The genre was, as far as is known, invented by the philosopher and scientist Theophrastus (*c*. 370–286 BC). His little work, the *Characters*, is probably a mutilated extract from a much longer original, with some moral tags added by a Byzantine scholar. There are some thirty sketches on a uniform plan: the name and the definition of a psychological type are followed by a list of symptoms and patterns of behaviour. The types included the Dissimulator (or Eiron), the Flatterer, the Gross Man, the Friend of the Rabble, etc.: they seem to be grouped into species, since there are kinds of talkative men – the Chatterer, the Loquacious Man, the Slanderer and the News-

Craniology Burlesqued (1818), a satire
of the widely accepted theories of
Gall and Spurzheim, who claimed to read
character from bumps on the skull.

Specimens of Partial Genius.

Destructiveness.

Veneration.

Philoprogenitiveness.

monger. It must be supposed that the motive for this classification was scientific curiosity, since Theophrastus in two lost works classified plants systematically. One can also see that the work has a basis in the Aristotelian ethic of avoiding extremes; the various types also deviate in some way from the golden mean. But the main point of the work, it has been conjectured, is to compile material for a treatise on comedy: the sketches are of types who might easily appear in the 'New Comedy' of the day, as in the plays of Theophrastus' friend Menander. The descriptions are not remarkable for style or wit, but they have a sober charm in their scenes of city life, showing the Athenian middle-class citizens (the peasantry and slaves hardly appear) living their out-of-doors public existence. The tone is urbane, not indignant; the work cannot be called a satire but it provides a model for satirists to follow.

All later 'characters' descend from this book, after it was revived at the Renaissance. The most famous imitation which improves on the original is *Les Caractères de Theophraste* by Jean de la Bruyère (1645–96). This began as a 200-page addition to a very free translation of Theophrastus published in 1688; in seven later editions in 1694 La Bruyère increased his original work under headings like 'De la Societé et de la Convention', 'De la Cour', 'De la Mode', etc., and under each he combined aphorisms and short essays with short sketches of contemporary types under invented names. The aphorisms are excellent, the sketches beautifully written, with a marvellous sense of rhythm. Take his lover of flowers, a monomaniac in the age of the tulip:

Vous le voyez planté, et qui a pris racine au milieu de ses tulipes et devant la *Solitaire:* il ouvre de grands yeux, il frotte ses mains, il se baisse, il la voit de plus près, il ne l'a jamais vue si belle, il a le coeur épanoui de joie: il la quitte pour l'*Orientale*, de là il va à la *Veuve*, il passe au *Drap d'Or*, de celle-ci a l'*Agathe*, d'où il revient enfin à la *Solitaire*, où il se fixe, où il se lasse, où il s'assit, où il oublie de dîner: aussi est elle nuancée, bordée, huilée, à pieces emportée; elle a un beau vase ou un beau calice: il la contemple, il l'admire. Dieu et la nature sont en tout cela qu'il n'admire point; il ne va pas plus loin que l'oignon de sa tulipe, qu'il ne livrerait pas pour mille écus, et qu'il donnera pour rien quand les tulipes seront negligées, et que les oeillets auront prévalu.

(You see him planted and taken root in the middle of his tulips and before his 'Solitaire'; he opens his eyes wide, rubs his hands, bends down, looks more closely at it, he has never seen it looking so lovely, his heart is in an ecstasy of joy; he leaves it for 'Oriental', thence he goes to the 'Widow', he passes on to 'Cloth of Gold', from that to 'Agatha', then returns to 'Solitaire', where he stops fixed, is tired out, sits down, forgets to dine: it is so admirable in shade, shape, colour, sheen and edges; it has a beautiful flower, a beautiful calyx: he contemplates and admires it. God and nature are not at all in his thoughts; they do not go beyond the bulb of his tulip, which he would not sell for a thousand crowns, and which he will give away for nothing when tulips are out of fashion and carnations have won the day.)

If Theophrastus is drawing on the comedies of Menander, this is also dramatic, a little mime in words. Not only in technique but in outlook La Bruyère approaches Molière; both speak with the voice of the intelligent and critical bourgeois, becoming bitter under the restrictions of the *ancien régime*. La Bruyère worked in the household of the Condé family, and had an excellent opportunity to observe the nobility and the court; he valued the politeness of the 'honnête homme', but he does not belong spiritually to this milieu. He criticises the affectations of courtly life and the hypocrisy of a rigid society with as much freedom as he dare. He used fictitious names and other cautious devices to evade censorship, but was certainly understood in his day as a serious critic of social institutions. His work is satire disguised as moral treatise and manual of conduct.

La Bruyère was the first to revive Theophrastus in France, but he did not invent the character-sketch or portrait. This had been popularised a few decades earlier by Jean Regnault de Segrais (1624–1701). While Segrais was secretary to the Duchess of Montpensier he collected the character-sketches composed in her salon and started a fashion. The 'portrait' became part of *précieuse* culture; it was partly a social genre and partly an aid to self-correction and to the formation of social ideals.

The English composers of prose-characters are even earlier, but it must be confessed are far less interesting. They contain some lively documentation of Jacobean life, but they are too rigidly moral and too full of the traditional stiff attitudes of the formal satirist to make attractive reading. One of the earliest was in fact a formal satirist, Joseph Hall (later Bishop of Exeter and of Norwich) whose *Characters* of *Virtues and Vices* (1608) shows some knowledge of Theophrastus but small descriptive skill. There are some delightful pieces here and there in the *Characters* attributed to Sir Thomas Overbury (1614); the most extensive collection is *Micro-Cosmographie* (1628) by John Earle. The tradition was contained by Butler, author of *Hudibras*, without the success or verve of his poetry, and then was given a new lease of life by Addison and Steele. In the *Tatler* and *Spectator* they used the 'character' as part of their programme for educating the public by very mild satire of social absurdities. One of these targets was the old-fashioned Restoration rake, the young blood who lives it up:

> I remember a young man of very lively Parts; and of a sprightly turn of conversation, who had only one fault, which was an inordinate Desire of appearing fashionable. This ran him into many Amours, and consequently into many Distempers. He never went to Bed till two o'clock in the Morning, because he would not be a queer Fellow; and was every now and then knocked down by a Constable to signalize his Vivacity. He was initiated into half a Dozen Clubs before he was one-and-twenty, and so improved in them his natural Gayety of Temper, that you might frequently trace him to his Lodgings by a Range of broken Windows, and other like Monuments of Wit and Gallantry. To be short, after having fully established his Reputation of being a very agreeable Rake, he died of old Age at Five and twenty.
>
> (*Spectator* 576)

This is almost as elegant as La Bruyère and to my mind much funnier. The strength of Addison is that he is a very close observer of London life, and has a wonderful ear for contemporary speech.

The 'character' appears and flourishes in two successive centuries in which writers were fascinated by the problems of moral

The figure of the mercenary soldier returning from the wars is common in sixteenth-century Switzerland. This caricature by Urs Graf (1519) is analogous to the 'types' of stage comedy of the sixteenth century and to the literary 'characters' of the seventeenth century.

behaviour, and when literary critical theory stressed the didactic function of art. It is probably no accident that this period also shows the flourishing of moral formal satire in verse. The 'character' declines when people become less interested in the norms of social behaviour and in social types as deviants from these norms, and more interested in the peculiarities of the unique living individual. This shift of interest began in the second half of the eighteenth century, when there appeared the first great autobiographies (i.e. Rousseau's *Confessions*), biographies (such as Boswell's *Life of Johnson*) and works of historiography (Gibbon's *Decline and Fall of the Roman Empire*). It was not a sudden shift, since it had been anticipated by earlier writers of journals and memoirs, the greatest of whom was the Duc de St Simon; and it came into full flower only in the Romantic era. It became and it has remained much more interesting for most readers to learn about the passions, motives and eccentricities of individuals in their historical contexts than to go over the old generalisations about vice and folly, however skilfully presented. Literary traditions, however, die hard; and there was a curious overlap between the old and the new in the writing of history and memoirs, which is part of the story of satire.

To describe a living or dead person critically, to paint his portrait realistically 'warts and all', is not necessarily satirical; but to impose the pattern of a character or type on this portrait may well be. The practice of inserting 'portraits' into a narrative is an old one, and has been followed by many historians since Thucydides. The master of the critical portrait, incisive and cruelly final, was Tacitus; he transfixes his subjects with deadly wit, as when he ends his portrait of the Emperor Galba: 'et omnium consensu capax imperii nisi imperasset' (by common consent capable of ruling, if only he had not ruled). This is allied to the satirical device of the mock-epitaph. Gibbon was also a master of this summary ending to a portrait; his style is inscriptional, his beautifully balanced sentences are fit to be carved in monumental marble: there is no appeal from his verdict. This is one of the reasons why so much of Gibbon's history reads like satire.

Allegory

There is a more primitive kind of satirical typing than the Theophrastian 'character' or the historical portrait: this is the allegorical representation of the vices and virtues, which flourished in the Middle Ages and survived in later centuries. It is of course only one aspect of medieval allegory, which is a huge and complex system of thought. Briefly, it may be said to have begun with the interpretation of the Bible; to every part of the Old Testament there had to be assigned a correspondence with the New Testament. From this there developed the four-fold significance of every sentence in the Bible: literal, allegorical, moral and anagogical. This method of interpretation was later applied not only to the Bible but to all serious literature, whether classical or newly written. We are here concerned with the moral 'significance': the medieval theologian spent a great deal of effort both in discovering hidden moral meanings everywhere – even in so unsuitable a poet as Ovid, who was *moralisé* – and in inventing narrative forms to carry such meanings everywhere – even in so unsuitable a poet as Ovid, who moral allegory in their sermons, in a way that offered an opening for simple forms of satire. These sermons are full of *exempla*, or 'examples', which might be animal fables or folk-tales, or even rather gross anecdotes. These caught the attention of the congregation who were then treated to an exposition of the Christian doctrine hidden in the *exemplum*. The friars, who made a special effort in missionary preaching, were particularly free with the use of exempla; the sermons of Cardinal Jacques de Vitry, a thirteenth-century cardinal, are richly studded with folk-tales and anecdotes. Among the techniques of the preachers was the representation of the vices in human form, that is, the invention of realistic figures drawn from contemporary life, which would also represent the Seven Deadly Sins. There were more subtle methods of classifying vice: Dante used an Aristotelian scheme of ethics for the different groups of sinners in the Inferno, but the Deadly Sins – Pride, Envy, Anger, Gluttony, Jealousy, Lechery, Sloth – were more easily memorable and explicable to popular audiences. Sloth (or *accidia*), wrote Baudelaire, is the sin of monks; but the whole scheme is essentially monkish. These sins are the opposites not of the public, political and worldly virtues extolled by the Greeks, but of the monastic Christian ideals of humility and austerity. It was possible, however, in personifying them to give a very lively and realistic picture of the world.

Some of the best examples are in the fourteenth-century English poem *Piers Plowman*, attributed to one William Langland. In one section of this religious vision, which owes much to the sermon tradition, the Deadly Sins appear as real people in low life; Gluttony is pictured with coarse vigour as a drunkard in a London tavern, Sloth 'comes all be-slobbered, with two slimy eyes'. This is the verbal equivalent of the grotesques of medieval carving and illuminated manuscripts. For the moment the preacher's moral intent is lost in the poet's delight in describing the unregenerate world. Simple satiric allegory disappeared from literature at the end of the Middle Ages; it is found for the last time in the Scots poet William Dunbar. But it survived in the preaching of the sectarians who kept the medieval tradition alive well into the seventeenth century; and then it returns to literature with a preacher who was a great unconscious artist, John Bunyan. The episode in *Pilgrim's Progress* dealing with 'Vanity Fair' is a magnificent satiric allegory, while in *The Life and Death of Mr Badman* he passes from preaching to a brilliant preview of the satirical novel.

Fable

The fable is a story in which the non-human behaves like the human, and a simple moral point is conveyed. It descends from the folk-tale, in which it is quite common for the non-human to speak and act intelligently: helpful animals guide the hero in his quest, maidens are transformed into swans, and the fox outwits the bear. But the fable is a transformation of the folk-tale for the sake of moral instruction: like wisdom literature it is pedagogic and

Krylov's Fables (1852): 'the dogs' friendship'.
Polkan and Barbos, beneath the kitchen window, swear
eternal canine friendship, which they acknowledge to
be as rare as that between humans. The cook's offer of
a bone leads at once to a fight. Krylov concludes that
human friendships have a truly canine quality.

clerkly, first produced by the literati of the ancient urban civilisations. Primitive man sees himself as part of the animal world in
many ways: as a hunter he pits his skill against the animals' speed
and cunning. It is only at a fairly high stage of social evolution that
men can see themselves as essentially different from beasts, and
take the relatively sophisticated step of portraying men in the guise
of beasts in order to say something about the conduct of men –
which is the central point of the fable.

It is not necessary for fables to be about animals, but the
animal fable is the basic type used by the satirists: it corresponds
most usefully to the satirical device of reduction, of revealing the
non-human drives behind human pretensions to grandeur. Animal
stories are found in all primitive literature: some are etiological
like 'How the Bear lost his Tail', but many of them are trickster
stories, like the American Indian tales about Coyote or the west
African ones about the Clever Spider. We have seen (in chapter 1)
that the trickster story in which the serious institutions of society
are often parodied, is the simplest version of the travesty theme
which keeps appearing in all satire. The world is turned upside-
down, there is a retreat into a world of childish make-believe as a
relief from the tensions of the adult code. But the primitive animal
tale also leads to moral satire, by a more circuitous route: first it is
moralised to become a lively lesson, secondly, the moral is itself
treated either ironically, to convey a humorous attitude to life, or
the moral lesson is transformed into satirical polemic, usually in the
form of political or social protest.

The earliest fables, like the earlier wisdom literature and the
imaginary voyages, are found in the literature of ancient Egypt.
These antedate Aesop by a thousand years; and it can be presumed
that all ancient oriental civilisations produced a store of fables. The
short Indian collection, the *Panchatantra*, is of uncertain date,
probably about the fifth century AD, but there is no reason to doubt
that the fables it contains are much earlier; or that the Greeks took
some of these stories, as they did some of their myths and legends,
from the ancient East. Aesop is a semi-legendary figure: he is

Собачья Дружба.

'The Birds and the Quadrupeds'. One of Aesop's Fables.
the richest source of animal figures for the satirists.
From a sixteenth-century Latin edition
published with woodcuts by B. Benasium in Venice.

supposed to have been a Phrygian slave in Athens about 620–560 BC but if he existed he may not have been the author of all the Aesopian fables that have come down to us. The Greeks may merely have attributed the whole body of this half-folkloric literature to a man who was a skilled story-teller in the market-place. In any case, we know the Aesopian fables only from much later versions: from collections made by later Greek and Latin versifiers. The fables were rendered in verse not before the second century BC and translated into Latin by Avianus in the fourth or fifth century AD. A prose translation by Phaedrus appeared in the early Middle Ages. The Aesopian fables had a huge expansion between the twelfth and the fifteenth centuries; they were much used in the Schools for moral instruction as well as literary exercises, and they were taken up by the preachers for their sermon exempla. The Greek lore was again added to from oriental sources; this was part of the flood of stories brought back from the Middle East by traders and pilgrims. Indian stories reached Europe through the Persians and the Arabs by oral transmission, long before the first printed translations. Other stories were drawn from native Euro-pean folklore, that is from Indo-European and Germanic tales about the fox, bear and wolf. At the same time as the growth of the fables, the animal stories were elaborated into mock epics, first in the *Ecbasis Captivi*, the *Ysengrimus* and later the *Renart* cycle – described in chapter 2 as the vehicle for political satire in the Middle Ages. The beast epic is the first major transformation of the fable into satire and had great popularity as a means of comic protest against the power of the church. The elaboration of the Reynard stories became more and more didactic, came to an end with the Low German *Reinike de Vos* (1498), and then went out of fashion. The Aesopian fables continued to have a separate life. There were many reworkings in the main European languages: Marie de France (*c.* 1200) wrote a *Ysopets* (or 'little Aesop') which has some charm, but the best versions are by the Scottish poet Robert Henryson (1430?–1506), the *Moral Fables of Aesop the Phrygian*. Henryson is both a naive pious moralist and a vigorous satirist, who showed much courage in attacking the misrule of the church and nobility of fifteenth-century Scotland; with grave humour he represents the rapacious clergy as the wolf and fox of Aesop and the Renart cycle. He is one of the few medieval writers to sympathise with the peasants: and he writes with unfailing charm and sharp realism.

From the medieval traditions all later fabulists draw their material. The master of the art is Jean de la Fontaine (1621–95), whose *Fables Choisies mises en vers* were published between 1668 and 1694. La Fontaine has the most perfect style of all fabulists, a marvellous mixture of spontaneity and formal balance; he must have been one of the most attractive human beings who ever lived, who looked on the world with saintly gentleness and acuteness. He is not at heart a satirist or a moralist: he is an ironist, taking a gently rationalist view of the absurdities of a society that he could not imagine ever changing. This has remained the classic stance of the ironic fabulist ever since, from John Gay and Lessing in the eighteenth century down to James Thurber (*Fables for our Time*, 1940).

The satiric fable is rather rarer in the last two centuries. The best examples are Russian, perhaps because the peasant tradition of proverb and folk-tale has remained stronger in Russian culture. Ivan Andreyevitch Krylov published his *Basni* (Fables) in 1809, and these remain the classic modern examples of the genre. Krylov, who transformed the language of folklore into a style of great purity, was essentially a conservative but attacked the Tsarist bureaucracy. Saltykov-Shchedrin imitated him in his *Basni* (1880–3) which are wholly political; his tales of stupid bears and the like are direct radical assaults on the autocratic regime. They are chiefly remarkable for the way in which they escaped the censorship and reached the liberal reading public. It is ironical that the last first-class fable should be about Russia. George Orwell's *Animal Farm* (1945) is a beautifully explicit allegory of the Russian revolution and the rise of Stalin. The farmyard animals, tired of their subjection to a human master, revolt and start to run the farm themselves; but they fall into worse servitude under their new leaders, the pigs. The pigs' slogan – 'all animals are equal, but some animals are more equal than others' – is a classic parody of all revolutionary cant since Rousseau, which has been repeated with dismal monotony up to the present day. Orwell, a dissident man of the Left, who hated tyranny in any form, was the last of the traditional satirists of England – a free spirit.

Imaginary voyage and utopia

Man is a voyager through time and space; though his span on earth is limited, his physical stature minute, he reaches out into the void of uncertainty in hope and fear. One of his responses to the challenge of the unknown universe is religion, another is exploration, which began as soon as primitive man was forced to change his hunting ground. The world of ancient literate man was at first confined to the valleys of the Nile and Euphrates and the fertile crescent between; outside were the terrors of desert and sea, mountain and swamp. The Mediterranean and its surrounding lands were gradually explored by Egyptians, Mesopotamians, Minoans, Phoenicians, Greeks and Romans: each of these must have left factual records of their discoveries, for the benefit of colonists and traders, and some of these have survived. But every factual record has a penumbra of speculation and error, of tall tales about the anthropophagi and the men whose heads do grow beneath their shoulders, of Arimaspians who stole the griffins' gold, of basilisks and unicorns. The basis of the imaginary voyage is the real traveller's tale, part true and part false. The earliest literary voyages were probably serious epics, which combined travel with mythology and historical traditions: gods and heroes wander from the known to the unknown, like Gilgamesh in the Akkadian poem. At a later stage they were told for entertainment: the Egyptians of the Middle Kingdom (first half of the second millennium BC) were provided for in the tomb with light reading to pass the time in the next world. This seems to be, if not the origin, at least the earliest record of the romance and the novel. Among these Egyptian romances is the *Tale of the Shipwrecked Sailor*, who lands on an enchanted island, and is befriended by a huge snake. This story is said to be the source of parts of *Sinbad the Sailor* and of the Phaeacian episode of Homer's *Odyssey:* it is also the prototype of all Utopias. The *Odyssey* is of course partly a serious epic, based on the heroic legends of the Myceneans, and partly a fantastic traveller's tale, based on Egyptian, Minoan or Phoenician accounts of Mediterranean exploration; it also took some features from *Gilgamesh*. Other Greek stories, like those of the Argonauts and of Herakles' travels, lie on the borderline between fact and fiction. Herodotus combines reliable observation with wild speculation and entertaining narrative. The Romans were too preoccupied with the serious business of conquering and surveying their expanding empire to spend much time on fiction of this kind; but the genre reappears in the Middle Ages. The Arabs were the first serious travellers after the ancients: the frivolous side of this exploration is recorded in Sinbad and other stories of the *Arabian Nights*. The Irish created the story of St Brendan's voyage in search of the Earthly Paradise, which was supposed to be situated on an island in the Atlantic. *The Travels of Sir John Mandeville* (about 1371) purported to be a guidebook for pilgrims to Jerusalem, but includes a collection of the wonders of Africa and the Orient. The discovery of the New World and the exploration of the East in the sixteenth century produced successively accurate factual records (by the great Spanish explorers and chroniclers), serious epics (notably Camoens's *Lusiad*) and exotic romances. Shakespeare's *The Tempest* which is related to the romances and travellers' books, is the outstanding imaginative response to the excitement of the new discovery. Defoe's *Robinson Crusoe* (1719) is solidly based on the realistic details of actual travellers' accounts, like those of the explorer William Dampier; it is no less a work of the imagination, written to gratify the fantasies of its author and intended to deceive the public into accepting it as true. Because it contains a powerful set of myths, which express universal ideas and feelings about the primitive and unknown world, it has had an extra-ordinary appeal to the European imagination for over two centuries. If *Crusoe* is the peak of the fictional traveller's story, the genre continued to flourish into the nineteenth century, by the real discoveries which have gone on until the surface of the globe has been almost completely explored. In this century the genre has given way to science fiction: Jules Verne has been succeeded by H.G.Wells and thousands of imitators. In exploration of outer space and of space-time, fiction has usually preceded scientific accomplishment, but has not yet reached literary maturity. With very few exceptions straight science fiction remains at the level of popular mass-culture: it cannot be taken seriously as imaginative literature, but it has already offered itself as a splendid vehicle for the serious satirist.

The first satirist to exploit the possibilities of the imaginary voyage was Lucian, who wrote in Greek about AD 120. His *True History* is a joke at the expense of the classical travel writers, particularly Herodotus, and a parody of Homer. The hero sets out with fifty companions, and sails beyond the Pillars of Hercules for eighty days; they reach an enchanted island where an inscription marks the limits reached by Herakles; they are carried by a whirlwind and by monstrous birds to the moon, where the people are at war with the people of the sun over the colonisation of Venus – a foretaste of a basic science-fiction theme. The ship returns safely to the sea, but is next swallowed by a gigantic whale which has a complete sea and islands in its belly. They escape by lighting a forest fire; later, like Odysseus, they visit the region of the dead. This is a gay and playful spoof, which uses only some of the possibilities of the voyage: it burlesques the lying tales and exaggerations of the voyagers but it does not make the fantastic narrative into an image of the real world. Lucian used other vehicles for his satire, as we shall see. The *True History* was imitated by Ariosto in Astolfo's journey to the Moon on the hippogriff – largely a burlesque – and by Rabelais who transforms the idea into satire in book IV of *Gargantua and Pantagruel* (Le Quart Livre

1552). In book II Pantagruel had already reached Utopia by sailing round the Cape of Good Hope; now Panurge persuades Pantagruel and Friar John to go in quest of the Oracle of the Holy Bottle (L'Oracle de la Dive Bouteille), situated 'near Cathay in Upper India', to learn whether Panurge should marry. This time they take the north Atlantic route, following the French explorer Jacques Cartier: Rabelais took a serious interest in the new voyages of discovery. He now saw the opportunities in this kind of narrative for satire: when his travellers visit several islands on their way, they find strange inhabitants who are modern Europeans in disguise – the Papimanes (Papimaniacs) who live in hope of seeing their idol, the Pope, and have the Papal decretals as a holy book; and their equally ridiculous Protestant opponents the Papefigues (Pope-figs). For its attacks on the church this work was condemned by the Sorbonne; the satirical voyage was continued by Rabelais or an imitator in the *Cinquième et dernier livre* (book V 1564).

The evolution of the genre from burlesque to pure satire is continued by Cyrano de Bergerac (1619–55). A philosophical free-thinker or *libertin*, seriously interested in the new science, he held subversive views about the institutions of the *ancien régime;* in his anti-clericalism he is a forerunner of the critical spirit of the Encyclopedists. He did not dare to publish his satire in his lifetime: *Voyage dans la Lune*, the commonly used title of the first part of *L'Autre Monde, ou les États et Empires de la Lune et du Soleil* was printed posthumously and at first incompletely. Cyrano reaches the moon propelled by rockets to find a world of apparent absurdity: the young make the laws and are revered by the old; the learned language is music, and the classics are published in the form of musical boxes which may be worn as earrings (an anticipation of the transistorised tape-recorder!) and the people use their large noses as sundials. Nevertheless the moon philosophers hold forth lucidly and forcibly on the subject of Lucretian physics and the impossibility of miracles and even deny the existence of God; Cyrano adds ironically that these diabolical and ridiculous opinions made him shudder. ('Ces opinions diaboliques et ridicules me firent

Cyrano de Bergerac, with his famous nose,
as portrayed on the frontispiece
to his works (Amsterdam, 1699).

La terre me fut importune,
Ie pris mon effort vers les Cieux.
Iy vis le foleil, et la lune,
Et maintenant Iy vois les Dieux.

naître un frémissement par tout le corps.') He is one of the first to use the satirical device of reporting heterodox opinions while pretending to be shocked by them. So Gulliver is shocked by the downright condemnation of European culture by the King of Brobdingnag and by the Houyhnhnms. Swift was the first to perfect the use of the traveller as *persona*, as simultaneously mouthpiece and butt. The traveller is peculiarly suitable for this role: typically he is courageous, resourceful, stoical, like Odysseus himself. But he is inclined to be arrogant, both in his dealings with the natives and on his return to civilisation. He is observant but also at times credulous, and will slide from truth to half-truth, and from rumour to fiction. Both at home and abroad he remains an outsider. Swift built up the character of Gulliver from a careful study of the travellers whose accounts he had read as carefully as Defoe had. He even uses some of Crusoe's psychological make-up for his hero; and to complete the illusion he exactly catches the style of the voyagers, inserting a passage verbatim from a real sailor's account at one point without disturbing the level of style. This matter-of-factness strengthens the impact of the marvels when they first appear; it is also essential for the persona not to appear too intelligent, though he must seem a reliable observer. At the same time the traveller hero must be a target of satire, in so far as he is representative of the European civilisation which is under fire. The perfect travel-introduction to a Utopian satire is the early part of Samuel Butler's *Erewhon* (1872), which is a careful and solemn pastiche of Victorian explorers' narratives, based on his experiences of the wilds of New Zealand. Satirists who neglect this realistic preparation, like Voltaire in *Micromégas* (1752) and Anatole France in *Penguin Island* (*L'île des pingouins*, 1908) – do so at their peril.

Utopia is the goal of satirical travellers, the civilisation beyond the wilderness. The essential feature of utopia is that it is not primitive, not an earthly paradise, but an ordered society of people, a settled city state which is a mirror-image or distortion, for better or worse, of our own urban culture. The usual modern meaning is 'a place or condition of ideally perfect government', but if we are to use it as a literary term it is better to go back to the original meaning, which is the same as Erewhon – nowhere. The word was coined by Sir Thomas More from the Greek *ou* 'not' and *topos* 'place', for the imaginary island in his political romance of the same name (1516). The alternative to using the word in both good and bad senses is to adopt the awkward modern coining 'anti-utopian'. In this subject the satirists have again followed the serious fantasists, who in turn have used travellers' accounts of strange civilisations. As we have seen, the earliest hint may be found in the Egyptian tale of the shipwrecked sailor, and this is slightly ex-panded in Homer's Phaeacia, where Odysseus is entertained by Nausicaa and her father. The later Greeks knew of a fabulous and wealthy island-city called Panchaea in the Erythrean sea, which is described by Diodorus. But the true parent of all utopias is Plato, who describes his Atlantis briefly in the *Timaeus* and *Critias*. An Egyptian priest told Solon that there was a large island in the western ocean, with great natural wealth and a population of wealthy traders, who had built an artificial harbour and fine temples; but 9,000 years earlier it had been overwhelmed by an earthquake and sunk into the sea. Plato gives so much circum-stantial detail that scholars have been searching ever since for the identification of the lost island, recently with some success. Many scholars now think that Plato intended it as a myth or a playful fable, at most drawing a few details from travellers' reports. Although Atlantis is a physical idea, not enough information is given about its inhabitants for it to be called a social utopia. But Plato also invented that genre, with the ideal commonwealth described in his dialogue *The Republic:* an unpleasantly puritanical and communistic state, ruled by philosophers or 'guardians', the other two classes in a rigid system being the soldiers and the writers. Plato should be held in suspicion by all writers, since his Socrates would banish from this state all literature except hymns and patriotic songs, a hideous condition perhaps reached today in China. But again this description may be not a social blueprint but an allegory of the human soul, a metaphysical way of defining true justice. Whether that is the case or not, *The Republic* and the account of Atlantis, singly or in combination, have had a huge progeny of imitations. More's *Utopia* is the first famous one of the Renaissance. It is not a satire, but a serious indictment of the evils of English economic and moral life, at a time when the medieval social structure was being broken up by a new mercantile and individualistic trend. Book one is a dialogue on these evils, which included the latest 'enclosures' or seizures of common land for the benefit of private sheep-farming:

Your sheep, that were wont to be so meek and tame, and so small eaters, now, as I hear say, be become so great devourers, and so wild, that they eat up and swallow down the very men themselves.

In the second book More describes his ideal country where the problems of poverty, crime and social injustice have been solved. Curiously, though More writes from the standpoint of a devout Catholic, his utopians are not Christians but have reached their high level of justice simply by means of human reason: the implication is presumably that Christian Europeans ought to be able to do still better, instead of making the world a hell for the poor. Although More writes with some humour and irony, and can produce noble invective, as in the sentence about the sheep, he is a controversialist, even a preacher, rather than a satirist.

More's first notable imitator in England was Francis Bacon, whose *New Atlantis* was published posthumously in 1607. Again there is a voyage to an island, here called 'Bensalem', used as a framework for the exposition of Bacon's ideas about the fostering of natural science. This fable was an influential work of propaganda: the description of the island's institution for scientific study, 'Solomon's House', is said to have given some encouragement to the founding of the Royal Society sixty years later. The emphasis on science is the link with later utopian fables, such as Cyrano's and Voltaire's; and later with H.G.Wells' *A Modern Utopia* (1905).

A high degree of scientific and technical knowledge is indeed demanded of the creator of utopias. In his blueprint of the future he must suggest that he understands the technological basis of his imaginary society; unless he does so he cannot make convincing its economic and hence its social structure. This is why the best of English socialist utopias, William Morris's *News from Nowhere* (1891), is disappointing: it begins with a highly realistic account of the future proletarian revolution, but in the ideal communistic state that follows there is no explanation of where the fuel, power and machinery come from to make the good life possible. Butler's *Erewhon*, despite its convincing beginning, is also unsatisfactory on this score. Swift again provides an object lesson: he worked hard to acquire a sound knowledge of the science of his day before parodying it in the Laputa of the third voyage; and he always suggests that he knows how his people earn their livings technically. Swift's best modern follower is Aldous Huxley: in *Brave New World* (1932) he shows an amazing grasp of the science of his day (he used to read the *Encyclopedia Britannica* on railway journeys) and his extrapolations into the future have either come true, like the embryos in bottles, or remain likely possibilities. It does not matter whether the basis of the satire is pro-scientific or, like Swift's and Huxley's, an attack on scientific humanism; in either case the writer must do his scientific homework with enthusiasm and precision.

It is a relatively simple matter to pass from utopia to anti-utopia. The utopia makes a criticism of the irrational present-day world by offering a rational contrast; the anti-utopia is a grotesque vision of our world in the guise of a logical extrapolation. Swift in fact mixes both together in his Lilliput, as Samuel Butler does in *Erewhon*. The latter is utopian in his paradoxical reversal of society's attitudes to crime and to sickness: the Erewhonians treat physical disease as a punishable offence, but sympathetically give medical treatment to thieves and embezzlers. Here history has overtaken Butler, since today this is in fact the attitude to crime of many soft-centred liberals, and one itself deserving satirical attack. He is anti-utopian in his account of the musical banks which deal in invisible currency but have to be supplemented by the ordinary banks dealing in real money: it is an excellent allegory of the way conventional religion approaches the other-worldly injunctions of Christianity ('Lay not up your treasures upon earth'). The rest of Butler's attacks on Victorian morality are amusing but somewhat dated. His greatness as a satirist is not to be judged from *Erewhon* alone, but from his highly intelligent aphorisms and some bitter and uproariously funny pages in his autobiographical novel *The Way of all Flesh*.

The two outstanding anti-utopias of this century are Huxley's *Brave New World* and George Orwell's *1984*. Huxley's fantasy is set in the year 632 AF (After Ford), when the techniques of mass-production invented by Ford have reached perfection. His prognosis is not scientifically accurate but it is socially convincing: in the passivity of the masses, the endless watching of sport on television, the 'sexual revolution' (polite licensed orgies made possible by contraception), and the intellectual segregation into classes labelled alpha to epsilon – in these, if not in other respects the Western world has come to look remarkably like Huxley's vision. Into this world of perfect material comfort and philistinism there arrives the last primitive man left alive, the 'Savage', a Red Indian from New Mexico. He educates himself entirely by reading Shakespeare, in the last copy to survive, and comes to believe passionately in art, romantic love and the spiritual life: finding no place for such things in the millennial society, where they are considered incomprehensible by the masses and subversive of order by the Leaders, he commits suicide. This is a most ingenious variant of the primitivist strategy of traditional satire, since the 'savage' is not only the innocent eye, but the bearer of the aesthetic and spiritual ideals of Western civilisation up to the present day: his fate is a horrifying fable of the death of art.

Orwell's *1984* is less convincing as a vision of the future, partly because of its lack of scientific expertise; but in its wildest distortions it is a true account of Stalin's empire as it was at the time of writing (1949), and perhaps also of the heyday of Chinese communism. It is physically a picture of England at the end of the last war: the intellectuals working in government services, the awful canteens, the ruined cities, the proles interested only in gambling. Truth has vanished from public life: all historical records have been destroyed and all communication is propaganda. Supervision of private life is total, since 'Big Brother is watching you'; the attempts of his hero Winston Smith to escape from thought-control into love and private spiritual life are hopeless. The weakness of the book as satire lies in Orwell's handling of sensational incident, such as torture; he cannot make tragic episodes real or consonant with the purely satiric inventions in which the book abounds. These however are so rich in themselves that they have become and are likely to remain part of the armoury of liberal protest. Critics have been appalled by Orwell's bleak pessimism and have accused him of lack of humour; but they have often missed the fantastic wit that illuminates his vision of blackness. He is particularly good, for example, on the corruption of language under totalitarian régimes ('double think', 'newspeak'). *1984*, even if it images a condition that no longer exists in the West, remains the most impressive political fable of our time.

6 Satire in drama

We must now take up the history of satire in drama where we left it with Aristophanes. It is hard to find his true successors anywhere in the classic conventional drama. This is partly because great art is unrepeatable: the history of any art form is not a series of more or less good performances, but a series of once-and-for-all discoveries. The joy of artistic creation lies in the making of these discoveries, and the audience's pleasure comes largely from sharing this joy. It is also partly because the political, social and cultural situation of fifth-century Athens was unique. But there is a deeper reason for the absence of successors to Aristophanes; simply that pure satire is very rare in the drama. The normal way of expressing the laughable and ridiculous is through comedy, and comedy tends to drift away from satire. Comedy uses the devices of satire, typing of character, reduction parody and so on – and indeed satire has often borrowed such devices from comedy – but comedy uses them in a different spirit and for different ends. The usual sphere of comedy lies somewhere between the romance at one pole and the realistic picture of social life or 'manners' at the other. The former repre-sents an escape from the pressure of real life: the lovers are separated, undergo various trials and are brought together again for the closing triumph of youth in some kind of festivity. The latter, the comedy of manners, concerns individuals who deviate more or less seriously from an established code of behaviour, are punished, not too painfully, by being made to look ridiculous and are usually brought back repentant into the fold. The object of the comedy of manners is to create a style of living, to inculcate 'good form', tact, politeness and wit in conversation and behaviour – elegant wit and intelligent conversation are themselves part of polite behaviour in most societies. It does this by giving examples of gentility and boorishness, honesty and deviousness, and other opposites. Thus Molière puts forward the ideal of the *honnête homme*, Congreve the ideal of the gentleman: and so it is with the classics of the novel which correspond most closely with the stage comedy of manners (e.g. Jane Austen). But satire has different ends from this; the formal satires of the seventeenth and eighteenth centuries obviously overlap a good deal with comedy (as in the case of Boileau's and some of Pope's works), but the spirit of Aristophanes, Rabelais and Swift cannot be contained within their bounds. Comedy accepts the rules of the social game, satire does not: it is a protest against the rules as well as against the players, and it is much more profoundly subversive than comedy can afford to be. True satire offers both a more fantastically distorted vision and a sharper criticism of life than the traditional stage comedy can support if it is to meet its audience's expectations. As I suggested, one is more likely to find the essentials of satire in tragedy or tragi-comedy than in comedy proper: Shakespeare's greatest satire is in *Hamlet*, *King Lear*, *Troilus and Cressida* and *Timon of Athens*, not in *As You Like It*.

The other difficulty about combining satire with the stage is that all satire is to some degree allegorical; its characters have to stand for something beyond the literal level. They may be personae for the satirist himself or they may be fantastic monsters cloaking abstract moral ideas. Now, stage drama tends to avoid allegory, for good reasons. The very circumstances of play-acting are allegorical in themselves – everyone in the audience knows that the actors are literally people dressed up and declaiming lines, and that what takes place on the stage is on a different plane from ordinary life. The actors are clearly symbols. In this case it is difficult for the audience to accept yet another level of allegory, or to enjoy with comfort the spectacle of an actor representing a 'character' that represents an idea. Most conventional or 'legitimate' drama is more or less fully committed to realism. Given the unrealistic, quasi-symbolic circumstances of play-acting – and the unrealistic requirements that plot makes on real time – the author and the actors have to create the illusion of reality in some dimensions, as of emotion, language, logical sequence of events or physical setting. The naturalistic drama of the nineteenth century laid down much stricter criteria for judging the illusion, but the earlier drama, whether classical or Renaissance, also had strict rules aimed at producing some kind of realism. Hence the normal drama has been too confined a medium for satire, which has flourished best on the

διαβάλλεταί σ᾽ ὁ θεῖος, ὦ πονηρὲ σύ.
τῶν γὰρ πατρῴων οὐδ᾽ ἀκαρῆ μέτεστί σοι
κατὰ τοὺς νόμους· νόθος γὰρ εἶ κοὐ γνήσιος.

stage in forms of entertainment less bound to the rules, that is,
ballad-opera, revue or the like. Aristophanic comedy is after all a
kind of ballad-opera, in which the action is interrupted by song and
dance: at one point the chorus even stop pretending that they are
characters and address the audience directly. It seems essential for
satire that the steady illusion of acting be broken from time to time;
only thus will the wild fantasy and its allegorical constructions
become acceptable. Later we shall return to ballad-opera and
'entertainment'. For the present one may suggest that conventional
comedy is likely to contain elements or episodes of satire rather
than to embody a complete satirical plot; just as the conventional
novel may be satirical in part, but only the fantastic *conte* or fable is
likely to be a completely formal expression of the satirical vision.

The exceptions to this rule are relatively few. Although
Machiavelli's *La Mandragola* (The Mandrake, 1504), is sometimes
quoted as the first satirical comedy of the Renaissance, the true
beginnings of dramatic satire in modern Europe would seem to be
in Ben Jonson. As we have seen in chapter 2 there is a strong
connection between his plays and the fashion for formal satire which

Aristophanes, *The Birds;*
Robert Farren's etching of the
production at Cambridge University,
in the original Greek, 1883.

191

swept England in the late 1590s. His first famous work *Every Man in his Humour* was performed in 1598, with Shakespeare in the cast; this is a comedy with a standard classical plot, concerning the efforts of two young men to escape from the hostility of their relations. On to this framework Jonson built a series of characters, carefully worked out according to his theory of 'humours' or ruling passions, an elaboration of a basic satirical device. The most interesting of these type-characters is Captain Bobadil, a contemporary version of the *miles gloriosus*. The year after this play came out, the Bishops' Ban on printed formal satire was imposed, and had the effect of driving some of the verse satirists into the theatre; and the literary war between them was transferred to the stage. John Marston attacked Jonson in *Histriomastix* (1599), and Jonson replied in *Every Man out of his Humour* in the same year. This has an even looser plot and as well as type-characters contains recognisable lampoons or caricatures of his literary enemies. Jonson continued the war in *The Poetaster* (1601), and Dekker came to Marston's aid in his reply *Satiromastix* (1602), which includes a caricature of Jonson. The formal satirist himself appears on the stage to denounce his opponents; so Macilente in *Every Man out of his Humour*, Crites in *Cynthia's Revels* and Horace in *The Poetaster*. This fierce literary in-fighting was popular with the London public for a few years, but is not very interesting today except to specialist readers. Jonson's real achievement in satirical drama came a few years later when he moved further away from the aims and methods of formal satire. *Volpone* (1606) is a brutal treatment of the vices of hypocrisy and greed: the characters are the pure embodiments of animal drives, combined with immense human ingenuity. Jonson, instead of the railing monologue derived from satire, uses a highly sophisticated version of that primitive satire form, the beast-fable. Volpone the Fox is the cunning imposter, who plays on the greed of the rascally Voltore (vulture, a lawyer), Corbaccio (carrion crow, a miser), and Corvino (raven, a crooked merchant): the fox shams dying as these birds of prey cluster round his body. What makes Jonson unique among comic dramatists is the power of his verse. All these characters, both the gulls and the sharks, live an intense life of fantasy: their lusts and their self-congratulatory raptures are expressed in wonderfully fluent rhetoric and in poetic images which lift them on to the plane of creative delirium; all satire tends to present human beings as monomaniacs, Jonson's creates the essence of paranoia. Volpone flings himself into his schemes with appalling energy but is surpassed by the vitality of his clever servant Mosca, the fly. After these demonic creatures have entertained us with their verbal ballet, it seems hard, even sadistic, on Jonson's part that he should have them so severely punished by the law at the end. The moral message is perfectly clear without insisting on the criminal nature of the actions; he has also broken out of the cardinal principles of satire, which is to deal with the folly and vice and leave crime alone as an unmanageable subject. This ending has evidently worried audiences: in 1928 Jules Romains and Stefan Zweig wrote a new ending for a production, in which Mosca inherits Volpone's money by a false will, and Volpone, who has to sham dead in earnest to avoid legal execution, creeps off empty-handed. Apart from the ending, *Volpone* is the greatest of all satiric comedies, a triumphant combination of moral realism with creative fantasy. Since a famous study by Professor L.C.Knights, there has been much discussion about the moral basis of Jonson's satire: is it social in direction and concerned with the new acquisitive ethos of growing capitalism, or is it simply an expression of the classical ethos of the golden mean, and of avoiding excess? My own view is that Jonson held the Renaissance ideal of the all-round man, who should fulfil his potentialities in action in every noble pursuit: anything that hinders man's self-expression, whether capitalistic greed or restrictive puritanism, is an offence against the vitality of the human spirit.

The lust for gain appears in an even more imaginative form in *The Alchemist* (1611). Among the gullible knaves who are exploited by Subtle and Face, the outstanding monomaniac is Sir Epicure Mammon, in whose fantasies sex, food and money are powerfully interlocked. The Puritans, who were becoming a serious political and social threat, are satirised in the hypocritical brethren Ananias and Tribulation Wholesome; but Jonson did even better in *Bartholomew Fair* (1614) by creating the superbly funny figure of Zeal-of-the-Land Busy. There is very little plot in this prose comedy; the centre of interest is the string of characters who pass before the background of the fair with its puppet-show and booths. Zeal-of-the-Land would have all such things suppressed as 'dominations' and 'idols' – Jonson gives a wonderful parody of the biblical speech of the preachers, as he does of all kinds of contemporary jargon and slang. In the end the spirit and vitality of the fair (which represents the sacred cause of unedifying entertainment) triumphs over the Puritan. Would that England herself had been more fortunate! The greatness of Jonson's plays comes from his grasp of the English language through its range from the vulgar to the learned, and from his ability to present images of the physical world with extraordinary immediacy.

In the same period satire also found its way into Jacobean tragedy. Apart from Shakespeare's, the best tragedies are Webster's *The White Devil* and *The Duchess of Malfi*, and Tourneur's *The Revenger's Tragedy* (all between about 1607 and 1614). It is a remarkable sign of the persistence of formal satire that in each of these plays is a leading character who not only speaks passages very similar in tone and matter to the verse satire of the previous decade, but also acts out the traditional role of the satirist, as un-masker of vice. This character is known generally as the malcon-tent, from the play of that title by the satirist Marston (1604); he finds the times to be out of joint and hypocrisy prevailing everywhere. He is melancholy and frustrated but lashes out with savage wit: so Flamineo in *The White Devil*, Bosola in *The Duchess of Malfi* and Vindice, the hero of *The Revenger's Tragedy*. In the last, many of the characters have the names of moral types, such as Lussurioso (Lecherous) Ambitioso and Supervacuo, the sons of the wicked Duke. The revenger stalks among them, plotting their destruction and uttering long and eloquent diatribes on the

If graphic satire has often taken its inspiration from literature,
the reverse has sometimes happened too. This particular engraving,
'Le Juge ou la Cruche Cassée', after the painting by Debucourt, is said
to have inspired Kleist to write his play *Der Zerbrochene Krug*.

satirical topics of lechery and avarice. *The Revenger's Tragedy* has
been shown to be in the tradition of the medieval satirical allegory,
and it can also be seen as a prolonged formal satire interrupted by
sensational (and not very dramatically convincing) incidents. This
is not true of Webster's two great plays, which have moments of
grandeur and pathos and more authentic characterisation; but even
in them the action is broken up by satirical aphorisms or harangues
of doubtful relevance. Thus in *The White Devil* (act III) at the trial of
Vittoria, the prosecutor Monticelso begins his case by saying 'Shall
I expound whore to you? – I'll give their perfect character', and
does so at some length and with much brilliance in the traditional
manner of a satirical character, without however coming very close
to the actual case of Vittoria. In *The Duchess of Malfi* Bosola is
'the only court-gall', the scourge of vice, who rants at the hypocritical vices of the great in bizarre witticisms. Bosola is not only an
agent of evil in the play, he is also a representative of the satirists of
his age, the poor and discontented scholars who found relief for
their frustration in aggressive wit. It is the way in which the satire
overflows the dramatic situation that helps to give these plays their
disturbing quality.

After Ben Jonson, the plays which are completely successful
embodiments of a satirical vision are relatively few. In England a
minor successor to Jonson was Thomas Shadwell, who combined
the tradition of the comedy of humours with realistic description of
low life in *The Squire of Alsatia* and *Bury Fair* (1689). The latter is
possibly the original of the famous episode of Mrs Leo Hunter and
Count Smorltork in Dickens's *Pickwick Papers* (also set in Bury St
Edmunds), and Dickens learned something of the techniques of
creating satirical characters from Jonson's and Shadwell's comedy
of humours. The Restoration dramatists on the whole abandoned
the tradition for the comedy of manners, but William Wycherley
kept closest to the old satiric attitude in *The Plain Dealer* (1677),
which is a very free adaptation of Molière's *Le Misanthrope*.
Manly, an honest sea-captain, returns from a voyage to find that he
has been betrayed by his best friend Vernish (the name implies the

varnished surface) and by his love Olivia. His disgust with the
treachery and deception of the world makes him produce a version
of the Stoic diatribe favoured by the verse satirists, sturdy and
original enough to redeem an otherwise conventional romantic
comedy. 'Plain-dealer' is in fact an excellent general term for the
satirist's persona.

The drama of the early nineteenth century includes two famous
satirical comedies, *The Broken Jug* (Der zerbrochene Krug, 1803)
by Heinrich von Kleist, and *Woe from Wit* (Gore ot uma, 1823–4)
by Griboyedov. In the latter (also known as *Too Clever by Half*) a
young nobleman comes home from a foreign tour to discover the
pettiness of Moscow society; his outspoken comments get him into
trouble and he ends in isolation – a symbol of the satirist's predica-
ment. A much greater Russian comedy and one of the finest of all
satiric plays is Gogol's *Revizor* (The Government Inspector, 1836).
Khlestakov, a minor civil servant, is stranded in a provincial
town without money; the local officials think that he is the government official whose arrival is expected and feared, and start to

bribe him into overlooking their corrupt administration. Khlestakov grasps the situation and exploits it, until he is living off the fat of the land and making love to the mayor's wife and daughter. He is exposed when the postmaster reads his letter to a St Petersburg friend boasting of his exploits, but escapes in time, just before the real inspector arrives. In a marvellously economical sequence of hilarious scenes, every kind of human corruption, greed, fear and vanity, is given its perfect embodiment: the device of using a rogue to expose worse rogues has never been more skilfully used. The play is a convincing indictment of the political system which makes such corruption inevitable: but it is more than a denunciation. There is an extra dimension in Khlestakov, a quality of wild fantasy which lifts him above the level of a satirist's persona. Gogol's sympathy with human weakness and his powers of imaginative travesty (which appear in the great satiric scenes of *Dead Souls*) make his play unique.

In the much larger group of comedies which contain a satirical element, Molière must be given the first consideration. It is not difficult to see the main point of his comedy of manners: he accepts the ethos of his milieu, part courtly and part bourgeois, and presents deviations from the norm, which if allowed to get out of hand might destroy the delicate balance on which the good life rests. Good sense must triumph over eccentricity, triviality and boorishness. But there seems to be a deeper level of satire half-hidden in some at least of his plays. Comedy is a self-contained system, even when it reflects social norms; it offers a style of living, not a philosophy. Satire is open-ended, and looks out from the theatre to the social and political problems of its time. Critics have been unable to agree as to whether *Tartuffe* (1664) is satire in this sense: is it an attack on religious hypocrisy or a mockery of religion itself? Certainly Tartuffe is never revealed as a hypocrite by any of his own words; he uses the language of mystical devotion apparently in real earnest when trying to seduce Elmire; and the play was heavily attacked by all the clerical authorities. It took Molière five years of hard work to get it produced on the public stage; he would surely not have been so persistent in the face of ecclesiastical criticism if he had not been trying to say something he felt to be important and true. At a time when it was impossible for a free-thinker to speak out openly, Molière went to the limits of daring in burlesquing the practices of piety. It makes better sense to see him as belonging to that very large half-underground resistance of the seventeenth century, the movement known as 'libertins', which included Epicureans, deists and anti-clericals of all kinds. A clerical writer, Pierre Roulé, described Molière in 1664 as 'a demon in the flesh, dressed in men's clothing, the most impious, libertine spirit of all time ...' – and from his point of view he may have been right: the laughter released by the spectacle of Tartuffe at his devotions was re-echoed in the satire of Voltaire and the overt anti-religious critiques of the Enlightenment. The implications of his less famous play *Don Juan* are also significant. *Don Juan ou le Festin de Pierre* (the stone guest) was dropped from the stage after only fifteen performances in 1665. Here he presented a libertin and free-thinker in action, and not altogether unfavourably. Of course the Don is damned at the end, but only by the ludicrous device of the statue, drawn ultimately from a naive medieval legend. Without the assistance of Mozart's trombone chords this episode cannot be taken very seriously, and gives no indication of what Molière really thought of his hero. In fact Don Juan behaves wickedly for only part of the time: he is arrogantly hardhearted in the manner of a grand seigneur to his women, but against that he unselfishly and courageously saves a man's life from the bandits. That he is capable of such disinterested behaviour would seem to imply that morality is possible without religious belief, a thesis which has always been vigorously opposed by the clergy. This may seem a roundabout way of expressing subversive views, but it was the only way open to a writer of that period, apart from circulating libertine tracts in secret. The ambiguity of *Don Juan* prevents it from being effective propaganda, but it seems calculated to cause dangerous doubts, and succeeds in producing a disturbing impression.

A clearer example of satire escaping from the bounds of comedy

and becoming a powerful political influence can be seen in Beaumarchais' *Marriage of Figaro* (Le Mariage de Figaro ou La Folle Journée, 1784). His earlier play *The Barber of Seville* is a straightforward comedy of intrigue; but when Beaumarchais took up the adventures of the clever servant nine years later he made them into a vehicle for political protest. The Count is in favour of Figaro's marriage to Suzanne provided that he can exert his feudal rights over her; he is frustrated by Figaro's ingenuity and openly attacked as a representative of the reactionary nobility. Beaumarchais brilliantly expresses both the prerevolutionary mood of the times and his own disgust at social stupidity, through Figaro's monologue in act v, scene 3, addressed to the nobility in general: 'What have you done to deserve such wealth? You took the trouble to be born and nothing else.' Beaumarchais' daring led to the play being suppressed for three years, and he was even put in prison for a few days. The play's popularity in its day was immense and had an incisive effect on the climate of opinion; its abiding greatness as satire comes from its combination of lucidity, gaiety and scorn.

Henrik Ibsen, *Et Dukkehjem* (*A Doll's House*): 199
a scene from the second act in a production of 1879
at the Royal Theatre, Copenhagen.

The finest satire of the nineteenth century is in Ibsen's mature drama, although Ibsen's genius is too great to be confined to satire at any single point. The closest he came to a straightforward satirical attack on bourgeois stupidity was in his earlier *Love's Comedy* (*Kaerlighedens Komedie*, 1862); later his satire is always set in a frame of pessimistic irony and directed at himself as much as against his enemies. It is easy to forget in the context of these overwhelmingly dark fables of human fate that Ibsen is a superb comic writer: but he proves himself to be a master of ridicule in his portraits of Parson Manders in *Ghosts*, Hjalmar Ekdal in *The Wild Duck* and Tesman in *Hedda Gabler* – the last being such a deadly type of academic vice that no professor can see it without shuddering. *An Enemy of the People* (1882) was his reply to the outcry raised by *Ghosts*. Ibsen portrays himself as Dr Stockmann, the honest doctor who insists that the town's water supply is infected, against the efforts of the local conservative politicians to silence him. This play is an excellent fable for political propaganda, and as such it is even more effective in the recent adaptation by Arthur Miller; but it is too angry and self-righteous to be great satire. In a mood of self-revulsion Ibsen next pictured himself as another kind of truth-seeker in the ineffectual Gregers Werle in *The Wild Duck*. The 'claims of the ideal' cause Gregers to bring to light the sordid truth about the Ekdal family; but the effect of his meddling causes the death of one wholly innocent person in the story and leaves everything else as it was before. Stockmann is one version of the satirist's persona of 'plain-dealer' or unmasker; Gregers is an ironic travesty of this very role, mocked at the end by Relling's cynical advice, that people should never be told the truth but merely be given an anodyne 'life-illusion'. The subtlety of *Hedda Gabler* lies in Ibsen's unique ability to see all the characters as butts of satire, contemptible and predictable, and simultaneously as suffering and even tragic human beings.

George Bernard Shaw was a self-styled disciple of Ibsen, but moved more deliberately in the field of politics. He was an active polemicist and pamphleteer as well as dramatist: one would therefore expect his satire to be more sharply directed on to the problems of society, but today it no longer looks like that. Ibsen's ideas are still highly relevant to the world of today, Shaw's are curiously dead. Despite his keen intelligence, his satire nearly always lands just off the target. Unlike the great satirists Shaw is not at all disturbing to read or to see on the stage: he is a great entertainer, the licensed buffoon of the powers that be – and he admired most of the centres of power in his day, even fascism and Stalinism. Reversing the normal direction of satire, which proceeds from fantasy to reality, Shaw turns every real issue into a pure abstraction, creating a music of ideas which he orchestrates with superb skill. He remains, with Wilde, one of the greatest of pure comedians, and nowhere does his genius for abstract wit appear more beautifully than in *Heartbreak House*, which is meant to be a parody of Chekhov but can just as well be read as a parody of satire itself. There are two striking exceptions to Shaw's normal run of non-satirical satire: the Devil's harangue in the Don Juan episode of *Man and Superman*, and *John Bull's Other Island* (1904). Although he often pretended indifference or contempt, Shaw was deeply involved in the political and social troubles of his native Ireland, and he shows in this last play feeling and insight as well as precise knowledge. The main issues of Ireland are brought into sharp focus – the peasants' land-hunger, the Catholic church, nationalism – and Shaw's analysis is informed with contempt for the stupidity of the natives and for the absurdity of English liberal attempts to cope with a situation they can't understand. He builds up with great dramaturgic skill the contrasts between the absurd Englishman Broadbent (an idealist with an eye to making money) and the realistic exiled Irishman Doyle, between the power-loving priest and the unfrocked mystic. There is one scene involving a slapstick accident with a pig, where Shaw emphasises the cruelty of Irish laughter usually masked by naturally good manners; and something of this cruelty affected Shaw in the writing of this play. But it is cruelty tempered with compassion for the hopeless plight of the Irish peasant.

Shaw was the master of Sean O'Casey, who learned from that

'You eat your daarlin' sassidge and never mind the exile of Sibeyria'. Boyle and Joxer reflect on the wonders and ironies of life, in an early production of *Juno and the Paycock* by Sean O'Casey.

play in particular how to deal with the tragi-comedy of Irish politics. O'Casey was a lesser dramatist but a potentially greater satirist than Shaw, although his gifts only came to fruition in two outstanding plays, *Juno and the Paycock* (1925) and *The Plough and the Stars* (1926). They deal with political themes from the immediate past (the first set in the Civil War of 1922, the second in the Easter Rising of 1916) and show the slum-dwellers of Dublin caught up in terrible conflicts which are beyond their understanding. *The Plough and the Stars* contains some of the finest comic scenes in the English language, as well as some of the most touching.

O'Casey's unsentimental and satiric picture of his countrymen in their most heroic moment caused riots in the Abbey Theatre. When O'Casey left Ireland, largely because of this play's unpopularity, his writing lost its immediacy; but here and there in his *Autobiographies* (1939–54) there are spontaneous and vivid passages which equal the best satire in his early plays.

No English dramatist has since appeared to rival the great Irish writers of the last generation. John Osborne is a master of the tirade (as in *Look Back in Anger*, 1956, or *The Entertainer*, 1957) but has so far produced accomplished invective rather than satire. The English, like the French, theatre seems to be moving away from the traditional forms, such as satirical comedy and tragi-comedy, into the new realms discovered by Beckett and Ionesco which are beyond the limits of this survey.

The popular theatre

Beneath the 'legitimate' theatre of every age there has always been a vast amount of popular entertainment in the form of miming, song and dance, and this has been the main vehicle for the simplest forms of satire. From time to time the legitimate theatre has been closed down altogether by the civil authorities, often under ecclesiastical pressure, or it has been subjected to strict control and made into a legal monopoly – hence the term 'legitimate'. But such is the love of the human race for entertainment that the 'illegitimate' theatre has never ceased, although it has taken many different forms. The mime has been variously known as the Roman *mimus*, medieval minstrel, strolling player, comedian and so on; his productions have included the Roman Atellan playlets, medieval and modern farce, the *commedia dell'arte* and its descendants like harlequinades and pantomime, burlesque and vaudeville, music-hall, cabaret review and ballad-singing. Such things have been performed at any suitable occasion, from village fairs to television programmes; they are by their very nature the most fugitive forms of art, and therefore the hardest for the historian to record. The most permanent form of these popular arts is probably the broadside ballad, which implies a printed text; but most other forms have faded into oblivion until very recent times, when some have been preserved for posterity by means of cinema, television and the long-playing record.

The mime's art is extemporary. He makes people laugh by the gestures of slapstick, verbal mockery and by the mimicry of individuals or social types. There is inevitably a certain amount of lampoon-satire somewhere in his repertoire, although the proportion will vary according to popular demand. At the most primitive level of entertainment, the amount of crude satire demanded and offered is probably rather high, since jeering mockery is the simplest way of raising laughter. As the audience's taste becomes a little less crude, the proportion will tend to decrease and be replaced by spectacle, pathos and sentimentality and straightforward slapstick, which in many periods make up the staple fare of the popular theatre. But in times of political and social tension, when there is a large enough public interested in public affairs and sophisticated to the point of enjoying barbed allusions to public figures, the amount of satire in the mime's repertoire will tend to increase again. It is at this point, when the popular stage becomes more involved with politics, that it has the greatest influence on literary satire. The mime's art at its simplest level also tends to be obscene and irreverent; he is inevitably a breaker of taboos, and a mocker of established institutions. Because there is so much bawdry in the comedian's art he is always coming under the fire of the official guardians of morals. The complaints of the medieval churchmen against minstrels and mummers, the hostility of the English Puritans to any form of stage entertainment are signs of the disquiet caused in the hearts of the godly by the mere presence of the entertainers, those agents of the Devil and seducers of the weaker brethren. The association of the mime with irreverent bawdry and social unrest is the main reason why actors in general have enjoyed such low status until recent centuries, and have often been treated like potential criminals and vagabonds. The amount

204

of bawdry demanded or tolerated by the public also seems to fluctuate in roughly the same cycles as the rising and falling tide of political and social satire; but obscenity and blasphemy have never disappeared from the popular stage, even in the most puritanical periods, just as under the more authoritarian regimes the flag of satire is kept flying somewhere at the lowest level of entertainment.

The names for the mime's art are legion, and keep changing confusingly. We shall mention only a few. *Vaudeville* is said to be derived from the Val de Vire in Normandy, where one Olivier Basselin was possibly the author of humorous and satirical drinking songs, about the middle of the fifteenth century. These songs became popular all over France, and were imitated in satirical songs to popular tunes, known as Vaux-de-vire. They were written in couplets and in the sixteenth and seventeenth centuries were the medium for political comment, being roughly the equivalent of the English broadside ballad. The term was used in the 1670s to describe songs in this vein written by Boileau. In the early eighteenth century the word changed its meaning: it was used for the plays in pantomime (comédies-en-vaudeville) put on by strolling players to get round the monopoly of the Comédie Française. The word now lost its satirical associations, and still later changed its meaning again in the USA where it became the equivalent of the English music-hall. So with the word *burlesque:* in the theatre originally it meant a satirical parody of the serious genres (like Villiers's *Rehearsal* or Fielding's *Tom Thumb*); later simply a light entertainment with music, as in Victorian England; and still later in the USA it was used for another kind of music-hall, with a stronger tradition of obscenity than vaudeville, and in fact the ancestor of modern striptease.

These are two examples of both the word and the form of entertainment losing their connections with satire: *Revue* is a third. Like many other excellent kinds of popular entertainment it was a French invention, springing from the irreverent *esprit gaulois*. The word meant a plotless theatrical performance which passed current affairs in review. Traditionally this was done at the annual street

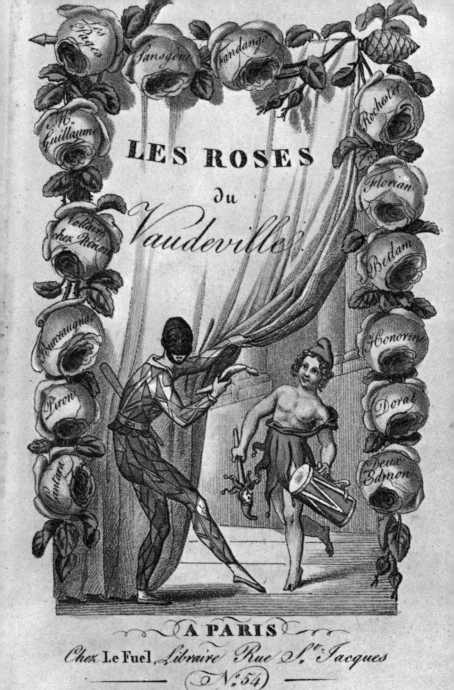

Yvette Guilbert by Lautrec: a tribute from one great ironist to another.

fairs at which the players commented on the events of the year in comic songs and improvised sketches. This was taken over from provincial to Paris life, and adapted to a more sophisticated audience in the early nineteenth century, at a time of unsettled political conditions. The original revues were full of satirical remarks on current politics, in songs, sketches and impromptu comedians' acts; and this distinguished it from the other kinds of 'variety' or 'music-hall' flourishing simultaneously in France and other European countries. The *revue* was first developed at the Paris theatre Porte Saint Martin by the brothers Cogniard, and it was not accidental that it grew up at the same time as the French satirical periodicals and cartoonists. It did not cross the Channel successfully or have much effect elsewhere in Europe, presumably because the right degree of political sophistication in the wider public was lacking. In England the masses were long faithful to the more naive and sentimental art of the music-hall, and revue only made an appearance just before the 1914 war, and then in an attenuated form; it came to mean an organised sequence of songs, dances and sketches put on by a company, rather than the solo turns of music-hall. Although there were some elegant and witty London revues in the twenties and thirties, notably those put on by Charles Cochran or written by Noel Coward, they did not keep the satirical spirit of their French originals but reflected the uncritical mood of the middle-class public. In the even more complacent USA the revue proper had even less success, until the spread of left-wing political ideas, during the depression. In 1937 *Pins and Needles*, put on by the Garmentworkers' Union, had great commercial success. This was a curiously direct return to the political roots of the genre: the title of one of its numbers, intended to be half ironical, 'Sing me a song of social significance', conveniently illustrates this point. The stage revue has withstood the onslaught of the cinema and television better than music-hall or variety, and it is still a living art-form, if only for the more educated minority.

The stage revue is not the only means by which satirical entertainment can be presented. If we return to nineteenth-century France,

(*left*) 'At the top of the uniform is situated the head, to inform the soldiers of the height to which his salute should be brought'. Bruno Paul, in *Simplicissimus* (1904).

(*below*) Germany after World War One: an acid comment by Georg Grosz from *Der Spiesser Spiegel* (1928).

Polly and her parents Peachum.
A production by the Berliner Ensemble of Brecht's
Dreigroschenoper (*Threepenny Opera*).

we can notice the development of other frameworks for the same kind of song and sketch: the *cabaret*, the *chansonnier* and the *café-concert* are less formalised ways by which the artist, whether singer, *diseuse* or comedian, could reach an intelligent public. These lively popular arts fermented vigorously in late nineteenth-century Paris, then the capital of the world for the serious arts of painting and poetry. We know this dazzling and sordid world, which ran from the criminals and whores up to the intellectuals, from the paintings and posters of Toulouse-Lautrec. He caught the image of the most famous *diseuse* of all, Yvette Guilbert, in her yellow dress and black gloves, from all accounts a brilliant mimic and satirist of Paris life. (I heard her only in her old age when she had changed to a more respectable repertoire.) Her success depended partly on the excellent songs written for her and partly on her ability to improvise realistic sketches. This tradition has never died out in France and the links between the night-club, cabaret and café and the best writers of the day have never been broken.

The most interesting export of the Parisian tradition of cabaret was to Germany, and this proved to be the most fruitful for serious literary satire. There had long been a German genre of light quasi-satirical revue on a high level, beginning with Heine and continuing to Wilhelm Busch and Christian Morgenstern at the end of the nineteenth century; but this genre had been rather detached from the world of the theatre. There was a new beginning when the *chansonnier* was imitated in Germany. In 1900 Bierbaum's *Deutsche Chanson* were published and in 1901 a cabaret called *Die Elf Scharfrichter* (*The Eleven Executioners*) was opened in Munich. It has close connections with the Munich satirical journal *Simplicissimus*, which published powerful cartoons, verse and prose in protest against German imperialism and militarism. Wedekind wrote for the journal and performed in the cabaret, and established a tradition of popular political satire which survived the 1914–18 war. There was in the 1920s a powerful growth of the serious night-club, especially in Berlin. Again there was collabora-

tion between an intelligent periodical (Siegfried Jacobsohn's *Weltbühne*, later edited by Carl von Ossietsky, who won the Nobel Peace prize in 1935), satirical cartoonists and illustrators (George Grosz and Neher), poets (Kurt Tucholsky, Erich Kästner). The poets wrote their social criticism to be sung in the cabarets by first-class singers and to be sold in large cheap editions: their satire was intelligently written and singable and reached a wide public[24].

Bertolt Brecht began by setting his own poems to his own tunes and performing them, it is said, in Munich bars. He soon found the perfect collaborator in Kurt Weill and the perfect performer in Lotte Lenja who came from the circus and ballet, not from the legitimate theatre. The great ballad-opera, *Die Dreigroschenoper* (1928) and *Aufstieg und Fall der Stadt Mahagonny* (1930) are marvellous imaginative expansions of the cabaret entertainment full of the best popular satirical songs ever written. Whatever Brecht's later political outlook, these songs do not express the party line; at once they attack the conventions of society from the anarchic Bohemian viewpoint of a Villon and a Rimbaud (both of whom he admired and adapted), and show a deep sympathy for the obscure and oppressed which has never been equalled in left-wing verse. It is worth noting that he also used Kipling's *Barrack-Room Ballads*. The perfect balance between these two approaches is reached in songs like *Seeräuber Jenny* and *Wie man sich bettet*. It may well be that Brecht is overrated as a dramatist, but he seems to me one of the best song-writers of all time, and within his limits a great satirical poet. *The Three-penny Opera* was also made into one of the finest of satirical films; and more than twenty years after it was written it has become a classic of the world theatre.

The German milieu in which Brecht created his best work did not survive the coming of Hitler; the satirists were driven into exile, Tucholsky dying in Sweden. It does not seem to have been re-created in Western Germany, nor has this kind of collaboration between writers and the entertainment world ever again reached such a high level. There have been signs of something like it developing in the United States; in the fifties and early sixties the songs of Tom Lehrer and the monologues of Mort Sahl and Lenny Bruce revived the art with varying degrees of sophistication and brutality. They were followed a few years later by the sudden flowering of political and topical satire on British television; and it is with this medium that the future of this genre seems to lie.

7 Satire in the novel

The novel, that 'loose, baggy monster' as Henry James called it, is notoriously difficult to describe in generalities. It is so loose that as an art form it can hardly be said to exist. Under the heading of prose fiction a vast number of types have appeared during the last two centuries, when the novel dominated Western literature. A principal type has been the romance, which offers escape into a world of fantasy through close identification between the reader and the characters: a story of love or adventure or mild comedy, now largely replaced as mass entertainment by its equivalent in cinema and television. There is an element of pure entertainment and fantasy in all novel-reading, but the serious novel aims at a different goal, which is understanding. The novel in this sense is an explanation of how society works, and how individuals are related to society; since it is an imaginative interpretation of history, every novel is a historical novel. The novel in Stendhal's well-known phrase is a 'mirror walking along a highway' – and the highway leads from the obscure past to our complex present and on into the doubtful future; the reader looks into the mirror to learn who he is, and who his contemporaries are. We demand many things simultaneously of the novelist: he must give us a realistic transcript of life as it is lived, provide models for behaviour, both in morality and in style of life; and at the same time he may give his narrative a structure of myth or symbolism to give a more than literal meaning to the events he describes.

If we demand and receive from even the simplest classic novel so many different things, this is inconsistent with the simplicity of satire. Whereas the novelist aims at understanding the complexities of life, satire aims at simplification, at a pretence of misunderstanding and at denunciation. The sheer size of the open-ended form of the novel has also much to do with the difficulty that satirists have in using it: satire seems to require a light and closed form which helps to make a simple point effectively – the form is itself a component of the wit without which satire is unbearable. It follows that no full-length novel is likely to be satirical throughout, and indeed not one example among the classics comes to mind. Satirical

THE SPLIT-MAN.

Wyndham Lewis himself illustrated his satirical novel *The Apes of God*, in curiously abstract style for such a personal view of the literary scene.

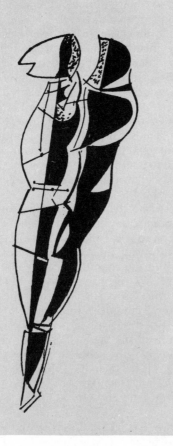

fiction if it is to be successful needs to be short and also to approach one of the traditional forms discussed above – the folk allegory, imaginative voyage, utopia or some version of these genres. At the same time, satire may appear at almost any point in a serious novel, to provide extra attack on one of the main themes, to emphasise one of the moral points or to change the level of representation from factual documentary to imaginative travesty. This is to say nothing of the straight lampoons or attacks on real people, which appear in many novels: novelists evidently cannot resist the temptation to pillory their acquaintances, especially their literary enemies. Thus D.H.Lawrence gives a serious but distorted picture of Middleton Murry in *Women in Love*, Aldous Huxley has a hilarious caricature of Murry in *Point Counter Point*, while Wyndham Lewis assaulted the Sitwells in *The Apes of God*, a mountainous, sprawling and hardly readable work of genius which demonstrates the difficulty of writing fictional satire at great length. The lampoon or malicious caricature can be expected to continue as long as novels are written, since it is the simplest way of working off literary aggression and rarely risks prosecution for libel.

Satire in the novel should not be confused with propaganda, of which prose fiction has been a powerful instrument. The novelist may want to draw attention to social evils and to call for reforms; and he can best do so by drawing an accurate picture, fully documented with telling detail of the conditions of the poor. The first effective use of the novel for propaganda was by Dickens in *Nicholas Nickleby* and *Oliver Twist* (1837–8); and there is a long tradition of left-wing naturalistic novels through Zola and Maxim Gorki, which has the responsibility of fathering the monstrously dull 'socialist-realist' novels of the Stalinist era. Nor should satire be confused with the use of grotesques in the novel, with the distorted monsters who make their first brief appearance in Richardson and stalk in full magnificence across the pages of Balzac. Satire uses the grotesque but only as a means to heighten ridicule and fantasy.

There are, however, two special traditions of the novel which have close affinities to satire and have provided fruitful media for novelists during the last three and a half centuries. The first is the quixotic, which uses variations of the persona created by Cervantes. *Don Quixote* (El Ingenioso Hidalgo Don Quixote de la Mancha, 1605, 1615). Alonso Quijano, a poor country gentleman, has lost his wits by reading too many romances of chivalry. He begins to interpret every experience in terms of romance, and sees himself as a knight errant called upon to redress the wrongs of the world, and changes his name to suit his new character. He rapidly runs into the cruel blows of reality, and is soon beaten up by some merchants whom he challenges to knightly combat. He sets out on his journey again, taking with him the peasant Sancho Panza as his squire: Sancho's common-sense and folk-speech at first make a wonderful contrast with his master's fantastic idealism, but after he has been promised an imaginary governorship, he succumbs to the same illusions. After many adventures, in which the Don and Sancho are brutally deceived by their observers, the Don recovers his sanity, abjures romance and dies. The greatness of this novel lies in its immense variety, its digressions, its absurd and profound comments on human life, its realistic descriptions of contemporary life; it offers such richness of content and style that, not surprisingly, a great many conflicting interpretations have been produced during the last three centuries. It obviously begins and ends as a straightforward satire on the chivalric romances; but is the central part of the book to be taken as satire, and if so against what targets is it directed? Cervantes has been seen as quasi-Protestant, even a free-thinker; he has been supposed to have hidden in his narrative an attack on the church and the Spanish political system. But since these esoteric meanings are not available to the majority of readers, it is safer to leave them to the experts: the book is satisfying enough without them. What matters more for the history of satire is the persistence of interpretations or mis-interpretations which have set up the Cervantic tradition; it is this that has influenced so many later writers. Here the essential point is that the hero should be in some respects a simpleton or a monomaniac who fails to

Lazarillo de Tormes: the boy picaro,
captured in a net, is exhibited by the fishermen
as a sea-monster (from the English edition
of 1726). This is a world of cruel reverses.

come to grips with reality and suffers accordingly; but also that he should be spiritually superior to the rest of the world. The people who understand and can handle reality successfully are seen to be knaves, otherwise they could not be the masters of this wicked world: the sacred fool cannot cope with the simplest demands of reality, but so much the worse for a world that favours deceit and chicanery. The figure of the noble idiot keeps reappearing in the eighteenth-century novelists influenced by Cervantes: he is reborn in Fielding's Parson Abraham Adams in *Joseph Andrews* (1742), who is hopelessly lost in a dream of the classics and incorrigibly absent-minded, but by far the most unselfish and altruistic person in the story. Other variants can be found in Goldsmith and Smollett, but the finest flower of the tradition is Dickens's Mr Pickwick, a wholly good man in a fairly wicked world of politicians, snobs and self-seeking lawyers. The quixotic hero is related to the satiric device of the innocent eye, and is particularly suited for attacks on the complexities and selfishness of competitive civilisation.

The other tradition which began a little earlier than the Cervantic is the picaresque. Here the moral position is reversed since the hero, the *picaro*, is himself a kind of rogue. He is the outsider or misfit, a bastard or a boy too intelligent for his station in life, who can find no regular occupation or fixed place in a stratified society. He is forced to move out on the road and to keep moving both horizontally in the novel and vertically in society. He meets with as many cruel blows of fate as the Cervantic hero but he gives as good as he gets, outwitting cunning knaves by even greater cunning. He lives by his wits and just gets by when he learns the hard lessons of the world. The picaresque novelist takes an amoral cynical view of life; he is unsentimental, realistic in his description of the social scenes, and basically anti-heroic. The genre began with the anonymous *La vida de Lazarillo de Tormes* (1554), a bitterly funny tale of a poor boy and his various masters. If it cannot be said with certainty that *Don Quixote* is a criticism of contemporary life, there is no doubt about *Lazarillo:* it certainly makes acid if indirect comments on the church and the semi-feudal order. In a short space it presents a

brilliant collection of satirical types, including a miserly priest, a greedy friar, and a seller of indulgences, seen against a realistic background of town life. *Lazarillo*, though never surpassed, was much imitated, notably by Mateo Alemán (*Guzmán de Alfarache*, 1599–1605), by Cervantes in his 'noveles exemplares', and by Francisco de Queredo (*Historia de la vida del Buscon*, 1626). For a century it remained a purely Spanish genre, perhaps because of a peculiarly Spanish tension between the survival of the medieval and the new colonial economy. The French then began to imitate the picaresque, the most famous example being Le Sage's *Gil Blas* (1715–35). The genre was adapted for spiritual and metaphysical ends by Johann Jakob von Grimmelshausen in his *Simplicissimus* (*Der abentheurliche Simplicissimus Teutsch*, 1669); this classic of German prose describes the hero's search for religious truth in the context of the Thirty Years' War, which is described with satiric realism. Later the genre was imitated, as Cervantes was, by the English comic novelists of the eighteenth century. Smollett's *Roderick Random* is the purest example of the tough, amoral picaresque. Fielding's *Tom Jones* belongs to the genre only to a limited degree, since the toughness has been softened by a benevolent and almost sentimental view of humanity; it remains in parts an effective attack on hypocrisy and hardness of heart, as personified by Blifil, Thwackum and Square. The greatest version of the picaresque in the nineteenth century is Mark Twain's *The Adventures of Huckleberry Finn*, (1884), which is also the outstanding use of the innocent eye in all North American fiction. Twain, rather a crude and facetious humorist when he turned to straight satire (as in *A Connecticut Yankee in King Arthur's Court*, 1889), produced in the narrative of Huckleberry Finn an extremely subtle and humane indictment of slavery and of the colonial society of the South, in the purest and most expressive colloquial idiom. Picaresque satire depends to a very large degree on a mastery of spoken idiom since any artificiality of diction spoils the effect of casual throwaway comment. This spoken idiom need not be lower-class speech; it can just as well be the conversational style of the upper-class 'barbarians'. The master of this style is Evelyn Waugh, who is also the most elegant and lucid picaresque satirist of the twentieth century. *Decline and Fall* (1928) has not been equalled for its exquisitely distorted picture of English upper and middle-class life; but his finest *picaro* is Basil Seal, the Etonian adventurer who is the hero of *Black Mischief* and appears again in *Put Out More Flags*. Waugh had the perfect temperament for a picaresque satirist: he was in love with the absurdities of contemporary England, yet alienated from both the worldly and liberal values of his culture by a deep pessimism; he judged the world from the standpoint of a conservative Roman Catholic, which in his day had the effect of new and radical judgment. His sharpness as a satirist fell off in his last novels, but at its best it was heightened by his economy and sense of form. *Decline and Fall* has a perfect circular form: it ends just where it begins, having moved with an absurd inevitability which is the satiric equivalent of tragic fate. This circularity of plot which appears in so many good satiric narratives (compare Flaubert's *Bouvard et Pécuchet*) is the ideal embodiment of the stoic resignation of the picaresque satirists; his fable of escape and voyaging ends with the discovery that escape is impossible.

This brief glance at the picaresque and the Cervantic would suggest that the most promising types of narrative fiction for the satirist are those which possess a strong formal element, so as to set up a tension with the realistic description of the world. Pure picaresque is too loose a form to make a powerful satiric point: it can make a general comment, amoral or cynical, on the hypocrisy and folly of the world; but any more definite idea may become lost in the amusing transcription of reality. A formal pattern may help to turn the narrative into a fable, changing the hero's voyagings into a quasi-allegorical Pilgrim's Progress, towards the goal of self-discovery or worldly wisdom. Another way of formalising narrative is to present it as dialogue, that is, in a semi-dramatic form. This is especially suitable for the satirical comedy of ideas. By observing some of the conventions of stage drama, the satirist reduces his characters to voices, who proclaim their obsessions and explore some field of contemporary thought. The trick is to make abstract ideas much more real and compelling than they can ever be in life, and to demonstrate their absurdity by drawing out their logical consequences. The credit for inventing the dialogue satire, or for the imaginary voyage, must be given to Lucian (*c.* 120–200). Lucian's *Dialogues of the Gods* treat classical mythology and religion in an engagingly lighthearted manner, which makes them perhaps the earliest examples of free-thinking satire. There is of course a wide gap between these dialogues, in which the narrative element is slight, and the dialogue novel; this was successfully bridged in the early nineteenth century by Thomas Love Peacock. Drawing heavily on the classics and on Rabelais, Peacock gives an incomparable survey of the intellectual life of his time. His technique, first shown in *Headlong Hall* (1816), is to collect a representative group of intellectuals at a house-party, and then make them engage in conversation; the ideas they put forward are brilliant parodies of current views on philosophy, politics and literature, close enough to the originals to make them true intellectual history and yet so representative in their absurdity of permanent modes of human thought as to make them of universal satirical validity. Peacock is at his best in his savage caricatures of Wordsworth and Coleridge, whom he detested as political reactionaries and obscurantists, and in his affectionate portraits of Byron and Shelley, with whose radicalism he was in sympathy. His masterpieces are *Nightmare Abbey* and *Crotchet Castle; Melincourt* is more overtly political in its satire, describing how an ape called Sir Oran Haut-Ton became elected as a Member of Parliament, but it fails to keep the even tone of derision and delight in logical absurdity which make the others such triumphs in the satire of ideas. This genre can only be attempted by writers who combine great learning with lightness of touch: Peacock's only gifted disciple in English is Aldous Huxley, who in his earlier works like *Antic Hay* showed a mastery of the ideas of the 1920s and gay irreverence in expounding them. From *Point Counter Point* onwards, with the exception of *Brave New World* he began to throw away his gift as he turned himself into a middlebrow chronicler of the pseudo-spiritual life.

The outstanding satire of ideas remains Flaubert's little-read *Bouvard et Pécuchet*, not quite finished at his death in 1880. His two clerks, set free by a legacy to embark on a life of study, are archetypal figures of intellectual folly. They take up one subject after another with enthusiasm, from agriculture to archaeology, only to become muddled and disillusioned. In despair they think of suicide, but the rope breaks; they turn to the consolations of religion, only to become bored with that. At the end they return with relief to their old job of copying (once again, the pattern is circular). In their voyage through the world of ideas these clowns make every sort of error; Flaubert documented the workings of their utterly commonplace minds with every kind of rubbish drawn from the popular and pseudo-science of the nineteenth century, and adorned their discourse with the clichés of 'bourgeois' opinion which he collected with loving horror for his *Dictionnaire des idées reçues*, which was to have formed part of a second volume of *Bouvard et Pécuchet*. From this aspect of Flaubert's satire Joyce took the hint, when he came to illustrate the interior monologue of his self-educated clown-hero Bloom. But it must not be thought that *Bouvard et Pécuchet* is simply an attack on the follies of vulgarised learning or on the intellectual rubbish of the time. Many readers perhaps approach it as such and are repelled by the ferocious pedantry with which Flaubert ridicules pedantry. But in fact the satire has a wider and more universal application; it is a paradigm of all learning except the highly specialised and professional. Once outside our own fields of expertise, we are all like Bouvard and Pécuchet, trying hopelessly to understand a universe of which we know very little except at second-hand, or even tenth-hand, and failing miserably to grasp even the essentials of (say) cosmology or molecular biology. Yet unless we are content with ignorance we have to try to understand the world, in the certainty of making fools of ourselves. Flaubert's last book is a wry comment on the years of historical study that went into his earlier books; and it

Bouvard dressed as warrior, with pot for helmet; Pécuchet
as monk. The indefatigable pair, in their tour of all sciences,
have now arrived at 'archaeology' and Medievalism.
The widow Bordin is not amused. Drawing by Stanislaus Gorski
from a nineteenth-century English translation.

remains a salutary warning to all authors.

Yet even the warmest admirers of *Bouvard et Pécuchet* must admit that the joke goes on too long. The perfect length as well as the perfect form is found in Voltaire's *Candide*, which also combines the other devices that we have considered – the picaresque, the innocent eye, the voyage into the world of ideas, and the fable. *Candide* is a comic vision of disaster. With immense verve it looks at the awful possibilities of human fate; it is a horrifying picture of the condition of embattled humanity, in which war, destruction, syphilis, oppression and torture are accepted as normal. Yet Voltaire's gaiety is a talisman against the worst that this irrational universe can do. He insists on the indifference and casual malevolence of this universe and protests that any attempt to justify the ways of God to man is nonsensical. The starting-point of the satire is an attack on Leibnitz who figures as Dr Pangloss, and stands for all theologians and metaphysicians who have tried to explain the existence of evil. Leibnitz had invented the term '*théodicée*' ('theodicy' from *theos*, 'god' and *diké*, 'justice') and used it as the title of a book published in 1710. Whether Voltaire misrepresents Leibnitz's arguments is beside the point: Pangloss's cant of 'sufficient reason' and 'the best of all possible worlds' is an apt parody of any optimistic system which sees a beneficient providence behind the sufferings of humanity. Another such system was used by Pope in his *Essay on Man* ('Whatever is, is right'), a poem that Voltaire once greatly admired but had come to reject, especially since the appalling Lisbon earthquake of 1755. Voltaire demonstrates by his fable that there is simply no way of reconciling the idea of an omnipotent and just God (or gods, or Providence) with the undeserved punishment inflicted on the innocent. What Nature does by way of earthquakes and shipwrecks is complemented by the equally disastrous works of man, whether feudal or colonial oppression, war or religious persecution. Voltaire ingeniously compresses his favourite range of satirical targets into the framework of Candide's adventures: the Inquisition and the Jesuits in Paraguay represent the follies of religious zeal, the execution of

Admiral Byng the cruelty of irresponsible politicians. He runs through nearly the whole range of the satirist's devices, introducing a utopia (Eldorado), the innocent eye in the corrupt capital (Candide's naive comments on the literary critics and journalists of Paris), the destruction of clichés by their reduction to emptiness. But one senses Voltaire's superiority to most other satirists: he knew how to fight public battles at his own risk, and he knew how to live. His vitality and his enjoyment of the pleasures that this world can give, even in the midst of its cruel blows, comes through in every line. If you face the universe with irreverence, gaiety and courage, he implies, you may survive to cultivate your garden. *Candide* also solves the problem faced by every satirist – that of combining a low and brutal content with elegance of form and style. The satirist's art, as practiced here, is in itself an effective armour against the malevolence of destiny.

It has been observed that Voltaire, like Swift, sometimes seems to be attacking the wrong century. The Age of Enlightenment, after all, was a reasonably pleasant interlude in human history; the horrors described in *Candide* lay both in the past and in the future, that is, in our own century. There is no nineteenth-century equivalent to Voltaire's fable, while the twentieth-century experience of war and revolution and genocide has been embodied not so much in satire as in the haunted parables of Kafka and Samuel Beckett. The closest equivalent to Voltaire's spirit is probably to be found in Brecht's play *Mother Courage;* the closest to the form of *Candide* is in some of the stories of the American writer Nathanael West (Nathan Wallenstein Weinstein, 1903–40). *A Cool Million* (1934) is almost *Candide* brought up to date; the hero is also a Mark Twain innocent and as appears from his name, Lemuel Pitkin, something of a Gulliver. The basis of the satire is the all-American success-story or 'poor boy makes good'; as Pitkin goes through one misfortune after another, dumbly suffering mutilation of his spirit and person, he gradually ascends the political scale; after his assassination he is acclaimed by a cynical party boss as a heroic symbol of America. *Miss Lonelyhearts* is an even more powerful expression of his pessimism. A newspaper man writes a column of advice to troubled readers; at first he is cynical about his work, then comes to take it in deadly earnest, identifying himself with his readers' sufferings and developing a 'Christ complex'. His pilgrim's progress and struggle with his Apollyon, the ultra-cynic Shrike, ends in an irrational martyrdom, proving the impossibility of spiritual life in this milieu. *The Day of the Locust*, his last novel, is closer to traditional satire; the target is Hollywood in its greatest days, when it was the ultimate expression of the people's dream. Hollywood and Californian satire is of course a huge topic in itself (the best-known British treatment of it is Evelyn Waugh's *The Loved One*). The difficulty about handling this subject is that in California reality easily outstrips fantasy, the monstrous becomes the normal; and indeed this is one of the themes of West's last novel. His hero is an observer-satirist, the painter Tod Hackett, who is planning a huge canvas called 'The Burning of Los Angeles'; in a terrible and ludicrous riot his vision comes true. West writes in an extremely economical and lucid style; his blend of irony and compassion, his outraged moral sense and fascination with absurd details, places him in the line of the great satirists, and his work demonstrates that the short *conte* or expanded fable is still the best medium for satiric fiction.

Novels which exceed *Candide* and its successors in length, realism or scope are not likely to be pure satire – indeed, I cannot think of any exception to this rule – but they may contain satirical episodes of the highest quality. Some of the finest political satire ever written is embedded in Dostoevsky's *The Devils* (also translated as *The Possessed*), which shows a profound insight into the nature of both revolutionaries and liberals, as well as a marvellously acute sense of comedy, as in the episode of the literary fête. Part one of Nikolai Gogol's *Dead Souls* contains a fine grotesque picture of the petty swindlers of provincial life. But these great books go well beyond satire; nearer to the central tradition is a lesser but still most impressive novel *The Golovlovs* (1872–6) by M. Saltykov-Shchedrin. This was one of the last of the nineteenth-century realist novels of Russia to be translated and become known in the West. It is a black picture of country life, describing a decaying family of small landowners. Saltykov, a Liberal who also wrote political fables (*Fairy Tales*, 1880–5) is attacking the ascendancy of the land-owning classes, but goes beyond politics in his nightmare vision of stupidity and corruption. This novel contains perhaps the greatest proportion of pure satire of any of the classics; but many of the other Russian, French and English classics contain some satirical writing of a high level. Since it is impossible to discuss them all, I propose to discuss four of the novelists who have done most to widen the range of narrative satire – and the greatest of them is Charles Dickens.

The special quality of Dickens's satire can be partly explained by his extraordinary relationship with the English public. On the one hand, he was the great entertainer, who could make a huge number of readers laugh and cry as no other author has ever been able to do. On the other hand, he was a man of affairs and of a public conscience, a journalist deeply involved in the political and social questions of his day; a radical, actively concerned with exposing the evils of industrialism and in promoting reforms of various kinds, such as the laws affecting debtors. As an entertainer he felt it his duty to give his readers what they wanted, and since his personal tastes did not differ greatly from the general popular tastes of Victorian England he knew exactly what to give. Dickens is therefore an unabashed purveyor of sentimentality, melodrama and farce, and none of his books is wholly free from these forms of entertainment which are related to the traditions of the popular theatre. He developed another theatrical tradition to the highest degree ever seen in the novel: that of the 'humour' character, possessed by monomania or obsession, often known as the Dickensian caricature. Dickens was the greatest of all natural humorists in this sense, producing with amazing facility the immortal Sarah Gamp and dozens of other creatures of his imagination, whose only purpose and only effect are to cause pure delight in the vagaries of human nature. Now these aspects of Dickens's demonic genius have little to do with satire, nor have his brilliant powers of describing the physical life of the city. The satire in his novels is intermittent: it wells up under the pressure of his indignation and then subsides into pure entertainment. There is no one novel which approaches the consistency of a satiric fable; the nearest approach is *Hard Times*, but even there he digresses into melodrama. On the other hand there are early and late novels, from *David Copperfield* to *Great Expectations*, in which the satiric element is very slight. But Dickens is the master of the satiric episode, and the loose structure of his novels made it possible for him to insert such episodes at random without damaging the plot.

He was not greatly interested in the comedy of manners or in moral satire. His villains are usually total villains, criminals and violators of the human decencies, beyond the reach of ridicule. Their callousness or brutality is exposed and punished, but this is denunciation rather than satire. One of the few personal vices that Dickens treats satirically is hypocrisy, as in the splendid Tartuffe-like figures of Uriah Heep and Mr Pecksniff.

But usually the topics which set Dickens's imagination working satirically are political, in a broad sense, rather than moral: the characters against which he uses his vast powers of ridicule are representative of economic and social evils, which can be swept out of existence by radical reform. The kinds of human folly and vice that he lampoons are those left free to flourish or those positively cultivated by an iniquitous and stupid political system. Reduced to its simplest terms, this means the rule of the landed aristocracy, which had worked well enough in the eighteenth century but which was incapable of coping with the problems of industrial England. The share-out of power between a few great families, Whig or Tory, has its classic description in *Bleak House:*

England has been in a dreadful state for some weeks. Lord Coodle wouldn't go out, and Sir Thomas Doodle wouldn't come in, and there being nobody in Great Britain (to speak of) except Coodle and Doodle, there has been no government.

Dickens returns to the problems of political power and administration in *Little Dorrit;* the Circumlocution Office is the perfect satirical case against an inefficient bureaucracy: 'Whatever was required to be done, the Circumlocution Office was beforehand with all the public departments in the art of perceiving – HOW NOT TO DO IT.' It is run as a family monopoly by the Barnacles, effete at everything except clinging to power, procrastination and dealing with importunate enquirers who want action: as Barnacle Junior says 'Look here. Upon my soul you mustn't come into the place saying you want to know, you know.' Dickens accurately diagnosed the paralysing effect of the English class system, even when he admired the eccentricities of the gentry whom he had observed very closely: the Dedlocks' relations in *Bleak House* and Cousin Feenix in *Dombey and Son* are the best examples of his social mockery. When he turns from the old landed ruling class to the newly rich, his tone becomes more bitter, his satirical techniques more deadly. In describing the milieu of high finance in *Little Dorrit* he uses the device of reduction with extreme force: Mrs Merdle becomes a bird in a gilded cage, the great financier himself gradually turns into an automaton, and the eminent guests at his house, corrupted by money, reduce themselves to the depersonalised abstractions of Bar, Bishop, Bench. Even more awful examples of the *nouveaux riches* are the Veneerings and Podsnap in *Our Mutual Friend.*

The American section of *Martin Chuzzlewit*, his longest and most offensive satirical episode, is also political in outlook. The Americans are not primarily attacked for their boastfulness or crudity of manners; their barbarity comes from the corruption of their system, which encourages bribery, ignorance and violence. After politics, Dickens's chief targets were the law, religion and education. The workings of the law being commonly one of the most unpleasant or irritating parts of human experience, it is curious that so few other satirists have been able to cope with this subject. This is perhaps because it is so technical and dry, that only an expert such as Dickens was can grasp its essential idiocies and turn them into comedy. The case of Bardell versus Pickwick is only surpassed by that of Jarndyce and Jarndyce in *Bleak House* which 'still drags its weary length before the Court, perennially hopeless' until the costs eat up the whole estate. The London fog becomes a metaphor for the fog of law: by this and by his other central symbols, like the prison in *Little Dorrit* and the dust heaps in *Our Mutual Friend*, Dickens extended the range and imaginative power of prose satire beyond 'humours' and caricature. His descriptions of the city scene are rich in poetic images which embody the central satiric issue – usually an irrational restriction of human freedom in one way or another. The law and bureaucracy are the most obvious and powerful means of repressing man's creative energies: but education, with which Dickens deals masterfully in *Nicholas Nickleby* and *Hard Times*, is just as an effective and cruel way of crippling the spirit. In each of his topics Dickens goes to the heart of Victorian England, and in nothing more closely than in his treatment of religion. Dickens, himself a liberal Christian, detested the Evangelical puritanism that paralysed the imagination and taste of the working and middle-classes; the living symbol of this paralysis is the grimly Calvinistic Mrs Clennam in *Little Dorrit*. Here Dickens had to be careful not to antagonise his public; but, using some discretion, was able to produce a gallery of Tartuffian villains, beginning with the greedy humbug Stiggins of *Pickwick Papers*. The most effective attack is on the hypocritical Chadband in *Bleak House*, where he produces a beautiful parody of the non-conformist sermon without once using the name of God: 'What is peace? Is it war? No. Is it strife? No . . .' 'It is', says Chadband, 'the ray of rays, the sun of suns, the moon of moons, the star of stars. It is the light of Terewth.' Dickens's chief weapons are his powers of verbal parody and his eye for the unexpected and telling detail: the fork pinning together the curtains in the neglected household of the pious and philanthropic Mrs Jellyby, who is busy with 'educating the natives of Borrioboola-Gha, on the left bank of the Niger', while her own children fall unheeded into the basement area. Sometimes careless about his novelist's art, often ambiguous in his attitude to social problems, Dickens threw out of the volcano of his demonic temperament more creative sparks than any other satirist in literature.

Some of the finest satire of the twentieth century is to be found in James Joyce's *Ulysses* (1922). *Ulysses*, of course, contains many other things besides satire: it is a naturalistic novel which describes in loving detail the sights and sounds of Dublin in 1904, where Leopold Bloom, Stephen Dedalus and other characters pass a day; it is a psychological study of great complexity, in which the thoughts and feelings of the characters are presented as a 'stream of consciousness' and it is an elaborate mythical structure, in which the lives of Bloom and Stephen are paralleled with situations in the *Odyssey*, *Hamlet* and Christian theology. Joyce's attitude to his subject is far more sympathetic and his comprehension of the human condition far wider than those of the traditional satirists; but *Ulysses* does contain many of the basic concepts and techniques of satire pushed to the ultimate limits of ingenuity and poetic intensity.

The lampoon, for example, is a conspicuous ingredient of *Ulysses* and even of the earlier short stories called *Dubliners*. Joyce put his enemies and his false friends into his books, and held them up to derision for ever. Dr Oliver St John Gogarty as 'Buck Mulligan' is the most famous, but there are dozens of other real people under thin disguises or none at all. Bartell D'Arcy, the tenor, who appears under his own name in *The Dead*, though in no very unfavourable light, went straight to his solicitors after reading this story. If Joyce had stayed in Dublin after the publication of *Ulysses*, he would probably have had to face many lawsuits. One of the victims of the gossip so realistically recounted through the book did not even know that he had appeared in *Ulysses*, until thirty years later he heard a broadcast of the 'Hades' episode and promptly sued the BBC.

Ulysses is also a version of the most famous type of literary travesty, the 'mock-heroic'. The mock-heroic is a travesty of the classical epic, in which both epic style (long similes, elevated diction, etc.) and epic content (heroic combats, supernatural intervention, funeral games etc.) are parodied. The finest example in English is Pope's *Dunciad*, which replaces the incidents of Virgil's *Aeneid*, especially books v and vi, with gross and absurd fantasies about the Grub Street writers and Pope's literary enemies. Now it is often assumed that the purpose of mock-heroic is to mock the present, by contrasting the noble and heroic way of life with modern debasement and triviality. That was certainly part of Pope's purpose in the *Dunciad*, which like T.S.Eliot's *Waste Land* presents contemporary London as an image of hell: the *Dunciad* is a comic Inferno, to be set against the Paradiso of Virgil and Homer. But it would be wrong to suppose that such is the only purpose of mock-heroic. It may be just as much to mock the heroic, to offer relief from the extreme adulation of the classical epic, which has been the basis of humanist education since the Renaissance. When writers have been repeatedly told that classical epic is the un-repeatable perfection of literature, and that the heroic way of life is the supremely good one, they must have found an immense sense of release in burlesquing of the whole tradition, in a saturnalian revolt against the tyranny of Homer and Virgil.

This same double aspect of mock-heroic can be seen in Joyce's *Ulysses*. With extraordinary ingenuity he bases a day in the life of Leopold Bloom, the first advertising man in literature and the least heroic hero of all time, on the adventures of Odysseus: dozens of parallels are drawn, as is well known, from Molly the unfaithful Penelope to the lighted tip of Bloom's cigar, corresponding to the lighted stake used to put out the Cyclops' eye. Now, part of Joyce's intent is to show how vulgar and trivial modern city life really is. A chapter called 'Aeolus' is set in a newspaper office, kingdom of flatulence and rumour, and is interspersed with news headlines to ridicule the vulgarities of journalism. The chapter called 'Nausicaa' gives the monologue of Gerty MacDowell, a girl who thinks in the most sickly clichés of romantic novelettes, with overtones of popular pornography; this chapter is also a satire on the sentimentality of popular religion. 'The summer evening had begun to fold the world in its mysterious embrace', it begins, and

According to his biographer Richard Ellmann,
Joyce himself suggested the iconography for
this cartoon by César Abin (1932): the black bowler
with cobwebs (chronic dejection), the patches
(poverty) and so on. The globe shows only one
country, Ireland, with Dublin shaded black.

goes on to catalogue with the loving horror of a Flaubert every possible error of taste. But it would be wrong to conclude that Joyce idealised the glorious Homeric past and set it up against modern baseness or meanness. It appears from Joyce's comments on Homer (made to Frank Budgen) that he did not consider Odysseus a more ideally noble figure than Bloom: on the contrary, he thought that Odysseus showed the same mixture of rashness and cowardice, ingenuity and folly as his counterpart; and that in any period of history human nature and morals are very much the same. Joyce did not take the side of the Ancients against the Moderns in a 'Battle of the Books'; and he did not venerate Homeric style any more than Homeric matter. With vast and perhaps justified confidence in his powers as a stylist he felt sure that he could meet Homer as an equal.

If Joyce belongs in part to the traditional line of mock-heroic, he has also affinities with the burlesque tradition of Rabelais and the young Swift. As in *Gargantua* and *A Tale of a Tub*, the satire points in every direction; at literature itself, as for example in the *tour de force* known as *The Oxen of the Sun*, where he parodies with accurate ear the prose style of several dozen authors – this has the effect of making any set of historical mannerisms look absurd. Joyce's love of fooling and virtuosity with words, further developed in *Finnegans Wake*, bring him close to Rabelais. But he combines lampoon, mock-heroic and burlesque into a gigantic saturnalia which resembles and perhaps surpasses that of Aristophanes's comedies. At the same time Joyce is writing moral satire, admittedly from a rather special point of view, which also seems to be broadly Aristophanic. That is, *Ulysses* contains an indirect but cumulatively powerful attack on violence, whether in physical prowess, war or nationalistic politics, and by implication it is a panegyric of Leopold Bloom, the man of peace. Joyce hates the violence embodied in Blazes Boylan, Molly's coarse lover, and in the nationalist Michael Cusack, the Citizen-Cyclops, and he does everything in his power to make it look ridiculous, using the violence of the word against the violence of the body; and invoking peaceful,

natural, anarchic fertility, in the spirit of the *Lysistrata*, against the great restrictive institutions of church and State.

Ulysses is one of the most complex books ever written, and obviously contains many things besides satire. The chief concentrations of satire are in three chapters, called 'Cyclops', 'Circe' and 'Ithaca' respectively, which are among the best-written and most moving parts of the book. The first concerns the escape of Odysseus from the cave of the man-eating Polyphemus – literally, the confrontation of Bloom with Michael Cusack in Barney Kiernan's public-house which leads to political argument and Bloom's near escape from physical assault. Here Joyce uses a satirical technique which he called 'gigantism', that is, excessive inflation: everything is blown up to gigantic proportions, in the manner of Ben Jonson's comedies. The anonymous character who tells the story rambles on in a marvellous imitation of Irish pub-conversation, but when he reaches a significant point, concerning politics, executions, religion and so on, there is a digression with a sudden change of style. For example the first description of Cusack is a parody of Irish heroic legend and of journalistic exaggeration:

The figure seated on a large boulder at the foot of a round tower was that of a broadshouldered deepchested stronglimbed frankeyed redhaired freely-freckled shaggybearded widemouthed largenosed longheaded deepvoiced barekneed brawnyhanded hairylegged ruddyfaced sinewyarmed hero.

There is a discussion about the death and supposed ghost of Paddy Dignam:

Dead! says Alf. He's no more dead than you are.
Maybe so, says Joe. They took the liberty of burying him this morning anyhow.

This leads to a mock account of a spiritualist seance, in occultist language. The talk turns to capital punishment and hanging, with a long and fantastic description of a public execution, as it might appear in a newspaper; and then to games, especially boxing, emphasising the theme of muscle. Politics is the other main theme:

and the Citizen pours out violent imprecations on England and English civilisation.

> Their syphilisation, you mean, says the Citizen. To hell with them! The curse of a goodfornothing God light sideways on the bloody thicklugged sons of whores' gets! No music and no art and no literature worthy of the name. Any civilization they have they stole from us. Tonguetied sons of bastards' ghosts.

In the political discussion, Bloom does the rashest possible thing: he speaks up for liberalism, saying there is much to be said on both sides, thus irritating the Citizen still more.

> But it's no use, says he. Force, hatred, history and all that. That's not life for men and women, insult and hatred. And everybody knows that it's the very opposite of that that is really life.
> What? says Alf.
> Love, says Bloom. I mean the opposite of hatred. I must go now …

Bloom is absurd and bathetic, as the digression on love that follows makes clear. But then liberalism, pacifism, broadmindedness, *are* absurd, especially in tense historical situations. Joyce is implying that, but also stating clearly that liberalism and pacifism are the only possible political attitudes compatible with a humane view of life. They may be ridiculous, but they are the best we have got. Through the symbolic overtones of this chapter, which lead us into Judaeo-Christian as well as Homeric parallels, Bloom appears as an embodiment of Joyce's most deeply treasured values. He comes through his ordeal triumphantly thanks to his mildness and tolerance, and at the same time shows great courage in defending the Jews against the Citizen's rabid anti-semitism. In his absurd apotheosis at the end of the chapter he represents the triumph of mind over matter, of human kindness over brutality; as he is driven off he becomes the prophet Elijah in his chariot:

> And they beheld Him even Him, ben Bloom Elijah, amid clouds of angels ascend to the glory of the brightness at an angle of fortyfive degrees over Donohoe's in Little Green Street like a shot off a shovel.

238

After Joyce, the finest satirical writing in any novel of the inter-war years has been produced by Céline (Louis-Ferdinand Destouches). Céline's biography does not concern us, except in so far as his anti-semitism and collaboration with the Nazis caused his work to be neglected for many years; it is best to assume that he was deranged at the time, and certainly his two great novels are not affected by his later political opinions, but are inspired by a vast compassion for human suffering. *Voyage au bout de la nuit* (1932, *Journey to the End of the Night*) and *Mort à Crédit* (1936, *Death on the Instalment Plan*) are both autobiographical: the second describes his poverty-stricken boyhood, the first his experiences as a cavalryman in the 1914–18 War, his travels and his life as a slum doctor in Paris. *Mort à Crédit* is a powerful piece of grotesque, written in an energetic and colloquial style; the satire is concentrated on the figure of Courtial des Pereires, inventor, charlatan and balloonist. His office, where the hero works, is jammed full of pseudo-scientific rubbish, symbolical of the accumulated nonsense which has infected scientific and technical progress. To that extent it follows on from *Bouvard et Pécuchet*, but Céline manages more brilliantly than Flaubert the classic satiric device of crowding his canvas with fascinating and revolting junk, in a manner worthy of Ben Jonson. Courtial is a modern alchemist, duping and duped, disintegrating under the pressure of his monstrous schemes; he is also in his absurdity a truly Dickensian comic character. The background is a development of Dickens's more sombre town-scapes, drawn without sentimentality but in a tough-minded sympathy with poverty. This is expressed more purely in *Voyage au bout de la nuit*, a much finer novel. Céline is enraged with the stupidity and selfishness of the poor, but he suffers with them. He has been accused of nihilism and total pessimism, but much of this book seems to be an authentic account of the senseless waste caused by modern civilisation, and above all by modern war. No account of war has ever equalled the dreamlike sequences of the 1914 campaign, and no evocation of desolate city streets has surpassed Céline's in poetic intensity. The central figures are

Robinson – passive, drifting and half-criminal – and his mother-in-law to be, Mme Henrouille, who shows by contrast a demonic energy of speech. The best satire is in the brutally funny picture of life in French Colonial Africa (the section on America is disappointing), and in the sketches of Paris slum-dwellers. The style, based on an inspired use of colloquial idiom, is exactly suited to the ludicrous treatment of commonplace horrors. Céline's satire, like Swift's in *A Modest Proposal*, is informed with a noble disgust at the lies with which civilisation covers up its sores.

Jean-Paul Sartre has not only praised Céline but imitated him: some of the best satirical passages in *La Nausée*, like those describing the pictures of the bourgeois in a provincial gallery, owe a debt to the master. But Sartre is only rarely a satirist, and I do not know of anything else in modern French fiction to equal Céline.

The outstanding novelist of contemporary Europe who falls within the sphere of this study is the German Günter Grass (born 1929 near Danzig). *The Tin Drum* (1959) is told as the fantastic memoirs of the dwarf Oskar Matzerath, written from a lunatic asylum. As an idiotic child he played endlessly on his tin drum, and found this to have magical powers over people; he could even break up political meetings by altering the rhythm. Oskar's voice is also magical, since by singing he could smash glass, even windows, at a long distance. The book has a framework of witchcraft: but after all the power of the Nazi drum and of Hitler's voice were not less magical. The dwarf is not apparently interested in politics, since he is withdrawn into a lunatic sexual life; but gradually we begin to see the nightmare of German history through his eyes – the growth of the Nazi party, the invasion of Poland, the atrocities, the raping Russians who enter Danzig in 1945, and so on to the post-war 'economic miracle'; Oskar becomes a famous jazz drummer before he goes irrevocably insane.

Dog Years has a similar framework of travesty and fantasy. It is ostensibly the biography of Hitler's dog, a Danzig sheepdog presented to the Führer, which stayed with him to the last days in the Berlin bunker. Around this absurd story are grouped the more or less realistic lives of various Danzigers associated with the dog. One of them, a half-Jewish boy, has the gift of creating satirical scarecrows and snow-men which are almost as magical as Oskar's drum. Beaten up by storm-troopers he changes his identity, survives the Nazis and reappears as a rich man; now he has a complete underground factory for making his scarecrows, which represent the horrors of German history. Parallel to this there is the quasi-picaresque story of another dispossessed Danzig boy's wanderings in post-war Western Germany. This is the framework for witty though rather too diverse satire on the contemporary scene, but despite its brilliant parodies and burlesque the book goes on for too long. But like *The Tin Drum* this is a true and revealing picture of history: both books explain what it has meant to be German in this century. Grass is saying in effect that reality is more appalling and fantastic than any satirical invention can ever be. He gives us the authentic shock of great satire, which can make us see, as if for the first time, what the world is really like.

Postscript

Satire does not end with the novel or with the other forms of literature discussed in this book. It is not even confined to 'polite letters', that is, to the more conventional and dignified forms of literature. Excellent satire has always been found in journalism throughout the history of the periodical press; and journalism includes not only the newspaper and magazine but the popular song: as we have seen, the broadside ballad was once a most effective vehicle. This is to be expected: the political satirist in particular must try to reach a wide public if he is to achieve his ends, and any popular medium will serve his purpose. It would have been interesting, if there had been space, to follow the development of satire in modern journalism, from the reviews of pre-Hitler Germany, through the famous French weekly *Le Canard Enchaîné* to London's *Private Eye*, which is still with us, if it has not finally succumbed to multiple libel actions before this book is published. There has often been a close link between the satiric little magazines, the entertainers of cabaret and revue, and the cartoonists, as is the case with *Private Eye;* and it is likely that satire will continue to flourish in such mixed and complementary forms. The most fruitful extension of such kinds of informal satire has come about by means of the gramophone record and sound-tape, which can catch the spontaneous impromptu performance of the entertainer, and best of all by means of television. This medium, which is not yet satisfactory for formal drama, is highly suited to the intimacy and informality of the *chansonnier* style, to improvised miming and to the loose structure of the revue. Documentary illustrations and the art of the cartoonist, still or animated, can be interwoven with satirical songs, sketches and monologues. This mixture was first used successfully in Britain in the satirical programme *That Was The Week That Was*, which with David Frost as *compère* had great success in 1962–3 and has had several less entertaining sequels. This kind of programme presupposes a public that is fairly sophisticated about politics, as the British public of the sixties seems to have become, after a decade of education by television; and in turn it perhaps heightens the political awareness of the public.

Whether television can foster great satirical art is doubtful – that the cinema can is certain. The cinema has been used successfully to translate some of the classics of literary satire into a universal visual language, and it has produced satirical classics of its own. The medium offers many advantages for satire: in particular, the possibility of achieving the proper balance between fantasy and realism, which seems to be essential for the communication of a satiric message. The main disadvantage of the cinema is that it is vulnerable to censorship and, even more than television, to commercial pressure: a moving picture is a very expensive undertaking, and the sponsors may want to avoid taking risks with outspoken criticism. Satirical pictures about life in Russia during the Stalin era were forbidden and have been slow to emerge in recent years. An adaptation of Laclos' great satiric novel *Les Liaisons Dangereuses* was for a while refused an export licence by the French government on the grounds that it presented an unflattering and allegedly distorted image of modern French life. The brilliantly funny film about unofficial strikes *I'm all right, Jack* (Boulting Brothers 1959, with Peter Sellers) is said to have been made under protest from certain trade unions. Hence good satirical films have usually been made in fairly free political conditions or by independent producers with modest financial backing.

The classic of adaptation is Pabst's *Dreigroschenoper* (The Threepenny Opera, 1931), a free reworking of the musical play by Brecht and Kurt Weill. Some of the verbal wit and intellectual complexity of the original are lost, but the combination of elegant stylisation and low-life realism is beautifully realised. The anarchistic spirit of Brecht (and of John Gay and Villon, who inspired Brecht) comes across with great force, as does Pabst's addition of the final all-conquering march of the beggars.

The first and greatest name in original film satire is Charlie Chaplin. He has created the most moving and enduring image of the century – the little man lost in the alien world or the city jungle, surviving only by his ingenuity and stoic cheerfulness. *Modern Times* (1936) is his first full-length satire, on the theme of machine technology and mass production and their effect on the individual. The memorable opening uses a basic device of satire: sheep go down a gangway, cut to workers entering a factory. The machines take control: Charlie is fed by one and, driven mad by the assembly line, he turns into a machine. These despairingly funny scenes make a noble protest against dehumanisation. *The Great Dictator* (1940, but begun before the war in 1939) is courageous political satire, a marvellous burlesque of Hitler and a protest against the brutalities of his régime at a time when many Europeans and Americans were willing to tolerate Nazism. It could not have been made any later, since Hitler in the 1940s was no longer a subject for satire; but at the right moment Chaplin spoke for the world's conscience and made the world laugh. Despite the failure of his later films, Chaplin earned a place of honour in the history of political satire. There are not many other classics in this field. In Germany the tradition of Pabst was taken up again in *Wir Wunderkinder (Aren't We Wonderful:* Kurt Hoffmann, Western Germany 1958), describing the parallel lives of two schoolboy friends, one a Nazi, from the First World War to the 'economic miracle'; there are interludes in the action with songs in the style of the pre-war Berlin satirical revues, and this stylisation allows the subject of chicanery and graft to be presented with witty detachment.

There are many examples of 'sub-satire' in the cinema, including Hollywood comedies that offer ironic exposures of social abuses, the charming fantasies of René Clair (especially *À Nous la Liberté* 1931) and of Jacques Tati, and the surrealistic violence of Luis Bunuel. Finally one should mention the achievements and potential of the animated cartoon: Orwell's *Animal Farm* has been the basis for a cartoon film, and the imaginative possibilities of the form have been shown by Dick Williams in *The Little Island,* 1955.

Here we return to traditional visual satire, that is, to caricature and cartoon. I have not attempted to trace the origin and history of this art: the illustrations must tell their own story. Cartoon means a fantastic composition, often some kind of allegory and usually on a political topic; caricature is the distorted portraiture of individuals.

René Clair's *A Nous La Liberté* (1931)
a gay anti-Utopian satire on industrialism,
was a triumph of the early French cinema.

Goya, *El Buitre Carnivore* (The Carnivorous Vulture)
from *Disasters of War*, about 1813. The Cock of France
is swept away in disgrace by the Spanish people.
Goya's combination of fantasy and grim realism
begins with satire but often passes its limits.

In combination since the eighteenth century, they have probably
been the most popular and influential form of satire. This is
the most literary kind of visual art, intimately connected with
journalism. Most literate people in the world turn every day, or at
least week, to their favourite cartoonist for his comment on current
affairs. But even before the mass circulation of newspapers began,
cartoons could reach a very large section of the public through the
medium of woodcuts, engravings and lithographs. Like literary
satire, the art of the cartoonist is essentially ephemeral but occasionally, as with Hogarth, Gillray, Goya or Daumier, may ascend to
greatness. Again, as in literature, the dividing line between propaganda and imaginative creation is difficult to define, but in both
there must be a dimension of fantasy and travesty, and a spirit of
free criticism. The art of caricature and cartoon is obviously still

thriving, and in free societies its future seems as assured as any human institution can be.

It is not clear, however, that we can have the same confidence in the future of literary satire. In this survey I have not taken the history of literature up to the present day (apart from mentioning a few examples in poetry, drama and the novel); if I had done so, I should have been hard put to it to find many great satirists still alive and producing. But this is also true of other kinds of literature: there is currently also a shortage of first-class poets and novelists. We have passed through a great age, which reached its peak about 1910 to 1940, the age of Yeats, Rilke, Joyce, Kafka, Mann and Proust; and the contemporary scene in Europe is one of imaginative exhaustion and the exploitation of minor talents. Since this kind of trough has appeared many times before in history, it would be absurd to speak of the present or future death of literature. The printed word, in the service of art and the human spirit, is potent and will revive. But will satire also revive? As journalistic comment on the absurdities of politics and manners it has never been in danger of dying out except when political freedom has been in danger, and in the open society it should have as permanent a future as caricature and cartoon. But that satire will again cross the frontier into the enchanted realm of imaginative literature, as it has done many times in the past, is difficult to predict. It may be that the modern world makes too great demands on the writers; demands, that is, for understanding the ever more rapidly increasing changes caused by science and technology, and for flexibility in dealing with these changes. The satirist, after all, traditionally takes up a rigid stance in the face of change; he does not want to understand everything. He is committed to militant action, while the modern world increasingly asks for peace, negotiation and the often tedious examination of problems. Just as hot war has become too expensive a luxury for mankind, so the war of words may become too great an expenditure of effort for the writer. Again, the world is becoming de-ritualised. Throughout history men have defended themselves against a hostile universe, not just by their practical efficiency, but by the ritual forms they invent and preserve, in religion, politics and social life, forms of ceremony, dress and rhetoric. The satirists, as I have tried to show, have always attacked these rituals whenever they have found them absurd; and they have often invented mock rituals, parodies and travesties of ceremony, like mock-heroic poetry, to enshrine folly and vice. But ritual behaviour is now felt to be less and less appropriate to the conditions of our life; we are being forced into informality, whether of dress, manners or speech: in political debate and literature traditional rhetoric is going out of favour. So the satirist is becoming deprived of many of his favourite targets, and his readers may fail to enjoy or understand his elaborate rituals of parody.

The satirist, however, has always accepted the risk of failure: by committing himself to the exposure of public abuses, he allows himself to be caught up in the ephemeral and transitory events of his day. When these events have receded into the night of history – as many of the topics mentioned in these pages have done – his work may be overtaken by oblivion, or at best live on only for the antiquarian. The greatest satire not only fixes a moment of history in a frozen attitude of absurdity, and makes the event a permanent and ludicrous warning to the future, but it tells the truth about the depths of human nature, which do not change. Satire warns us that man is a dangerous animal, with an infinite capacity for folly; and when it has said that well, it has said enough. It is for the poets to speak of man's glory.

Notes

[1]*The World through Literature*, ed. Charlton Laird, 1959, p. 34.

[2]Adapted from Henry Rink, *Tales and Traditions of the Eskimo*, p. 67; cit. Paul Radin, *Primitive Man as a Philosopher*.

[3]H.Junod, *Les Chants et les contes des Ba-Ronga*, transl. and cit. Paul Radin, *Primitive Man as a Philosopher*.

[4]For this and other ideas in this chapter I am indebted to Dr J.R.Goody.

[5]Archilochus 97A; freely adapted from the translation in the Loeb Library edition.

[6]Paul Radin, *The Trickster: a study in American Indian mythology*, with commentaries by Karl Kerenyi and C.G.Jung 1956. Joan Westcott, 'The Sculpture and Myths of Eshu-Elegba, the Yoruba Trickster', *Africa* 22 (1962), pp. 336–54.

[7]F.M.Cornford, *The Rise of Attic Comedy*.

[8]Northrop Frye, *The Anatomy of Criticism*, 1934, p. 224.

[9]Aristophanes tr. Rogers *The Complete Plays of Aristophanes*, tr. Moses Hadas, Bantam Books 1962.

[10]Juvenal and Persius, ed. and tr. G.G.Ramsay, Loeb Classical Library, 1918, Introduction, p. xxiv.

[11]Julius Capitolinus, cit. Allardyce Nicoll, *Masks Mimes and Miracles* (1931), p. 124.

[12]Texts and discussion of medieval Latin satire may be found in the following: *Carmina Burana*, ed. Hilka and Schumann, Heidelberg, 1930.

Les Poésies des Goliards, ed. and tr. Olga Dobiache-Rojdestvensky, Paris, 1931.

F.J.E.Raby, *A History of Secular Latin Poetry in the Middle Ages*, vol. II, Oxford, 1934.

W.T.H.Jackson, *The Literature of the Middle Ages*, New York, 1960.

[13]*Epistolae Obscurorum Virorum*, the Latin text with an English rendering, notes and an historical introduction by Francis Griffin Stokes, 1909, 1925.

[14]'Complainte de Messire Pierre Lizet, sur le trepas de son feu nez', in *Les satires du XVIe siècle*, ed. F.Fleuret and L.Perceau, 1922.

[15]*Poems* on *Affairs of State*; *Augustan Satirical Verse, 1660–1714*, vol. I, (1660–78) ed. George de F.Lord, New Haven, 1963. Introduction p. xxvi. This is the first of six large volumes.

[16]*The Common Muse: an anthology of popular British ballad poetry xvth– xxth century*, ed. V. de Sola Pinto and A.E.Rodway, 1957, pp. 77–8. The first two sections of this anthology contain many political satires.

[17]*The Ancient Near East*, ed. James A.Pritchard, 1958, pp. 236, 251.

[18]*Greek Lyrics*, translated by Richmond Lattimore, Chicago, 1949.

[19]Jerome, *Adv. Jovinianum*, 47; Migne, *Patr. Lat.* vol. 23, col. 276; tr. G.G.Coulton, *Life in the Middle Ages*, vol. 4, pp. 22–5, Cambridge, 1930.

[20]See R.C.Elliott, *The Power of Satire*, p. 102, and G.L.Hendrickson, 'Satura nostra est', *Classical Philology* xxii, 1927.

[21]F.Fleuret and L.Perceau, ed. *Les satires françaises du XVI^c siècle*, 1922; *Les satires françaises du XVIIIe siècle*, 1923.

[22]Voltaire, *Discours de reception à l'Académie française*, 1746.

[23]J.P.Stern, *Lichtenberg: A Doctrine of Scattered Occasions*, 1959.

[24]See John Willett, *The Theatre of Bertolt Brecht*, London, 1959.

Acknowledgments

Acknowledgment – further to any made in the captions – is due to the following for illustrations (the number refers to the page on which the illustration appears): frontispiece M. Philippe Mousseau; 22 (*right*), 57 Musée du Louvre; 29 Royal Library Windsor (reproduced by gracious permission of Her Majesty the Queen); 43 Mr Walter Raeburn; 58, 59, 66, 69, 75, 84, 93, 96, 97, 103, 104, 114, 120, 136, 148, 149, 154, 164, 173, 174, 181, 190, 195, 205, 206, 208, 219, 224, 235, 246 British Museum; 88–9 Victoria and Albert Museum; 113 Biblioteca Nacional, Madrid; 116 Gabinetto Nazionale delle Stampe, Rome; 117 (*top*) Vatican Library; 117 (*bottom*) Staatliche Graphische Sammlung, Munich; 125, 244 Connoisseur Films Ltd; 145 Tate Gallery, London; 169 Kunstmuseum, Basel; 198 Nordisk Pressfoto, København; 201 Farm and Country; 209 The Estate of Georg Grosz, Princeton, N.J.; 211 Percy Paukschta, Berliner Ensemble; 215 Penguin Books Ltd; 239 Hermann Luchterhand Verlag; 245 Mr Charles Chaplin.

For permission to reprint text extracts the following acknowledgment is made: to the Bodley Head (for *Ulysses* by James Joyce), to Penguin Books Ltd (for *The Penguin Book of Japanese Verse*, translated by Geoffrey Bownas and Anthony Thwaite), to the University of Chicago Press (for *Greek Lyrics*, translated by Richmond Lattimore), to Methuen Ltd (for *The Threepenny Opera*, in *The Plays of Bertold Brecht*, translated by Desmond Vesey and Eric Bentley), to Cambridge University Press (for *Life in the Middle Ages* by G. G. Coulton).

Parts of the paragraphs on Jonathan Swift appeared in the *Irish Times* and in a broadcast talk on Radio Telefís Eireann (Thomas Davis Lectures, 1967), to both of whom acknowledgment is made.

Index

Aborigines, Australian 17
Addison, J. 105, 124, 167
Aesop 24, 51, 172, 175
Akkadian tales 151
Alemán, M. 220
Alphonsus, Petrus 92
American Indians 16, 20,
 172
Arabs 18, 19, 92, 175, 178;
 Arabian nights 178
Archilochus 18, 19, 134,
 160
Archipoeta 44–5
Ariosto, L. 138, 179;
 Satires 138; *Orlando
 Furioso* 138
Aristophanes 8, 23, 24, 28,
 34, 36, 37, 38, 56, 82,
 188, 189, 190, 234;
 The Acharnians 34–5;
 The Birds 36–7; *The
 Clouds* 35, 36; *The
 Frogs* 23, 28, 36, 37, 122;
 The Knights 35;
 Lysistrata 24, 37, 80, 82,
 236; *The Peace* 36;
 The Wasps 36; *Women
 in Parliament* 83
Aristotle 13
Auden, W. H. 119
Aurelius, Marcus 151,
 152
Austen, J. 131, 188

Bacon, F. 150, 155, 156;
 New Atlantis 184
Balzac, H. de 216
Basselin, O. 204
Baudelaire, C. 171
Beaumarchais, P.-A. C. de
 198
Beauvoir, S. de 80
Beckett, S. 202, 226

Beerbohm, M. 122
Belloc, H. 162
Bergerac, C. de 180–2, 184
Bèze, T. de 53
Bible 85–6, 87, 98, 130, 151
Bierbaum 210
Blake, W. 155
Boccaccio, G. 95
Boileau, N. 105, 135, 139,
 140, 143, 144, 189, 204;
 Sixth Satire ('Les
 Embarras de Paris') 135,
 140
Born, Bertran de 48
Boswell, J. 153; *Life of
 Johnson* 168
Brecht, B. 37, 212, 242;
 *Aufsteig und Fall der
 Stadt Mahagonny* 212;
 Die Dreigroschenoper
 101, 212; *Mutter Courage
 und ihre Kinder* 226
Bruce, L. 213
Bunuel, L. 243
Bunyan, J. 171
Burns, R. 162
Burton, R. 105
Busch, W. 210
Butler, S. (1612–80) 59,
 142, 167; *Hudibras* 59,
 142
Butler, S. (1835–1902) 150,
 182, 185–6; *Erewhon*
 182, 185–6; *Way of
 All Flesh* 186
Byron, Lord 73–4, 76, 159

Camoens 178
Capitolinus, Julius 39
Cardenal, P. 48, 51
Carmina Burana 44
Carroll, L. 124; *Alice in
 Wonderland* 31, 124

Catullus 161
Céline, L.-F. 238–9
Cervantes, M. de 92, 216,
 218, 220; *Don Quixote*
 115, 216, 218; 'noveles
 exemplares' 220
Chamfort, S. 152
Chaplin, C. 242
Chaucer, G. 37, 41, 51, 79,
 80, 92, 98–9; *Canterbury
 Tales* 90, 95, 98–9,
 120–1; *Legend of
 Good Women* 80; 'Sir
 Thopas' 122
Cheever, J. 107
Churchill, C. 60, 73
Clair, R. 243
Commedia dell' Arte 202
Congreve, W. 80, 188
Coward, N. 207
cummings, e. e. 163

Dante 48, 100, 120, 170
D'Aubigny, A. 54–5
Daumier, H. 76, 246
Defoe, D. 71, 178, 182
Dekker, T. 191
Democritus of Abdera
 156, 160
Denham, J. 143
Deschamps, E. 95
Dickens, C. 13, 121, 216,
 228–32; *Bleak House*
 229, 230, 231; *David
 Copperfield* 229;
 Dombey and Son 230;
 Great Expectations 229;
 Hard Times 229, 231;
 Little Dorrit 230, 231;
 Martin Chuzzlewit 230;
 Nicholas Nickleby 216,
 231; *Oliver Twist* 216;
 Our Mutual Friend 230,

231; *Pickwick Papers*
115,194,218,230,231
Diderot,D. 124
Diodorus 183
Diogenes 156
Donne,J. 134,141,142;
Satyres 141,142
Dostoevsky,F. 155,157;
The Devils 227
Dryden,J. 24,58,60,61–3,
73,85,135,142–3,144;
Absalom and Achitophel
24,33,60,61–4,142,143
Du Bellay,J. 139
Dunbar,W. 51,99,171

Earle,J. 167
Ecbasis Captivi 175
Egyptians 172,177,178
Eliot,T.S. 233
Empson,W. 72,124
Ennius 133
Epictetus 151,152
*Epistolae Obscurorum
Virorum* 53,55
Erasmus 52
Eskimos 14–15,17

Fielding,H. 37,72–3,204,
218; *Jonathan Wild* 72;
Joseph Andrews 218;
Pasquin 72; *Tom Jones*
220; *Tom Thumb the
Great* 204
Figueira,G. 48
Flaubert,G. 122,221,
223–4; *Bouvard et
Pécuchet* 221,223,238;
*Dictionnaire des idées
reçues* 223
France,A. 182
France,Marie de 175
Freud,S. 109–10

Galland,A. 92
Gay,J. 64,65,72,137,176,
242; *Beggars' Opera*
65,72; *Polly* 72;
Trivia 137
Gibbon,E. 157,168;
*Decline and Fall of the
Roman Empire* 168
Gillray 246
Godwin,W. 71
Gogol,N. 195; *Dead
Souls* 196,227; *The
Government Inspector*
195–6
Goldsmith,O. 126,218
Goliardic metre,song 44,
46
Gorki,M. 216
Gourmont,R.de 157
Goya,F. 246
Grass,Günter 239–40
Greeks 18; Old Comedy
23,37,38; tragedy 12
Griboyedov,A. 195
Grimmelshausen,J.J.von
220
Grosz,G. 212
Guilbert,Y. 210

Hall,Bishop J. 141,142,
167; *Characters of
Virtues and Vices* 167;
Virgidemiarum 141
Heine,H. 76–7,210
Henryson,R. 24,51,
175–6
Herodotus 178,179
Herrick,R. 162
Hippocrates 150
Hobbes,T. 56,57,63,
109,156; *Leviathan* 56;
On Human Nature 109
Hogarth 73,246

Homer 14,19,24,178,
179,183,233; *Odyssey* 178
Horace 133–4,137,138,
139,140,142,143,144,
146; 'The Bore' 134,139
Housman,A.E. 16
Hugh of Orleans
('Primas') 46
Huxley,A. 144,185;
Antic Hay 222; *Brave
New World* 185,186,
222; *Point Counter
Point* 216,222
Huxley,T.H. 157

Ibsen,H. 122,199,200
Indian stories 172,175
Ionesco,E. 37,202

Jacobsohn,S. 212
Johnson,S. 16,33,74,79
126,135,150,151–2,
153,155,157,158;
London 135,137
Jonson,B. 18,121,126,
142,190,191–3,194;
The Alchemist 126,
192–3; *Bartholomew
Fair* 193; *Cynthia's
Revels* 191; *Every Man
in his Humour* 121,191;
*Every Man out of his
Humour* 191; *The
Poetaster* 18,19,191;
Volpone 191–2
Joubert,J. 152
Joyce,J. 232–7; *The Dead*
232; *Dubliners* 232;
Finnegans Wake 234;
Ulysses 28,36,99,122,
223,232–7
Jung,C. 23
Juvenal 11,55,63,83–5,

92, 94, 106, 129, 132,
134–5, 137–8, 139, 140,
142, 143, 144; *Satires:*
III ('Rome') 129, 134–5;
VI 83, 138; X ('The
Vanity of Human
Wishes') 38, 138

Kafka, F. 155, 226
Kästner, E. 212
Kierkegaard, S. 155
Kipling, R. 162, 212
Kleist, H. von 195
Knox, J. 91
Knox, Father R. 115
Koestler, A. 111–12
Kraus, K. 39, 111, 150
Krylov, I. A. 176

La Bruyère, J. de 165,
166, 167
Laclos, C. de 80
La Fontaine, J. de 24, 176
La Fresnaye, J. V. de 139
Lai d'Aristote 94
Langland, W. 171
La Rochefoucauld, F. duc
de 151, 152, 155
Lawrence, D. H. 216
Lebrun, P. D. E. 162
Lehrer, T. 213
Le Sage, A.-R. 220
Lewis, W. 216
Leys d'Amors 48
Lichtenberg, G. C. 150,
153–4, 156
Lodge, T. 141
Lorenz, K. 108
Lorris, G. de 95
Lucian 24, 156, 179, 222;
Dialogues of the Dead
156; *Dialogues of the
Gods* 222; *True History*

24, 179
Lucilius 38, 42, 133
Luther, M. 53, 54

MacDonald, D. 122
Machiavelli, N. 56, 190
Malherbe, F. de 162
Manilius 16
Map, W. 94
'Marprelate, Martin' 54
Marston, J. 141, 142, 191
Martial 16, 161
Marvell, A. 60, 61, 64
Marx, G. 112
Matheolus 94
Menander 165
Mesopotamians 177
Meung, J. de 41, 95, 98;
Roman de la Rose 94,
95, 100; *La Vieille* 95
Miller, A. 199
Milton, J. 55; *Paradise
Lost* 62, 90–1
Molière 105, 131, 166
188, 196; Don Juan
197; *Le Misanthrope*
194; *Les Précieuses
Ridicules* 105; *Tartuffe*
196
Montesquieu, baron de
126
Montherlant, H. de 155
More, Sir T. 52, 183, 184;
Utopia 52, 184
Morgenstern, C. 210
Morris, W. 185
Mycenean legends 178

Nabokov, V. 107
Neher 212
New Yorker 115
Nietzsche 155, 158
Nivardus, Magister 42;

Ysengrimus 44, 175
The North Briton 73

O'Casey, S. 200–2
Oldham, J. 135
Olivier, J. 105
Orwell, G. 24, 126–9,
186–7; *Animal Farm*
24, 176; *1984* 128, 129,
186–7
Osborne, J. 202
Ossietsky, C. von 212
Overbury, Sir T. 167
Ovid 92, 168

Pacuvius 133
Pascal, B. 151, 152
Peacock, T. L. 222
Persius 38, 138, 139, 142
Philip the Chancellor 46
Phlyax vase painters 30, 118
Pins and Needles 207
Plato 183, 184
Pope, A. 15, 28, 65, 73,
105, 126–7, 143, 144–6,
156, 162; *Dunciad* 8,
16, 24, 27, 65, 129, 135,
144, 233; *Essay on Man*
153, 225; *Imitations
of Horace* 143; *Moral
Essays* 143, 144: II ('On
the Characters of
Women') 106; IV ('Of
the Use of Riches')
146–7, 150; *Rape of the
Lock* 27, 105
Pound, E. 162
Prévert, J. 163
Prior, M. 162
Provençal troubadours
46–8
Ptah-Hotep 81
Punch 115

Puttenham, G. 141

Queneau, R. 124
Queredo, F. de 220
Quintilian 133
Quinze Jours de Mariage
 99

Rabelais, F. 24, 28, 36, 52,
 56, 99, 122, 140, 179–80,
 189, 222, 234; *Gargan-
 tua* 52, 179–80;
 Pantagruel 179–80
Racine, J. 139
Régnier, M. 105, 139–40
Reinike de Vos 175
Richardson, S. 80, 216
Rimbaud, A. 212
Rochester, Lord 16, 45,
 58, 160
Rojas, F. de 99
Romains, J. 192
Roman de Renart 24, 51,
 175
Roman satire 12, 38
Ronsard, P. de 54
Rousseau, J.-J. 162, 168

Sahl, M. 213
St Augustine 91
St Jerome 86, 91, 94, 98
Saint-Simon, duc de 168
Saltykov-Shchedrin, M. E.
 227–8; *Fairy Tales* 39,
 176; *The Golovlovs*
 227–8
Sartre, J.-P. 120, 239
Satire Ménippée 54, 55–6
Scarron, P. 30
Segrais, J. R. de 166
Sercambi, G. 92
Semonides of Amorgos
 82, 138

Seven Sages 92
Shadwell, T. 194
Shakespeare, W. 13, 102,
 111, 131, 178, 193; *As
 You Like It* 189;
 Hamlet 102, 157, 189;
 King Lear 30, 189; *The
 Tempest* 178; *Timon
 of Athens* 189; *Troilus
 and Cressida* 102
Shelley, P. B. 74
Simplicissimus 210
Smollett, T. 218, 220
Spectator 105, 124, 167
Steele, Sir R. 105, 167
Stendhal 76
Stephens, J. 19
Strindberg, A. 80
Sumerian aphorisms 151
Swift, J. 11, 28, 30, 36, 38,
 64, 91, 105, 109, 122,
 124, 130–1, 150, 189;
 Conduct of the Allies 67;
 Drapier's Letters 60,
 67, 68, 70, 126; *Gulliver's
 Travels* 24, 39, 65,
 67–71, 77, 115, 126, 128,
 153, 182, 184; *Modest
 Proposal* 130–1, 239;
 Tale of a Tub 118, 123,
 234; *Thoughts on
 various subjects* 153
Swinburne, A. C. 130

Tacitus 168
Tati, J. 243
Tatler 105, 167
Theophrastus 86–7, 94,
 121, 163; *Characters*
 163; *On Marriage* 86–7
Thucydides 168
Thurber, J. 107, 176
Tourneur, C. 105, 193

*Travels of Sir John
 Mandeville* 178
Tucholsky, K. 212
Twain, M. 115, 220

Verdier 159
Verne, J. 179
Villiers, G. 204
Villon, F. 45, 100, 212,
 242; *Le Grand Testa-
 ment* 100, 101
Virgil 24, 30, 233; *Aeneid*
 233
Vitry, Cardinal J. de 170
Voltaire 38, 42, 77, 111,
 112, 140, 150, 159,
 160–1, 162, 184, 197;
 Candide 225–6; *Lettres
 philosophiques* 39,
 123–4; *Micromégas* 182

Waller, E. 61, 143
Walpole, Sir R. 65, 67,
 68, 72, 137
Walter of Chatillon 46
Waugh, E. 221, 227
Webster, J. 102, 193–4
Wedekind, F. 210
Wells, H. G. 179
Weltbühne 212
West, N. 226–7
West African tales 20–1
Wharton, Earl of 65
Wilde, O. 111, 158, 200
Wilkes, J. 72
Williams, R. 243
Wycherley, W. 126, 194;
 Plain Dealer 194–5
Wylie, P. 106

Zola, E. 216
Zweig, S. 192

World University Library

Some titles already published

001 **Eye and Brain**
R. L. Gregory, *Edinburgh*

002 **The Economics of Underdeveloped Countries**
Jagdish Bhagwati, *MIT*

003 **The Left in Europe since 1789**
David Caute, *London*

004 **The World Cities**
Peter Hall, *Reading*

005 **Chinese Communism**
Robert North, *Stanford*

006 **The Emergence of Greek Democracy**
W. G. Forrest, *Oxford*

009 **Palaeolithic Cave Art**
P. J. Ucko and A. Rosenfeld, *London*

011 **Russian Writers and Society 1825-1904**
Ronald Hingley, *Oxford*

013 **Education in the Modern World**
John Vaizey, *London*

014 **The Rise of Toleration**
Henry Kamen, *Warwick*

015 **Art Nouveau**
S. Tschudi Madsen, *Oslo*

017 **Decisive Forces in World Economics**
J. L. Sampedro, *Madrid*

018 **Development Planning**
Jan Tinbergen, *Rotterdam*

019 **Human Communication**
J. L. Aranguren, *Madrid*

021 **The Rise of the Working Class**
Jürgen Kuczynski, *Berlin*

022 **The Science of Decision-making**
A. Kaufmann, *Paris*

024 **Muhammad and the Conquests of Islam**
Francesco Gabrieli, *Rome*

025 **Humanism in the Renaissance**
S. Dresden, *Leyden*

028 **The Age of the Dinosaurs**
Björn Kurtén, *Helsingfors*

029 **Mimicry in Plants and Animals**
Wolfgang Wickler, *Seewiesen*

030 **The Old Stone Age**
François Bordes, *Bordeaux*

031 **Data Study**
J. L. Jolley, *London*

032 **The Civilisation of Charlemagne**
Jacques Boussard, *Poitiers*

034 **The Dutch Republic**
C. H. Wilson, *Cambridge*

038 **The Tasks of Childhood**
Philippe Muller, *Neuchâtel*

039 **Twentieth Century Music**
H. H. Stuckenschmidt, *Berlin*

041 **Witchcraft**
Lucy Mair, *London*

042 **Population and History**
E. A. Wrigley, *Cambridge*